Live From Your Centre

A Course for Life

Magenta Wise

"Genius is not simply the exceptional found in the few, but the way in which each finds the exceptional in themselves." - Michael Meade.

No part of this book, including text and images, may be reproduced in any written, electronic, recording or photocopying without written permission of the publisher or author. The exception would be in the case of brief quotations embodied in the critical articles or reviews and pages where permission is specifically granted by the publisher or author.

Copyright © 2020 Magenta Wise

All Images © 2020 Magenta Wise and © 2020 Dominic Sladden

All rights reserved.

ISBN: 978-0-9932262-2-9

Book and cover design by Magenta Wise

Also by Magenta Wise
Poetry- *Messages are Dancing in the Rain.*
Short Stories - *Kill and Cure.*

www.magentawise.com

Dedication

To Richard Gardner, whose light of remarkable genius was the dazzling spark which ignited these discoveries, nourished their development and whose capable hands delivered it to the world.

Also to Tammo de Jongh, Barry Slater and Kenneth Carter. Their individual genius and collaboration with Richard Gardner gave birth to this miracle we call The Work. In recognition of their remarkable insights, I give them my deepest thanks.

To my dear parents, Elpida Panayidou and James Mitchell Weir. Thank you for gifting me my life and for all that you gave me.

"Heed these words, you who wish to probe the depths of nature: if you do not find within yourself that which you seek, neither will you find it outside. In you is hidden the treasure of treasures. Know thyself and you will know the universe and the Gods." – The Oracle of Delphi

Contents

Dedication	3
Acknowledgments	8
Part 1	10
• Revolve to Evolve	11
• The Discovery of the Work	24
• Time, Eternity and the Quest for Truth	31
• Sex, Gender and Evolution	50
• Nationalities	56
• Why Is Change So Hard?	59
• Why Is Change So Frightening?	66
• The Magic of Twelve	75
Part 2 - The Practice	80
• The Four Elements	81
• Water	89
• Fire	96
• Earth	101
• Air	106
Practising the Archetypes	111
Why There are Twelve Archetypes	113

Living from Your Centre 117

The Water Archetypes 131

- The Child 132
- How to Practise the Child 141
- The Enchantress 146
- How to Practise the Enchantress 160
- The Actress 165
- How to Practise the Actress 174

The Fire Archetypes 179

- The Fool 180
- How to Practise the Fool 187
- The Joker 192
- How to Practise the Joker 198
- The Warrior 203
- How to Practise the Warrior 212

The Earth Archetypes 217

- The Worker/Slave 218
- How to Practise the Worker/Slave 225
- Mother Nature 230
- How to Practise Mother Nature 239

- The Wise Woman — 244
- How to Practise the Wise Woman — 252

The Air Archetypes — 257

- The Observer — 258
- How to Practise the Observer — 266
- The Logician — 271
- How to Practise the Logician — 278
- The Patriarch — 283
- How to Practise the Patriarch — 293

The Relationships Between the Archetypes — 298

- The Four Open States — 302
- The Four Closed States — 303
- The Four Cardinal States — 304
- The Six Complementary Opposites — 307
- The Six Conflicting Opposites — 312
- The Reconcilers — 320

Neurotic Solutions and Psychological Problems — 327

Sequences of Elements — 336

The End — 359

"Our greatest human adventure is the evolution of consciousness. We are in this life to enlarge the soul, liberate the spirit, and light up the brain." - Tom Robbins

"Man must evolve from human conflict to a method which rejects revenge, aggression, and retaliation. The foundation of such a method is love." - Martin Luther King Jr

"I think quite spiritually of myself. I feel like I'm here to support the human evolution."
- Alanis Morissette

ACKNOWLEDGMENTS

♥ Thank you to the love of my heart, my daughter, Alexa. You live with remarkable strength and love and have given me the best reason to live. I love your sweet heart, I love you the most.

♥ Heartfelt thanks to Dominic Sladden for your many insights, wonderful artworks and illustrations, which bring this book to life. They enhance and clarify the work beautifully and are a necessary addition to Tammo's original portraits. Also, for your on-going support and understanding of the Work, many years of creative sharing, and fun, happy times. I could not have asked for a more loyal or better friend. You're my Soul Brother.

♥ Thank you to my dear friend and author, Rohase Piercy for your insightful help and support in editing. You have made a most valuable contribution to the Work. Your friendship, empathy and understanding, and that of Leslie Bunker and dear Spike, were there when I needed them. Everyone should have friends like you.

♥ Thank you to my dear friend, Elyse Smith, you recognised my soul and have been to me the sister I always needed. You have one of the most beautiful hearts on earth. You're my Soul Sister. I love you Sissie.

♥ Thank you to Helena and Michael Salisbury, your kindness to me was so generously given at a crucial time. It means more to me than words can say and will forever remain in my heart. You are precious souls.

♥ To my childhood friend Margaret Deery. Thank you for finding me again and reconnecting me to happy times. I love you as much as ever.

♥ To all the people whom I have quoted throughout this book, their perceptions are jewels of truth.

♥ Thank you to you, the reader, and to all the beautiful souls who strive to heal our world. May the gift of this Work aid in your evolution, and further reveal the radiant light of your Centre.

Note; Any typos or errors of information are my own.

We Are the Music-Makers

We are the music-makers,
And we are the dreamers of dreams,
Wandering by lone sea-breakers,
And sitting by desolate streams.
World-losers and world-forsakers,
Upon whom the pale moon gleams;
Yet we are the movers and shakers,
Of the world forever, it seems.

With wonderful deathless ditties
We build up the world's great cities,
And out of a fabulous story
We fashion an empire's glory:
One man with a dream, at pleasure,
Shall go forth and conquer a crown;
And three with a new song's measure
Can trample an empire down.

We, in the ages lying,
In the buried past of the earth,
Built Nineveh with our sighing,
And Babel itself with our mirth;
And o'erthrew them with prophesying,
To the old of the new world's worth;
For each age is a dream that is dying,
Or one that is coming to birth.

- Arthur William Edgar O'Shaughnessy

Part One

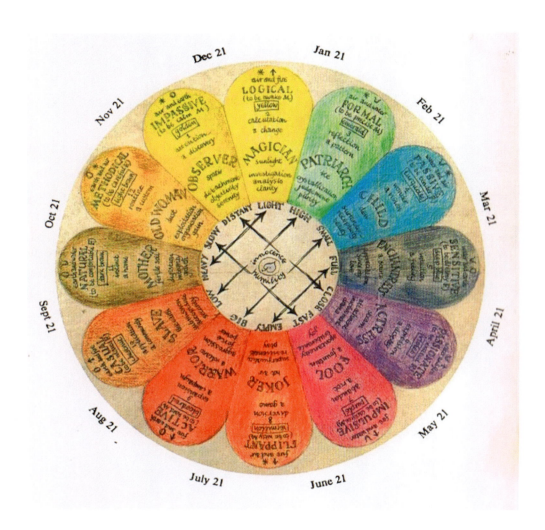

"Stay at the centre of the circle and let all things take their course." - Tao Te Ching

Live from Your Centre

Use ALL of yourself and Win the Life Game!

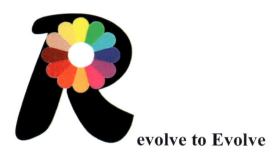 evolve to Evolve

This book is about YOU. It is a comprehensive identification of the nature of your consciousness in all its forms and how to recognise, develop and balance them. It celebrates who you are and shows you how to develop further into more of what you can become. Revolving the different aspects of our consciousness leads to our further evolution. Within you are many dormant powers, and through the practical application of the Archetypes on your Wheel of Life, your body, mind, spirit and soul can be vitalised and evolved. This Work can break the frustration of being stuck and free you in all areas of your life. It is a powerful tool that allows you to proceed at your own pace, on your own path. Part One covers some background, where I explore thoughts and ideas about our further development. Part Two is the Practice, where you will learn about each Archetype and how to develop it. You can read this book in any order you wish. If, however, you want to start practising right away, please read the chapter 'Living From Your Centre – The Practice' first, it gives important advice and instructions. Get to know all your Archetypes to establish a good overview and the practical reality of the Work. This is a Course for Life, in three senses. One, it will last you all your life, however long you decide to live. Two, it will bring you more of the energy of life. Three, it will take you on your own course, as in path, and as you criss-cross over the circle, your own pattern will appear, like a beautiful mandala.

This Work is all-inclusive, everything is represented. All cultures, peoples, types of societies, paths to growth, political systems, sciences, knowledge, wisdom and religions can be placed on the circle. It is completely unifying, which is what makes it so wonderful and so powerful. Although the Divine,

Goddess/God is mentioned, you don't have to believe in a Deity to use the Archetypes.

"I belong to no religion. My religion is love. Every heart is my temple." - Rumi

This is not just another way, another path. It is every way, every path. It is not an 'either/or' approach, it is all approaches. It is not one direction or another, it is all directions. The Archetypes described herein can be seen in ourselves and in the faces and behaviours around us. Maybe you think this is too simple, but the simpler a thing is, the closer it is to the truth. I'm not asking you to take my word for it; in fact, I'd rather you didn't. If you study and practise this Work you will see and experience it for yourself, and only then will it count. Otherwise it is meaningless. The only way to get into this Work is to live it and observe it alive in yourself and others. The Work is practical, it does not preach a belief system nor expect you to accept any truth without understanding it and making it your own. Nor is there any positive part of yourself that you have to give up. I simply explain what we call The Work, which comprises the Twelve Archetypes and how to develop them and thereby your Centre. I give you the means to practise it if you so wish. As Galileo Galilei said,

"We cannot teach people anything; we can only help them discover it within themselves."

"Life is like riding a bicycle. To keep your balance you must keep moving." - Albert Einstein.

Balance and movement are the basis of The Work. Movement is the key, the secret of self-growth, happiness and fulfilment. We need to keep the wheels of our consciousness turning, for without movement we lose our balance, become stagnant and open the door to misery, illness and disappointment. If you are intrigued by the idea of turning your own wheel of consciousness, then you'll find all the parts described here, together with the means of awakening and integrating them. Your real self is not the isolated parts of the circle with which you have become identified. You are the Centre. This is the most significant point. The information in this book defines and describes The Twelve Archetypes of the Wheel of Life, and gives you the means to apply them to yourself in a real and practical way, bringing them into your Centre, where they unite and bring you to your unique, true self. You can awaken and develop them all, expand your consciousness and enhance your life in limitless ways. You are not being asked to take anything on faith. Sincere practice will ensure that you see and experience for yourself.

"To live is the rarest thing in the world. Most people just exist." - Oscar Wilde

Applying the Archetypes will take us out of mere existence and into real living. It is a Work that is so simple it can be introduced to children from the age of three or four, and yet so sophisticated it can intrigue the most advanced minds indefinitely. Moreover, it can be enormous fun. This book contains all the information you need to further your process of growth and healing, leading to the unfolding of your true self. That's a big claim, but when these straightforward practices offered here are openly embraced, miracles and magic will abound within and around you. Even more so if you work with a group of others. You can go as far as you wish. Dip in your toe and enjoy enough insights and experiences to make small but fulfilling changes in your life, or go further and astonish yourself at what you can achieve. Greater objectivity, deeper insights and conscious choice are among the first gifts this Work brings. I give clear instructions on how to use it. I have included loaded invocation scripts that, properly practiced, will awaken you into each part of yourself. They give you the means to heal and reconcile the broken parts so that the joyful picture can be restored.

"You can't use up creativity. The more you use, the more you have." - *Maya Angelou*

"The object of Art is to give life a shape." - *William Shakespeare*

You are invited to become a practitioner of the highest art of all, which is the art of creating your magnificent, individual self. The twelve colours of consciousness and how they work in you are easily understood, and through their use, the portrait of your true self will emerge from the Centre. Each person is an artist who can personify a unique portrait of authentic beauty and extraordinary individuality. The Work is like a flower with twelve different coloured petals, uncurling each one bit by bit and adding them to your Centre of light. You truly become the captain of your own ship. Shakespeare, in identifying the seven ages of man, said, "All the world's a stage, and all the men and women merely players; they have their exits and their entrances, and one man in his time plays many parts..." Related to the Archetypes presented here, I hope you will see how they are like twelve actors, each with their role to play. Unlike Shakespeare's, which chart the average lifespan, these will promote your youthing, further growth and evolution.

The Work is beautiful in its logic, enchanting in its poetry and dynamic in its creativity. It is like an unbreakable twelve faceted diamond, reflecting all the colours of light. It is the Philosopher's Stone against which the false will shatter. Picture a beautiful chandelier in a darkened room; how dull it is, yet switch on the light and it twinkles with rainbows. This is true of us; our real selves are made of light. We have allowed our diamonds to become dull and lacklustre because our societies do not encourage the full extent of our beings. Our task is to polish them with our enlightenment until each facet glows and glitters, and we shine with pure light. If enough people embrace this, it will lead to a major step forward in human evolution. We will be the pioneers of a new, healthy, loving, harmonious world. I have tried and tested this Work over many years and have not been able to break it, only verify it to myself and significantly contribute to it. Richard Gardner (one of the four discoverers of the Work) advised me to make a small spinning top. I cut some stiff cardboard into a small circle and then snipped equally round the edges to make it twelve-sided. I then divided it into twelve parts, faithfully filled in the colours of the Archetypes as accurately as possible and stuck a small stick though the middle. I spun it, and as it sped up, the colours merged and became white. This deceptively minor test was one of the things which began to convince me that if we turned our own circle of colours, we could turn into beings of light.

You probably already have some understanding about what archetypes mean and may be wondering what's different about these. The answer is that the Twelve Archetypes described herein are based on real, visible and demonstrative energies. Carl Jung made explorations into Archetypes, identifying mainly four, naming them The Self, The Shadow, The Anima or Animus and The Persona, although he suspected that there may be others, possibly twelve. Other people have developed their own systems, but this Work is by far the most advanced, in that the Archetypes are not theoretical, subjective, nebulous or speculative. They are based on real living energies - the Four Elements; Earth, Water, Fire and Air, the basis of all life on earth. At this point, some may decide to dismiss this Work, considering the Elements to be an outdated approach, which has been superseded. This is merely the Air Element talking. I can assure the Air types that this work is perfectly logical and if they open their minds and practice as advised, they will see for themselves and be satisfied. Why am I so sure? Because the Air Element is strong in myself and I accept nothing until I have proved the logic of it for myself. Pause for a moment and consider what your life would be like without water, heat, oxygen, your body, a home planet. Do you still exist in your present form? Can you live without the Elements? If you think that none of it matters because you're going to die and move to a better place, then this Work probably won't reach you. I hope, however, that the fact that you hold it in your hands means you are willing to read on.

In part two you will discover who they are and how to bring them to life in yourself. Let me make this clear right away. The female ones do not apply solely to women, nor the male ones to men.

Using this work will break sexist stereotypes and free us to use all parts of ourselves. It will help to think of them in terms of Yin and Yang, opposite, dynamic energies which combine to make up a whole, whatever the biological sex. The purpose of this Work is to get our consciousness moving. I have sprinkled quotes throughout the book, which illustrate that others have shared many of the same insights. Here is a glimpse of the Twelve.

There are three Water Archetypes

The Child, the Enchantress and the Actress

CHILD   ENCHANTRESS   ACTRESS

There are three Fire Archetypes

The Fool, the Joker and the Warrior

FOOL   JOKER   WARRIOR

There are three Earth Archetypes

The Worker, Mother Nature and the Wise Woman

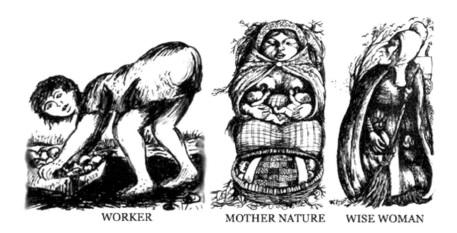

There are three Air Archetypes

The Observer, the Logician and the Patriarch

We don't want to be stuck on terminology before we've begun, which can limit our appreciation and understanding, so we don't always have to say 'Archetypes', we can also see the twelve states as:

12 Worlds

12 Functions

12 States of being

12 Shades of being

12 Energies

12 Vibrations

12 Frequencies

12 Dimensions

12 Facets

12 Colours of consciousness

12 Performances

12 Channels (like TV)

12 Spells

12 Petals of a flower

12 Facets of a jewel

12 Experiences

12 Personality types

12 Deities

12 Performances

12 Characters

12 Roles

12 Realities

12 Magic Potions

12 Remedies

12 Parts of You

Our understanding begins with the realisation of how fundamental the elements are to us. We all have bodies and live in an apparently dense, solid world, which is the Earth element; our bodies are largely composed of liquid, as the body of the earth is covered in seas, which is the Water element;

we have heat in our bodies, as does the earth deep in her bowels, and we have heat from the sun, which is the Fire element; we breath in oxygen, we and the earth are surrounded by various gases, which is the Air element. It is these four and their interactions with each of the three others which give a maximum permutation of twelve. I have often been asked, "Won't we all be the same if we use the same Archetypes?". I could say that we are already much like clones, with individual differences too small to make any great difference, yet deep down we know we are all unique. The problem is that we live within social constructs that are too narrow to allow us to fully develop and express ourselves. This work will break the chains that constrain us and free us to live in our light. We are already using these Archetypes, but **unconsciously.** Most people live in only two or three and say of people who are using different ones, "He/she is not my type". This means that we identify with the few that have got hold of us and believe them to be our true selves. We deny ourselves the gifts that the others can bring. The truth is that the authentic self lives in the Centre. By the **conscious** development of the different states of consciousness, we can connect with and develop ourselves at will. Just as water becomes stagnant when not moving, so does consciousness, so we often display more of the negative than the positive aspects of the Archetypes. Awakening dormant ones balances and automatically purifies others in which we have been stuck. Each culture throughout time has conditioned people into a small number of behaviours, favouring certain Archetypes over others. The result is that few people stand out; yet we know we are special in our own way, but we are losing our specialness. This Work will help you to uncover and recover who you really are.

"The most important kind of freedom is to be what you really are. You trade in your reality for a role. You trade in your sense for an act. You give up your ability to feel, and in exchange, put on a mask. There can't be any large-scale revolution until there's a personal revolution, on an individual level. It's got to happen inside first." - Jim Morrison

The Metaphysics of Evolution

"The world we are experiencing today is the result of our collective consciousness, and if we want a new world, each of us must start taking responsibility for helping create it." - Rosemary Fillmore

'Metaphysics' means 'beyond the physical'. It is time for humanity to participate in conscious evolution through understanding the metaphysical forces that influence us. When we look at the concept of evolution, most people look backwards and see apes. Look up the word and most dictionaries will give a definition like – 'The process by which different kinds of living organism are believed to have developed from earlier forms during the history of the earth.' It's always in the past tense, *'Have developed'*. There is no concept of the future. Who decided that the evolutionary process has ended? Who considers this to be good enough? Is it not short sighted and arrogant to believe that humans, arguably the most destructive and dangerous animals on earth, are the end result of the evolutionary process? We have furthered 'progress' on the outer world at the expense of inner development, resulting in regression in many areas and we are now endangering all life on earth. So far, evolution has been slow and unconscious. It now needs to be conscious, which will see more rapid changes.

"Until you make the unconscious conscious, it will direct your life, and you will call it fate."
- Carl Jung

We need to take control of the process whilst we still have time, and it can be done, we need not be disheartened. When people say that bringing peace and evolution will take a long time, I dispute it. Anything can happen practically overnight if we agree to it. Agreement is the thing. Look what happened in the UK when the last World War was declared; within a short time, thousands of men were sent overseas, children to the countryside, gardens became sources of growing food, food and clothes rations were imposed, a black market arose, pailings were removed from buildings for the metals to be used in armaments, women did the jobs of the men who had gone to fight, and many other huge social changes happened. In spite of the horrors that war brought, those who survived said it was the happiest time of their lives. Why? Because it brought change and excitement. People were moving in all kinds of ways, both within and without. If this can happen so rapidly in negative times, why could not many other changes be brought about in the positive? We can have anything on which we agree.

"The seed in its essence is all of the past evolution of the Earth, the evolution of human history, and the potential for future evolution. Our seeds of further evolution are already planted, they are waiting for us to cultivate them." - *Dr. Vandana.Shiva.*

The root of the word 'evolve' is from the Latin, evolvere, *to unroll.* I find that interesting, for it implies that we have 'rolled up' inside us further potential for development, and our cells are just waiting for the right conditions to show us what they can really do. That's exciting. With enough people developing themselves, I see the possibility, even probability, of an enormous paradigm shift, which will take humanity into a new phase of evolution. It is quite possible that our bodies will transform along with our increased awareness, and a new species of humanity would emerge, with a lighter, finer composition. Evolution has a future. Roll it out!

You will experience an exhilarating sense of freedom, as you realize that you no longer need to identify yourself with a small number of characteristics in yourself, thinking this is all you can be. You will see that it is an illusion, that your authentic self is much greater and resides in the Centre of the circle. You no longer need to choose one way of being over another, you can be all of yourselves and delight in the magic and power of experiencing each part of you merging into the real you. You can develop and bring forth each Archetype, each colour of your consciousness, and bring it to your Centre, where true control lives. Your wheel will no longer be stuck and as it turns, a more rounded, evolved, brighter YOU emerges, unique and truly YOU. This is a practical work, not a theory. Repetition is how we learn, and we need reminders in order to establish good practice and prevent us from falling into bad habits, threrefore I say some things more than once. I capitalise words like 'Archetypes', 'Centre', 'Elements', 'Water', 'Earth', 'Fire' and 'Air' the 'Work' to emphasise their importance. We call these discoveries 'The Work', not only because a great deal of work went into identifying them, but more specifically because working on ourselves is the greatest work we will ever do, and the most vital if we are to avert human extinction and prove ourselves worthy of being here. So, the purpose of the Work is to unfurl ourselves and evolve by connecting to our Centre through the practice of the Archetypes, awakening and developing dormant ones and bringing their energies to the Centre. Everyone will express them differently, and as your Centre grows, so will your uniqueness. We need to look at change and why we resist it, in the hope that it will encourage us to embrace it. You won't be changing the person you are, nor will you be giving up any positive aspects of yourself; the kind of change you will be bringing about is to add to yourself, increasing your range of qualities and abilities and thereby dissolving the negatives. Many of us have the illusion that growth is going further in the same direction, when in fact positive change can only come by going in the opposite. Then we attain balance. If you have the energy of anger in you for example, by learning to be softer and more peaceful you will transform it into strength and courage. If you are inhibited and over-restrained, you will be freer to express yourself and have more fun and so on. Practising the Archetypes will make this clear to you. You may find the chapters on Change helpful in preparing you to use the Archetypes. We will look at the Four Elements, the basis of the Work, and learn more about them and how they relate to us. You will learn how each element is paired with one of the three others, giving a maximum permutation of twelve. The Archetypes each have their own section which fully describes their world, with guidance on how to practise them, including the scripts which invoke them. It's easy to get to know all Twelve as they are grouped in their elements, three Water, three Fire, three Air and three Earth ones. It won't be long before you're familiar with them, you have the seeds of them all in you and are already using two or three, as are most of us. You won't find it too hard to know which you are using and which are dormant once you start working with them, and you'll start to recognise them in other people too. This work is not a creation, it is a discovery, like precious jewels that were lying in the dirt. The originators had the eyes to see them, polish them and bring them to the light.

"People often claim to hunger for truth, but seldom like the taste when it's served up."
- George R.R. Martin
"The truth will set you free, but first it will piss you off." - Gloria Steinem

Offering this Work to the world is a challenge. Opposition and resistance are common, because the Work is revealing. It breaks stereotypes, both on the personal level where there can be no more lies and pretence, and in the worlds of science, academia, religion, psychology, commerce, politics, business and so on. All are put in their place in their relevant Archetypes. Few of us like to be sussed, we prefer to hide behind masks and pretend to be more than we are. This means we can never be more. Our task is to use all we have learned from each Archetype so far, both individually and globally, and to bring it to a place of co-operation and equality, both within and without. If the world took up this Work, the nature of work would change and many jobs, with their financial arrangements and working hours would also change. We must go forward with humility and goodwill if we have the slightest hope of survival. Even the ego has a place in this Work, it is put where it can act as a tool for real achievement rather than for obstruction or conflict, as it is too often used.

"People don't want to hear the truth because they don't want their illusions destroyed."
- Friedrich Nietzsche

We shall have to learn to love and cultivate all Twelve States of our being in order to become whole, however much we may dislike any of them at present. This is difficult, because in my experience, we do not like any experience or information which is not supportive of the spells that are dominating us. By appreciating that the practice of the Archetypes will create a happier, more harmonious society, we can break the hold of the established order. In that sense, it is truly subversive. This work can bring understanding, peace and evolution to the world. It depends on which side we choose to be.

"Freethinkers are those who are willing to use their minds without prejudice and without fearing to understand things that clash with their own customs, privileges or beliefs. This state of mind is not common, but it is essential for right thinking; where it is absent, discussion is apt to become worse than useless." - Leo Tolstoy.

The Discovery of the Work

"May the sun bring you new energy by day, may the moon softly restore you by night, may the rain wash away your worries, may the breeze blow new strength into your being, may you walk gently through the world and know it's beauty all the days of your life." - Apache Blessing

People ask me how the Work came about and who created it. I have to emphasise that it is not a creation, as this implies it was invented by the originators. No, it was not made up, it was discovered. It is important to give a brief record of events in order to have the correct perspective on how the Work originated and the roles each person played so that recognition is given as is due. I give the following account as truthfully and accurately as possible. Although I have developed, contributed to, and significantly progressed this work, the original discoveries herein are not my own. They were made by a group of four in the 1960s, notably Richard Gardner, a metaphysician; Tammo de Jongh, an artist specialising in portraiture; Kenneth Carter, a historian and teacher, and Barry Slater, a mathematician and philosopher. I knew and worked with all four men in various ways and times, so everything I say I either observed for myself or it was told to me first hand by the four themselves.

It was Richard Gardner (1919-1997) who first planted the seeds of the work, through his extensive work on metaphysics, which led him into researching Archetypal patterns of behaviour based on the Four Elements. Richard was born in Belfast, Ireland and throughout his childhood he found the conflict there intolerable and left for Dublin as soon as he could. After travelling through Europe, he spent some time in Tangier. One day, in a bar, he turned to the man who took the seat next to him and said, "Turned out nice again". This amused the man, as it was hot and sunny there every day. He was leaving Tangier and had some things to sell. Richard bought a pack of intriguing Tarot cards from him. Richard then went to Majorca, and going to a post office to collect his mail, he was given a large package addressed to Richard Gardner, with a New York postmark. On opening it, he realised it couldn't be for him, even though the books inside were on subjects in which he had particular interest. Later, in Ibiza, Richard happened to meet the owner of the parcel, who was indeed another

Richard Gardner. They had a mutual female friend who told Richard that he and the other RG shared an interest in the Tarot. From this point on, Richard's pursued his studies on it.

Richard was living in Hampstead, London in the late 1950s when he was introduced to Tammo de Jongh by Hugh Levy, a friend and neighbour of Richard's. Tammo lived in Kentish Town, on the other side of Hampstead Heath, so the pair walked over to see him. Hugh was quite a character, he spoke fourteen languages, played the cello and violin, spending part of the year on cruise ships in an orchestra, and giving music lessons the rest of the time. It was a stroke of genius on his part to introduce Richard and Tammo, and so he played a vital role. The meeting came at a crucial time in Tammo's life when he was concerned for his mental wellbeing, feeling fearful and having thoughts and visions which he felt were taking him over. One of his visions was of a woman in blue. Sensing he could trust Richard, he confided in him. Richard immediately diagnosed the problem and told Tammo that he was not going insane, he was simply experiencing the Water Element and might be seeing the Virgin Mary. He need only balance it with other Elements to bring it under control. The realisation worked. At his home in Kentish Town, Tammo and I discussed this during a conversation about my own Water Element. Thus reassured, Tammo became fascinated with Richard's knowledge of the Elements, as his studies of the Tarot revealed many insights. As Richard imparted his discoveries, Tammo realised that Richard was right when he said that people who behaved alike looked alike, something he was able to see for himself through his work in portraiture. As a result of this meeting, the work in clarifying how the Elements influence people began.

Richard and Tammo were joined by Barry Slater, a gifted professor of advanced mathematics and philosophy, whose solid logic helped to accurately form the circle, and Kenneth Carter, a noted historian and teacher, who saw the relevance of how different cultures in different times and places were biased towards different Archetypal consciousness. They made a good mix of established thinking, logic, art and metaphysics. The initial insights began with looking at the sequences of Elements (Described in their own chapter). It is impossible to attribute specific parts of the work to any of the four, each contributed as the Twelve Archetypes began to emerge and reveal themselves, and for several years there were arguments, debates and difficulties as accuracy was paramount. No one was allowed to get away with anything, all four had to see it for themselves, and there were still some areas on which there was uncertainty and disagreement. Finally, Richard had the inspired idea of asking Tammo to paint them, in the hope that this might bring clarification. It did. Tammo did a brilliant job, and as a result changes, refinements and additions were made until finally all four were satisfied. They tried to break the work, they challenged everything; these four very different, brilliant brains hammered it out, they looked for flaws until they found none. Here was The Philosopher's Stone.

Richard Gardner published "The Purpose of Love" in 1970, which contains his insights into consciousness in general and the first explanation of the Twelve Archetypes. Without him, the Work would never have begun, he was its father, planting the seeds, helping them to grow, and he was its midwife, bringing it out into the world and doing all he could to further it. His genius should be recognised, he devoted his life to the Work and died disappointed that the world did not embrace and utilise it as he had hoped. It may never do so, but I offer this book with the wish that it may contribute to the healing of the world, and that his remarkable being, and that of the three others, did not live in vain. Tammo's booklet *"The Magic Circle of the Soul. The twelve aspects of the mind"* came out a year later, in 1971. It was written with the cooperation of Richard Gardner, Kenneth Carter and Barry Slater and is not solely Tammo's work. It should be clarified that Tammo was not the sole originator of the Twelve, everything in his booklet is the pooled work of the four. Richard Gardner published "The Wheel of Life" in 1980, a further description of the Twelve based on work he and I did together. I wrote a large amount of my insights about the Archetypes, and passed them to him to include, so in a way it was co-written, although my name is not on the book, but is dedicated to me. I have since extended the work, so in this sense, it is my work too. It belongs to me, as it does to anyone who appreciates and contributes to it.

I was born in Glasgow, Scotland, from a Scottish father and a Greek Cypriot mother and I began my search for answers as soon as I was able to think. I was lucky in that, because my parents belonged to different churches, I escaped heavy indoctrination. I became a 'hippy' in my late teens/early twenties, having decided that the 'normal' lifestyle was not for me, seeking an alternative and answers to my questions. I smoked dope, which I believe to be of a better and gentler quality in those days and it certainly expanded my consciousness. We original hippies did not take substances for escapism, or in order to numb ourselves, as often seems to be the way today. We did it to awaken ourselves, to see more, to be more, to do more, understand more. It was part of my journey towards expanding my consciousness, it opened new ways of seeing. When I found the Work in my early twenties, I had no further need for it, although, of course, there is a great deal of my consciousness that still needs to be expanded. This is not to say that I advocate taking drugs, things were different then, and these days there are far more drugs available, some addictive and dangerous.

I first came across the Work in 1970, by which time I was more than ready. I had an infant daughter, and worked as a live-in carer, first to a little boy and next as a general skivvy and nanny to a family. I had strong reasons for not wishing to remain in those houses and so moved again into a family with two little boys. There was a park nearby where I would take my daughter to get some peace and consider what to do. There was a little stream where we sat, and one day a group of people joined us a little distance away. Seeing me alone, one of them approached, offered me a drink and asked if I would like to join them. They looked interesting, colourful and friendly, proper hippies in fact, and they had three little girls with whom my daughter started to play. I met them several times and they came to know of my situation. Soon after that they invited me to move into their large house in Hampstead Garden suburb, which one of them owned. We had a happy, dynamic commune there, but change was coming. Shortly before we went our separate ways, Tammo's booklet arrived at the house. I was very interested in it, but it lacked a certain dynamic, so I moved back to Glasgow, Scotland and resumed my search, although it stayed in the back of my mind.

I had a collection of over 200 beautiful postcards, some of them old, with beautiful embroidery and pictures. I kept them wrapped up in a cupboard. I was living in a shared rented house, and one day I showed them to a girl who was there for a short visit with one of the other tenants. I didn't know her very well at all, but I sensed she would like my postcards. She fell in love with them and I saw that unlike me, she wouldn't shut them away, and would appreciate them more. So I gave them to her. She returned shortly afterwards with a book to gift me in return. It was *'The Tarot Speaks'* by Richard Gardner and told me how to read the Tarot cards. As I already had a pack, I got busy. It all made sense and I was able to follow it and learn, unlike other books which had merely confused me. It explained the philosophy enclosed within the Major Arcana which started to answer some of my questions. Not long after, I received a postcard, this one more precious and valuable than the ones I had given away. It was from one of the commune members, the man who had owned the house in London. He, his partner and their children had moved to Wales and invited me to visit. Thank goodness we had stayed in touch. The card asked me if I had heard of Richard Gardner. Of course I had, and it seems like the Work itself was sending me messages. I was impelled to get to Wales right away. I took my daughter, who was barely two at the time, and asked a male friend to come with me.

We hitch-hiked all the way, finding nothing but kindness, and we arrived safely. (Hitching lifts is not something I would recommend either these days). Within minutes I saw a book lying on the floor and I picked it up. It was *'The Purpose of Love'* by Richard Gardner, the first book about the work. I had read but a few pages when I knew my search was over. Even so, I started by trying to find the gaps in it. I was not going to take anyone's word for anything. I'd explored enough 'isms' and 'ologies' and 'paths' that led nowhere thank you very much - I was looking for something real. Before long, I realised I couldn't break it; Water exists, Fire exists, the Earth exists, Air exists, and our beings depend on and are shaped by them. It's interesting that Richard Gardner noted that he was most identified with the Earth element, Tammo de Jongh with Fire, Kenneth Carter with Water and Barry slater with Air. The combination of all four gave the work its strength. Richard said I was working for the Centre, that I pulled it all together and gave it life. It turned out he was right, but I didn't feel complimented to be honest, instead it felt like a massive responsibility. It still does, especially as I am the only one of the five who is still here. I strive to be worthy of the job.

Richard's address was on a sticker in the book, so as soon as I returned home I wrote to him. A few weeks later, on Burn's Night, he came to see me in Glasgow and we were together for twenty-seven years, until his death. fill out Finally, I put the Centre on centre stage when I wrote a play, *'The Wheel of Life'*, which brought the Archetypes to life, and in 1987 I published my booklet *"The Wheel of Life, the Practice"*, which contains the rhyming speeches of invocation I wrote for the play. I have since updated and polished them, and have included an improved speech for the Worker/Slave in this book. I played the Centre in the play, the light, the evolved being who rises from the middle of the circle, by no means because I was so far advanced, but simply because there was no one else who knew the Work well enough to be able to play it. It was hugely popular, people came again and brought others with them and we ended up with some sitting in the aisles and standing at the back. Audiences described it as a mixture of Ancient Greek Drama, Fairyland and Shakespeare. At the end of the play, it was magical, a golden glow filled the room, there was no division between the performers and audience, all basked in the beautiful energy created. People were excited, their faces beaming, as they began sharing with each other how they recognized themselves, their loved ones and friends in the Archetypes. I was asked why it wasn't on television or the West End. Unless the play was experienced, no one could see it for what it is, so money and sponsorship made it impossible for me to further it. I would love to be able to produce it again.

I had many daily experiences which proved that the Work works, small events that added up to major steps forward. One of the Archetypes in which I used to live too much was the Child, which was a bit of a nuisance. There was a small supermarket close to where Richard and I lived in Brighton, with an extremely nosy woman at the till. She was always asking me personal questions and the meek little Child in me had no option but to answer, even though I didn't want to. One day I practiced the Warrior and went out shopping. In the shop, an objectivity came over me, as I saw my usual performance in there. I was disgusted with myself for being so weak, so I brought on the Warrior, who stomped me round the shop at the double, marched me to the till and had me completely ignoring the woman's prying. I dealt with her politely, packed my things, paid and stomped out. She wasn't too pleased, but I laughed with elation. This was the first time I had consciously used an Archetype and I revelled in the little spurt of growth and freedom. I ran all the way home to tell Richard and we had champagne.

Richard could be very funny when he used his Fool. In a bus queue, instead of getting straight on the bus, he would run and skip all the way round it and have me convulsed with laughter at the shocked and puzzled faces around me. He loved to surprise people in the hope they might awaken a little. Sometimes Richard, Tammo, Tommy (Tammo's partner) and I would travel together on a bus in London. Tammo was always so loud and colourful in his robes, long white hair and beard. One day I couldn't sit with the others as the bus was full. I meekly listened to the criticism about him, nodding my head, pretending to agree. Such embarrassed faces when we reached our stop and Tammo called 'Come on Magenta darling', and we got off together. Me giving them all a big smile and a wave. We were very naughty. Tammo called me 'The Lady of the Twelve', and Richard had two nicknames for me - Portia when I argued with him until he got my point, and Columbine when I was being poetic and creative.

Richard and Tammo are dead, they went within months of each other in 1997, and it is likely that Kenneth and Barry have also passed on, as it is some time since I heard from them. I am the last living original authority of the Work, left to carry its light. It is my fervent wish that it travels far, igniting more light and enlightenment throughout the world.
Richard bought the copyright to Tammo's illustrations of the Work and the original paintings of the Twelve. I was bequeathed the copyright to Tammo de Jongh's paintings of the Archetypes and all of Richard Gardner's work, in the hope that I would continue to bring this knowledge forward, and so I

humbly present it to you that its brilliance will enhance your life and all on earth. Carrying the jewel that is the Work is hard, the responsibility is heavy, but I mean to keep going and to do better, to keep working on myself so that I continue to live, in spite of blows I have suffered. Most of us suffer sooner or later in the world as it is, but healing is always possible. The Work might take off and then I will be needed. You never know, miracles can happen. Humility is essential if we are to take any steps forward. All I can say is, if you're comfortable with where you're at, well and good. I wouldn't dream of persuading you otherwise. If you want to grow and be something special, use this work and be remarkable. I'm told that everyone thinks they have the answer and I'm no different; in fact people think I'm madder than most, but -

"People think you are crazy if you talk about things they don't understand." - *Elvis Presley*

Looking back, I see that my own role was as mother to the Work, to nurture and protect it, to help it fill out, to grow strong and healthy, to breathe life into the Archetypes, to put flesh on their bones, and bid them to arise and speak, to show their gifts clearly to the world that it may see their rainbow circle, its Centre shining divine light through the middle. I hope it grows and delights the world. By practicing this Work, you will be enabled to reach and shine your own magical light. It's the most exciting, proactive, multi-faceted journey there is. Self-evolution is the only way to go. Let us open our hearts and enjoy the trip together.

"If you wish to understand the Universe, think of energy, frequency and vibration." - *Nikola Telsa*

Time, Eternity, and The Quest for Truth

"There is a force in the universe which, if we permit it, will flow through us and produce miraculous results." - *Mahatma Gandhi*

Anything is Possible

"The problems of this world cannot possibly be solved by sceptics or cynics whose horizons are limited by the obvious realities. We need men who can dream of things that never were."
- *John Keats*

You may find some of these ideas outlandish, but then it's not so long ago when it was thought impossible to fly in the sky in a metal container. Leonardo da Vinci (1452 – 1519), was way ahead of his time, he designed flying machines, among other remarkable inventions. We need open minds and hearts and be prepared to expand our expectations and imaginations to accept that anything is possible. We have to realise how much we influence everything that happens to us, including illness, ageing and dying before we can be more objective about alternative possibilities. More people are coming to realise just how much power we have in and over ourselves. The form that further human evolution could take can only be known once we put this work into practice. So what are you thinking now? This is too simple to be real? Or could this be a Work of pure genius, just what the world needs? Are you sorry that the rescue formula has been found? Are you still clinging to the 'leave it to science' mentality? This work demands that we face reality, it gives us no more excuses. We are all exposed within this Work, all our current faces are on the wheel of consciousness. What are we going to do about it? See the light and evolve ourselves? Argue about it? Dismiss the Work? Live or die? Maybe something below will help you to make your choice.

Can we change our DNA? Possibly. There has been debate in recent years about stem cells (multi-potential cells) that are found in most tissues of the adult body. They have an amazing ability, which is to specialize into every cell of the body and replace those that are malfunctioning. Neuronal stem cells have been found, so even brain cells can be replaced. In 'What if?' the documentary movie (by

James A Sinclair), Dr Bruce Lipton, cell biologist, reports that through Epigenetic research they found that epigenetic techniques - perceptional shift techniques - create 30,000 variations on each gene blueprint. He says that "We are not victims of our genes – WE ARE THE PROGRAMMERS of our genes." Our brain capacity is enormous. These statistics were reported in the book 'The Brain that Changes Itself' by Dr Norman Doidge. "The human cortex alone has 30 billion neurons and is capable of making 1 million billion synaptic connections. Possible neural circuits: 10 followed by at least a million zeros...for comparison, there are an estimated 10 followed by 79 zeros particles in the known universe…" Therefore -

"Keep your thoughts positive, because your thoughts become your words. Keep your words positive, because your words become your behaviours. Keep your behaviours positive, because your behaviours become your habits. Keep your habits positive, because your habits become your values. Keep your values positive, because your values become your destiny." - Gandhi

Looking for Truth.

War

I arrived with a questioning mind and a 'what if?' approach to life. From the age of four I was asking questions. I was born soon after World War Two, which I heard referred to as 'The Great War'. This made no sense to me, as people spoke of the millions who had died and how much suffering had been endured. I asked "Why was it called a 'great war' when it was so bad?" The only answers I got were either an indulgent smile with a shake of the head or some rubbish about my being only a child and not old enough to understand. I asked men who had been in the war if they liked it, if it really was 'great' and they said it was a terrible thing and they didn't want to talk about it. Then I wanted to know why they went. I was told that only cowards refused to fight and were called conscientious objectors. Further investigation revealed that these anti-war people were despised by society and could be imprisoned for their beliefs in peace. It seemed to me that they had the right idea and that they should be the ones getting all the medals. By now I was convinced I had landed in a mad world. At the same time, the people who stayed at home said it was the best time ever, things changed and they felt like they were really living. So war was bad for those who fought it and only great for those who didn't? Yet I also learned that many who stayed at home were bombed and killed. It didn't add up. Later, I learned through this Work that conflict arises when the Warrior Archetype is out of control. Not only did I have to realise that killing was popular and peace was not, but that other things I perceived were unpopular too. I was in a maze of questions.

Strange Gifts

Suspend disbelief for the moment. From the age of three, I was able to astrally project at will. This is an Enchantress Archetype ability. People were amazed at what a good and quiet child I was, particularly when my mother took me visiting to see her friends. What they didn't know was that at the same time as I was sitting quietly doing and saying nothing, I was amusing myself by exploring their house and enjoying my wanderings. I made sure to stay indoors in case I was spoken to and needed to get back in my body in a hurry. One experience I had proved to me that this travelling around was real, but I was mistaken to think that everybody could do it as a normal thing. One day when I was four, my mother was taking my baby brother and I out, and took me downstairs to wait by the front door beside the pram while she went to get the baby. She seemed to be a very long time, so I went back upstairs and into the room where I thought I'd find her, but she wasn't there. Meanwhile, she went downstairs with my brother and went out. I looked all over the house and then sat down on my own little stool with my name painted on it, wondering what to do now. I expected I'd be in trouble for not doing what I was told. On finding me gone, my mother panicked. She locked up the house, with me inside, and went to look for me. I was nowhere to be seen, so she called my father from his work and a search party was organized. I got tired of waiting, so I went back downstairs, out the front door and soon found lots of people looking for me, calling my name. I thought they'd be pleased to see me, but everyone ignored me. I kept yelling "I'm here, here!" but no one seemed to hear me or see me. I ran around like this for some time but to no avail. Deflated, confused and not a little frightened, I went home and sat back down on my stool. Some time later, my distressed parents returned talking about calling the police, only to find me sitting quietly. As I expected, I was given a severe telling off for scaring everybody, but what was worse was that when I tried to tell them that I had been outside showing myself to them and telling them I was there, they didn't believe me. I was told I imagined it, even when I was able to describe exactly where they were and who said what to whom. They couldn't hide from me the fact that what I was saying was true, nor could they equate this with the actuality that I was physically locked inside the house with no keys to let myself in or out. I was forced to drop it and accept that I might be different and I had better be careful. Over the years, I lost the ability to astrally project naturally and developed a fear of it which lasted throughout my youth.

Life or Death?

When I was about eight, I had a vision, which was that everyone was born with a white heart and every lie we told and every bad thing we did made a black spot appear on it. When the black spots joined up and the heart was completely black, we died. I saw how unhappiness, anger and other negative feelings made black dots too. The only way to avoid it was to stay happy, kind and good. It made perfect sense to my young mind. It still does. As a teenager, I became fascinated by books I found in the library, particularly those on Alchemy, which spoke of The Fountain of Eternal Youth and the Philosopher's Stone, which I now realise is the true Centre in us all, that place within us against which anything can be touched and tested. The true will remain and the false will shatter. None of these books, however, told me how to achieve this eternal youth.

"Unable are the loved to die, for love is immortality.' - *Emily Dickinson.*

I continued my quest, subjecting myself to every 'ism', 'ology', religion and cult I could find and I learned something from them all, but was frustrated to find that they all ended up in the same dead end…stone cold dead. Not only that, but they all declared that other beliefs were wrong and only they had the one true answer. They all, however, shared deathism. I'd never heard other people talking about not dying, it was supposed to be a natural thing that happened to every living thing. I could see that it was true that people died, but I had also seen the way to avoid it. I naively thought that my explanation about how being good and loving would allow us to carry on living would be warmly received. No chance. No one taught how we could avoid death, although I knew Jesus said that his God was a God of the living, not of the dead and love was the answer. We know what happened to him for his trouble. I was not reassured.

This was the next hard lesson - people are committed to death and dying, and in the story Jesus was crucified for preaching Immortal life. Even the Old Testament tells us that "The wages of sin is death" - Romans 6:23. There are many references from ancient times about ending death, and if we view the New Testament as a new teaching, apart from the Old Testament, we might begin to understand it. I sometimes wonder if anyone has actually read it. If so, they certainly haven't understood it. Jesus could be regarded as a white magician. From across Greece to Israel and further into the Middle East, there was an expectation of the future healing of the body. Jesus spoke openly and directly of what His way of healing was about. He saw death as the thief of life. *"The thief cometh not, but for to steal, and to kill, and to destroy: I am come that they might have life, and that they might have it more abundantly." - John 10:10*

He claims to have the code to ending death. *"And when I saw Him, I fell at His feet as dead. And He laid His right hand upon me, saying unto me, Fear not; I am the first and the last; I am He who lives, and was dead; and, behold, I am alive for evermore, Amen - and have the keys of hell and of death." - Rev. 1:17, 18.* This is clear, though most people think he's talking about after they die. *"And God shall wipe away all tears from their eyes; and there shall be no more death, neither sorrow, nor crying, neither shall there be any more pain…He will swallow up death in victory…" 11.5 Isaiah 25:8.*

I thought good luck to them if they think they can ignore all the teachings and still arrive in some marvellous happily-ever-after place. The Bible, the Greek philosophers and many other nations' clergy spoke of the day mankind would end aging and death. We need not be limited to the Bible, research will disclose these kinds of thoughts in other times and cultures. I tried talking to adults about all this, but no one had any answers, just 'run along and play' or told repeatedly that I was going to die and that you couldn't get to heaven unless you were good. From that I surmised that most people were going the other way as they were creating Hell on earth with little sign of universal goodness. It still seemed to me to be the other way round, that being good kept you alive and badness killed you. I determined to prove them wrong and wondered how I could resolve certain difficulties, a main one being that by the time I reached 200, all those people to whom I was proving it would be dead, and no longer around to see it, so I'd have to start all over again with another generation. We had yet to reach the technological age, so recording the evidence was not going to be easy. This was coupled with the fear of what might happen to me if I claimed to be 200 plus and was observed for 50 years and found to be not ageing. I had seen how others had fared throughout the centuries for trying to enlighten humanity about evolution. I told my mother I was going to save the world through teaching Physical Immortality and to my amazement she didn't argue with me, she simply said "They'll kill you". I said that someone, sooner or later, must manage it.

Where is the Female?
As a child, the Church was of no use to me at all. It had no wish to address any of my questions, one

of the main ones being "Where is Jesus's mother?" "Mary" they said, "Mary is his mother". "No" I said, "Mary was his mother on earth and Joseph was his father on earth. He has a Heavenly Father, so where is his Heavenly Mother?" There was no satisfactory reply to this, leaving me with a feeling of deep frustration, as something was patently missing. Mary ascended to heaven they said, but I stubbornly clung to my feelings that there should have been a Heavenly Mother there in the first place. Years later, when I was privileged to become part of this Work, and then ventured into learning about the world of Goddesses, it was clear how most organized religions are dominated by the Patriarch, hence 'the old man with a beard' image of God. This Archetype has made God in his own image, but for thousands of years God was worshipped worldwide as female. Approximately 5,000 years ago, the patriarchal takeover began and almost all that is female power was oppressed. This has had a bad effect not only on women, but also on men, suppressing their emotions and feelings, cutting them off from their own inner female powers and encouraging mainly the male Archetypes. It has caused a great deal of unhappiness. Thus, we have increasing Warrior conflicts, 'progress' viewed from the purely scientific and technical viewpoint of the Logician, and the Joker lying and manipulating his way to 'success', all in the service of the Wise Woman who collects the money. There is a great deal of information about the ancient female-based religions if anyone one wishes to know more. The Pagan, Wiccan and Goddess movements are more egalitarian than the established religions, recognizing both the male and female aspects of deity, but being marginalized and ridiculed as they are, often they dip a mere toe in the waters of female powers. Having said that, you don't have to believe in Gods and Goddesses to practice this work, it's enough to have faith in your own potential. Encouraging the development of all the Archetypes in both sexes brings hope that we can bring peace and co-operation to earth.

When I was about thirteen, I invited some Jehovah's Witnesses to visit me, much to my mother's horror. They came several times, took me to a Kingdom Hall and proved as useless as everyone else, although rather persistent I have to say. I only managed to deter them by asking impossible questions such as "What is time?" and "Who is Goddess?" "Is sex good and when should I start?" I knew they couldn't answer and I never saw them again. They weren't the only ones, my young open mind was often considered ripe for conversion, but I could close it too when needed.

Answers

Before I reached my teens I learned these four things:

1 – The world prefers conflict to peace.
2 - There are other aspects of consciousness that are unpopular with the majority.
3 - People embrace death because they fear life.
4 - The female aspects of consciousness are oppressed in both sexes.

Through the years of my search, I had a reliable Geiger counter for truth. As soon as they told me death was inevitable, I moved on. When I found this Work in my early twenties, I knew my search was over, as Richard Gardner was the only person who answered my questions about life, death and evolution. I was then able to round out my insights a bit more.

1- People prefer conflict to peace because we favour the Warrior and other Yang, male Archetypes overmuch.
2 - There are other aspects of consciousness that are unpopular with the majority, which are mainly female, Yin ones - the Child, the Enchantress and Mother Nature.
3 - People embrace death and fear life more because they are disconnected from their Centres.
4 - The female aspects of consciousness are oppressed in both sexes because under a patriarchy the male archetypes are favoured over the female.

Is it possible that taken to its extreme we may be able to evolve onto a higher level where we would no longer need to die? Who knows where evolution will go next? If that's too far-fetched for you, at the very least it can heal on the personal, social and global areas through bringing greater understanding, health, harmony, excitement and peace. It's surely worth it for that.
"Death is a bad thing, for if death were a good thing, the Gods also would die" – Sappho
We mustn't deceive ourselves into thinking we have all twelve Archetypes already developed. To have all Twelve alive and working in us would mean that we were like Gods or Goddesses already, no longer subject to decay and death and with all magical powers at our fingertips. Evolution is not just looking backwards, it is looking ahead, realising the process has not ended and seeing the possibility of becoming greater. One of the ultimate aims of developing the whole spectrum of consciousness is the transformation of the flesh. The molecular structure of our bodies would vibrate at a higher frequency. We would be transformed. We have performed miracles and achieved so much in the outer world. It is time now to do the same in our inner world. Tom Fry, a physicist at the top of

his profession, believed that if we became worthy through further evolution, the flesh would transform during sleep. The 'impossible' is always possible. Aerodynamically, the bumblebee shouldn't be able to fly, but it doesn't know that, so it flies anyway.

What is Time?

"Surely God would not have created such a being as man, with an ability to grasp the infinite, to exist only for a day! No, no, man was made for immortality." - Abraham Lincoln

If we think about time we could ask, "What is it?" We might say it's something we take for granted, a clock by which we live our daily lives and an allotted span given to us to experience life on earth. We don't normally question it any further. We know that a second is part of a minute, which is part of an hour, which is part of a day - but what is a day? A day is the earth revolving once on her axis, so that each part is exposed to the sun giving us what we know as night and day. What is a month? A month is the full orbit of the moon around the earth which takes 28 earth days approx. What is a year? A year is the full orbit of the earth around the sun, which gives us our seasons. We could say that time is planetary movements. If you lived on Mercury your year would be 88 Earth days as it whizzes round the sun, but Saturn takes around 29 earth years and the outermost planet, Pluto takes 248 earth years. The experience of time, therefore, is simply where we are in space, relative to the planet on which we find ourselves, and is not universally fixed. This means that our idea of time is a human concept which negates our ability to see eternity. Yet we experience time differently according to how we feel in particular situations; time drags when we are bored, we speak of 'killing time' and 'time flies' when we are happy. We see that time is not fixed, it changes according to our perceptions. So is time an illusion? Are there other ways of measuring experience within our living framework? Is it possible that all time, past, present and future exists together all at once and that we are unable, with our present limited consciousness, to experience it?

I had a vision of time, where I saw two wheels with cogs around the outside, eternally turning. They made the Infinity symbol, (an eight lying on it is side), one went clockwise and represented the future, one turned anti-clockwise and represented the past, and where the cogs met on their way round was the present. It seemed that if I could be alive to these wheels inside myself, I would be in all of time and in eternity too. It has been said that if trauma is cleared from the present, it can change the future. This is indeed true, but it is also said that it can change the past, bringing healing to the ancestors. Can it be? I don't know, but I keep an open mind, as I have had experiences which have caused me to re-examine what I once thought about many things. The Tarot depicts Time as an angelic winged form with an urn in each hand, one containing male, Yang energy and the other female, Yin energy. She constantly pours one from the other to create the perfect blend and when this has been achieved, she will fly away. Eternity needs no time. Our present understanding of time as finite causes us to live our lives with the expectation of an end, so we say things like "How quickly the years go", "Life is short", we think of 'spending time' and 'wasting time', we say "For the rest of my life", "With my last breath", "I want to grow old with you", "A lifelong commitment" and the marriage service contains the words "Until death do us part". We use common phrases like 'retirement', 'middle age', 'a lifetime', 'a once in a lifetime experience', 'Time is a great leveller', 'It's all downhill after forty', and tell each other, "At our age we have to start taking things easy", and imagine it's too late to try new things and go in new directions. Many of us take life after death for granted and believe our loved ones will communicate with us 'from beyond the grave' and will be there to meet us. Deathist attitudes exist in many commonly used phrases – "I'm dying to do that", it's dead simple, it's dead easy, 'it's a dead weight', 'that's a dead cert', it's a dead end,' 'a deadline', 'Life's a bitch and then you die'. These concepts exert a powerful effect on our bodies, and therefore our ageing processes, and create destructive subconscious and self-fulfilling expectations of old age and physical decline. Our futures become full of anxiety and negative images and we programme ourselves to how much time we have left. We lose our joy, optimism and excitement about life. We ask "How old are you?", never "How young?" or "How long have you been here?" It's seldom that the media doesn't state a person's age, whatever they're reporting. In respect of life after death, I'm asking "Is there life *before* death?" Can we really call the struggle and pain-filled existence the majority of us are living 'life'? Of course we hope for a way out of it, but I'm pretty sure there's a better way than turning into a cadaver.

"I don't want to achieve immortality through my work; I want to achieve immortality through not dying. I don't want to live on in the hearts of my countrymen; I want to live on in my apartment." – Woody Allen

How can we be positive there is anything afterwards? I think there are many dimensions, but how do we know we won't be given a 'fail' on the other side and sent back here to try again, with another set of problems to deal with? Maybe it's just oblivion, in which case that might be okay, but is it worth the risk of it not being all over, of there being no permanent love and light on 'the other side'? Given a choice of how you'd achieve something, would you choose to try it as a healthy, living, breathing body or a stinking corpse? I don't think my rotting corpse could achieve very much at all, so I'd rather be alive and try to evolve myself, consciously and now. At the very least I'll live longer and better.

We don't have to wait until we die to experience Heaven or Nirvana. Our true magnificence exists right here, right now" - Anita Moorjani

What would happen if we changed our minds about time? Where did we get the idea that we have three score years and ten (70) as our allotted time and that's it? A major source is the Old Testament of the Bible, which has programmed us to expect to live this average time span, although science has pushed it a little further; yet the Bible itself tells of Methuselah who lived to be nearly 1,000 and there are many more stories in various cultures of people who have lived much longer than the usual. Here's a thought. What if we stopped telling our children they might be lucky to live past 80? What if we tell them instead that 300 years is the norm? I bet that within two or three generations it would happen. Is it not possible that sooner or later Time, or Temperance as she is also called, would call her work done and fly away, leaving us in a new dimension, one we may call Infinity or Eternity?

"Time is very slow for those who wait,
Very fast for those who are scared,
Very long for those who lament,
Very short for those who celebrate,
But for those who love, time is eternal." - William Shakespeare.

Living Forever?

"The last enemy that shall be destroyed is death" - Corinthians 1:15
"He is not the God of the dead, but the God of the living: ye therefore do greatly err."
- *King James Bible. Mark 12:27*

If you're young or remember being young, you'll know that feeling of thinking you're immortal. We pass it off as the illusion of youth, but what if we're right? What if we arrive with an innate knowledge that is ruthlessly bashed out of us from the earliest age? We see people going to some lengths to retain their youth, using cosmetic surgery, Botox and healthier approaches, such as a raw diet. We may dismiss this as vanity, and in many cases it is, with the added pressure of society's dictates in how we should look. Yet there is that underlying sense that staying young is better than ageing and dying. Of course it is. We are told death is natural, yet we resist it. The problem lies in humanity not having had true and lasting means whereby they can constantly re-energise themselves. I can guarantee that practicing this Work with sincerity will result in rejuvenation and more of the life force.

In a similar vein, I've wondered about the 'phantom limb' phenomenon. It's reported that when someone loses a limb they can still feel it and it often itches and hurts. So what if the feeling that the limb is still there is, in actuality, the energy shape into which a new limb could grow, but doesn't because we block it by thinking it's impossible? This might not be as outlandish as you think. Just like other life forms that live apparently forever, so can other creatures regenerate parts of themselves, so it is biologically possible. Unlike humans, these creatures are not burdened by conditioned thoughts that block the processes of life. Here are some examples –

* Lizards who lose all or part of their tails are able to grow new ones. Most lizards will regrow a tail within nine months.
* Planarians are flat worms. If you cut them into pieces each piece can grow into a whole new worm.
* It's the same with sea cucumbers that can grow to three feet long. Cut into pieces, each one can become a new sea cucumber.
* Sharks continually replace their teeth and could grow 24,000 new ones in a lifetime.
* Spiders can re-grow missing legs or parts of legs.
* When Sponges are divided, cells of the sponge will re-grow and combine exactly as before.
* Starfish that lose arms can grow new ones. Sometimes an entire animal can grow from a single lost arm.
* Salamanders and newts can regenerate almost any part of the body as long as it's not killed by the loss. They can regenerate their tails, spinal cord, parts of the eye, part of the heart, brain and more.
*The Turritopsis dohrnii, also known as the immortal jellyfish, is a species of small, biologically immortal jellyfish found in the Mediterranean Sea and in the waters of Japan. They are small, transparent animals who can turn back time by reverting to an earlier stage of their life cycle

What if we lived our lives tuned into a 'What if' attitude? Imagine how things might change.

"There are more things in heaven and earth, Horatio, than are dreamt of in your philosophy."
– Hamlet. William Shakespeare.

Most people want to live long, healthy, youthful lives but also claim that they don't want to live forever, and under present circumstances it's understandable. The reason that life becomes unbearable is the pain of our present way of existing, which brings about illness, grief and age which can only be tolerated up to a certain degree, so we'd rather die and end it. It is the presence of death itself that tricks us into not wanting to live. Let me ask you a question. If you were offered a potion that guaranteed physical immortality, would you take it? Are you more afraid of death or life? We need not worry about being forced into living interminably in the horrors of our present world because to break the grip of death would require an evolved species that replaces disease with health, suffering with joy, hatred with love and eventually, life with death.

"With love there is no death." - Prince

The Banquet There are two drawings. They are the same size and setting. We are in a banqueting hall, people are sitting around a large, round table which is piled high with delicious food and drink. One drawing shows skeletons slumped at the table, their clothes hanging off them and food all over the place. In the other drawing, the people are laughing, talking, well-filled out and happy looking. Both parties have been supplied with all they need to stay alive and well, but all have the same problem. Their elbows don't bend. In the alive version, the people have solved the problem by reaching their straight arms out and putting food and drink into the waiting mouth of the person next to them, and turn to the other side to be fed. The message is clear. Until we decide to help each other to use all of our talents to create a better world, we can never know what we could accomplish. The attempt itself would be a happier experience, however long we were able to live. The more love and goodwill we spread, the healthier we would be and longevity would increase. It's hurt that kills us, we are all suffering from not enough love. Even those who are happy now will eventually die because people are not giving out enough love to sustain life. Stagnation is a major killer. When our consciousness stands still we are on a downward spiral, sinking lower and lower until we become aged caricatures of ourselves. When we are moving we get onto an upward spiral.

We die in the Archetypes in which we are stuck. Life is in our Centres. Living from our Centres means that each Archetype becomes a life enhancer and movement becomes easier and joyful. There are people around who support that physical immortality is possible. It is wonderful indeed that so many are awakening to the idea of our further evolution, but it can only be thus if we use all our Archetypes to consciously make it happen. Just thinking it and saying it isn't enough, many practices need to be brought into play to effect real and lasting change. It will take all we have, collectively, to create a major shift. All too often, faith is again put into the Logician, believing that science will discover how to attain physical immortality. Is it as easy as popping pills? I have my doubts. Taking pills or having our genes manipulated will not bring lasting benefits. Of course science has a role to play, but the powers of the other Archetypes must be included. These pioneers of thought, however, are making superb contributions in challenging the existing belief systems. Rebirthing is one, and Sondra Ray, one of the original Rebirthers, says,

" ...who would want to live forever in a body that was old, decrepit, and full of pain? Nobody But do you know that your body is full of pain, or has any pain, because you are hanging onto the death urge in the first place? Trying to live while holding onto the thought that death is inevitable is like driving a car forward with the gears in reverse and/or with the brakes on. Eventually it just will not work. The body cannot resolve that conflict in the mind. It is getting mixed instructions. Since all pain is the effort involved in clinging to a negative thought, and since the worst anti-life negative thought is death (the opposite of life), then you can begin to see how death thoughts and old age thoughts lead to pain ..." - *"How to be Chic, Fabulous and Live Forever" by Sondra Ray*

We have the capacity to create miracles. What if we changed our minds about ageing and began to regard age as a chronic disease – dis-ease, a lack of ease within? If we believe that physical death is inevitable, we are either creating the way out slowly through dragging out an illness or we put ourselves in the wrong place at the wrong time to suffer a fatal accident and get out fast. Some of us deliberately commit suicide. Whichever way, we are programming ourselves with a 'death wish'. Think of water gushing out of a tap, you have the choice as to whether to keep it wide open and fully embrace the life force or you can turn it off a bit at a time, fading yourself out slowly. We are like barrels springing holes that we need to repair as soon as possible, we have to be vigilant to maintain our health and well-being and -

"Because the mind influences every cell in the body, human ageing is fluid and changeable, it can speed up, slow down, stop for a time, and even reverse itself. Hundreds of research findings from the last three decades have verified that ageing is much more dependent on the individual than was ever dreamed of in the past...to challenge ageing at its core, this entire world view must be challenged first, for nothing holds more power over the body than beliefs of the mind...We need to overturn the beliefs supported by fear. In place of the belief that your body decays with time, nurture the belief

that your body is new at every moment. In place of the belief that your body is a mindless machine, nurture the belief that your body is infused with the deep intelligence of life, whose sole purpose is to sustain you. These new beliefs are not just nicer to live with, they are true - we experience the joy of life through our bodies, so it is only natural to believe that our bodies are not set against us but want what we want." - Ageless Body Timeless Mind. - Deepak Chopra.

"'Tis very certain the desire of life prolongs it." - Lord Byron

Overpopulation

"Instead of controlling the environment for the benefit of the population, perhaps it's time we controlled the population to allow the survival of the environment." "The human population can no longer be allowed to grow in the same old uncontrolled way. If we do not take charge of our population size, then nature will do it for us" – David Attenborough

People say that there are enough people here already, some need to die to make room for the new ones. Overpopulation is out of control, terrifyingly so. We have not transcended to a higher level; we expect to die, we determine to die and we do, killing everything else with us as we go. We also do our best to ensure that we have added to the overpopulation problem before we go, thinking that is what is expected of us, and that passing on our genes is a way of achieving immortality. Considering that humanity is now also under threat of extinction, this is clearly a false premise. The only thing death does is create more death.

"Unlike plagues of the dark ages or contemporary diseases we do not yet understand, the modern plague of overpopulation is soluble by means we have discovered and with resources we possess. What is lacking is not sufficient knowledge of the solution but universal consciousness of the gravity of the problem." - Martin Luther King

Quantity and quality cannot exist together. We fail to live, so we pass the whole mess on to the next generation, which has increasingly worse problems to deal with. Have a fuck and pass the buck. We might speculate that there is a quantum amount of consciousness available to a maximum number of people and that we were once comprised of bigger souls which are becoming increasingly fractured, making increasingly smaller bits, resulting in less and less consciousness in each person. On the other hand, there is still an enormous amount of creativity, wisdom and intelligence in each of us, but we live in dumbed down societies, organised to schedules and mindsets that make it difficult for the true self to be reached. Perhaps as we evolve, numbers of us will find our group soul and then these reunited souls will unite with other group souls and so on, until we are all singing in the glorious harmony of oneness, whilst still retaining our individuality. In fact, it's only by fulfilling our individuality that we can attain true unity. The concept of 'dystopia' is swamping the culture; dystopian novels, dramas and art pointing the way things are going. The collective consciousness is getting fixed on it, and it's depressing and deadly dangerous. It comes forth from fear, anger, frustration, hopelessness and aggression. Can those who think my Utopian ideas are insane truly believe that I am the more mad? It seems to me that striving towards the actualisation of beautiful dreams is far saner than believing only in the perpetual horror of nightmares.

"History shows us that people who end up changing the world are always nuts, until they are right, and then they're geniuses." - John Eliot

"The saving of our world from pending doom will come, not through the complacent adjustment of the conforming majority, but through the creative maladjustment of a nonconforming minority." - Martin Luther King Jr.

Living fully and longer will mean fewer people, fewer babies being born, as there will not be the same urgency to breed. The environment will benefit too. It's easy not to care if you think you're going to die anyway and so you won't have to deal with it, but it's quite another matter if it's the world in which you intend to continue to live for a very, very long time, perhaps forever. This is similar to the difference between renting a house and owning it. Although by no means always the case, it can be observed that many who rent are less likely to care for a property than those who own it. This is how we treat our own bodies, our real homes. We see them as temporary, and therefore there is little point in caring for them as well as we could. Everyone accepts death, but no one wants to get old and ill. I can tell you that old age doesn't come alone. You will eventually suffer illness, aches and pains and die, for few are fortunate enough to die in perfect health. Those who remain in perfect health couldn't die. The fear of living forever in a decrepit body is an argument often heard, but of course it's not possible to exist like that. We would need to maintain our youth, which means the younger we start the better. We would need to transform our bodies with energy-filled youthfulness in order to prolong our lives.

"Every genius was first ridiculed before they were revered." - Robin Sharma

"Those who are unaware they are walking in darkness will never seek the light." - Bruce Lee.

Animal Life

Animals die too so it must be natural, right? Well it's normal but not necessarily natural and we don't know how long some species live. We are the most powerful animals on earth and all other creatures are subject to the energy we create. I believe that we take them up or down with us. As we evolved, we would emit wonderful healing powers which I am convinced would benefit all life forms, influencing their life spans and transforming them too. Perhaps nature need no longer be 'red in tooth and claw'. We don't really know what living organisms are capable of, some of them seem to be way ahead of us. Lobsters don't appear to age, they simply grow bigger and no one knows how long they can live. Some that have been caught and killed are thought to have been up to 140 years. Then there was a tortoise that died in 2006 and was so old at 176 that it was said to be a former pet of Charles Darwin. Apparently, biologically there is almost no difference between a juvenile turtle and one that's older than your great-great-grandparents, they seem to stop aging at some point. And then there's the amazing sea slug, which is solar powered. It eats algae and then incorporates the algae's chloroplasts into its own tissues until eventually it stops eating completely and lives off energy from the sun. There's a type of jellyfish that regenerates its cells indefinitely, the Planarian flatworm regenerates its cells and lives indefinitely and at 400 years, the clam may be the longest-lived animal known. It would appear that not all creatures have the same belief systems as humans regarding lifespan and the maintenance of life. As we become greater beings, we would start to live off the life of each other and not the death. As stewards of the whole planet, we would cease to drive other species to extinction, we would lift up the animal realms, and end the unbearable tearing of flesh in order to eat. The largest, strongest animals, such as the elephant, giraffe, hippo, rhino and gorilla are ahead of us - they are vegetarians. The large cats are an exception.

"The wolf also shall dwell with the lamb, and the leopard shall lie down with the kid; and the calf and the young lion and the fatling together; and a little child shall lead them." - Isaiah 11:6.

Has anyone actually read the Bible and all the other wonderful books of instruction? They sure didn't listen to my questions when I was a child and they've never listened to anyone before or since as far as I can see. We *can* live on Love alone; the promises of the great Masters and Mistresses are justified. Jesus, the Great White Magician promised us more LIFE. We would move into another dimension, full of bliss and ecstasy, where all our needs were satisfied and all our dreams came true.

"And death shall have no dominion." - Dylan Thomas

Life Through the Archetypes

"Within be fed, without be rich no more:
So shalt thou feed on Death, that feeds on men,
And, Death once dead, there's no more dying then." - Shakespeare. Sonnet 146

Oh ye of little faith. Due to the unbalanced influence of the Logician who rules science and the Patriarch who dominates organised religions, our imaginations and ability to have Faith have been seriously damaged. Our present leaders are simply pedlars of death on every level. This includes the majority of politicians, scientists and clergy. If you believe that we have the power to destroy our world, as we indeed do, then you should see that this is Black Magic at work. To transform ourselves to a higher level of consciousness is to become practitioners of White Magic and re-create the beautiful garden. There are no grey areas; those are illusions and cop-outs. We are either creating or destroying. We are so very powerful. It's hard living as we do, so why not try an easier, safer way? Isn't it better to end all the suffering and create happiness instead? What do we have to lose?...and how much there is to gain. Eternity may be too much for our minds to conceive at this point, but as our consciousness expands, more will be made known to us. Deep inside us we have a sense of this eternity, for we say "I will love you until the end of time". With enough love, I do believe we can end time and enter into a higher dimension.

"Life is better than death, I believe, if only because it is less boring, and because it has fresh peaches in it." - Alice Walker

Here is an important point. Both the Wise Woman and the Observer are composed of the two secondary elements, Air and Earth, which means they lack the two life-giving dynamics of Water and Fire. Our challenge is to repair this break in the circle and bring life into them, which can only be done by reconciling them with their conflicting opposites, The Actress (Water and Fire) and the Fool (Fire and Water), both of whom are composed of the two dynamic Elements. Looking at our present life cycle we see how we are on a deathist downward spiral. It's interesting that the veil that is said to divide the worlds of the living and the dead parts at Halloween, which falls in the month of the Wise Woman. Looking from an Archetypal perspective and going round the circle, we see that first there is conception, the beginning of new life in the Child. We are gestated in liquids in the Enchantress. We are created in the womb and enter the spotlight on the stage of life with the Actress. We respond to the environment with the Fool. We become aware and learn to manipulate our world with the Joker. We start going for what we want with the Warrior. We work and build our world with the

Worker/Slave. We make a home, with Mother Nature. Then we age and become a corpse in the Wise Woman. We turn into a skeleton with the Observer. We supposedly enter a tunnel of light with the Logician and we end up rigid in the rigor mortis of the Patriarch. Then we begin a new cycle and depending on what you believe this to be - simply a break up of our atoms, a going to a 'better place' or being reincarnated. To practise this Work and bring life into the Wise Woman and Observer would break this cycle, avoid many illnesses and significantly extend our life span.

As we evolve, we can lift ourselves to a finer vibration where we never suffer the lack of anything we need to keep us alive indefinitely. Looking at that part of the circle from the Wise Woman, to the Observer, the Logician and the Patriarch, rather than age when we arrive at the Wise Woman we can apply her wisdom to hold on to our lives by allowing the Fool to inject rejuvenation and we can move to the Observer and use his sight to look towards new enlightenment delivered by the Logician and really live it by reconciling with the Actress who, in her metaphysical womb, can aid in our rebirth. Then the knowledge we have gained can be held in the crown of the Patriarch and with renewed individuality we can begin anew on a life-affirming upward spiral with the Child. We would be constantly conceiving new life in our own bodies, growing ever more wonderful with each circuit. Up or down, we always have the choice. We just don't realise it. A woman in her forties, who is already looking older, can give birth to a perfect new human being. There is no reason she can't rebirth herself with the youth she has shown she can create. We perish in our Archetypes, that is to say we die because we get stuck in a very few of them. The states in which we have locked ourselves cause us to run out of energy, they wind us down. By keeping our Wheels of Life moving we can be constantly rewound, reborn, we can bring new energies in with each Archetype and fill ourselves with new life. This automatically makes us more loving. Then we can exchange these loving life energies with each other and create a world in which it is truly worth LIVING!

"Some pirates achieved immortality by great deeds of cruelty or derring-do. Some achieved immortality by amassing great wealth. But the captain had long ago decided that he would, on the whole, prefer to achieve immortality by not dying." - Terry Pratchett, *The Colour of Magic*

Here is an example of how our lack of imagination causes us to deny other dimensions because we exist in the dark. *(I'm sorry not to be able to give the unknown author credit.)*

In a mother's womb were two babies. One asked the other: "Do you believe in life after delivery?" The other replies, "Why, of course. There has to be something after delivery. Maybe we are here to prepare ourselves for what we will be later."

"Nonsense," says the other. "There is no life after delivery. What would that life possibly be like?"

"I don't know, but there will probably be more light than here. Maybe we will walk with our legs and eat from our mouths."

The other says, "This is absurd! Walking is impossible. And eat with our mouths? Ridiculous. The umbilical cord supplies nutrition. Life after delivery is to be excluded. The umbilical cord is too short."

"I think there is something and maybe it's different than it is here."

The other replies, "But nobody has ever come back from delivery. Delivery is the end of life. And what is life all about? Only a sad existence in the darkness, leading to nowhere."

"Well, I don't know," says the other, "but certainly we will see Mother and she will take care of us."

"Mother?? You believe in Mother? Where is She now, then?"

"She is all around us. We live through Her. Without Her all this world would not exist."

"Well, I cannot believe it! I never saw a Mom, therefore it's only logical that She doesn't exist."

To which the other replied, "Sometimes, if you are silent enough, you can hear Her singing, you can feel Her caressing our world."

What do you make of that? Did you translate it as a metaphor for dying, or does it symbolise faith in evolution and new levels of rebirth?

"I believe in the power of the imagination to remake the world, to release the truth within us, to hold back the night, to transcend death, to charm motorways, to ingratiate ourselves with birds, to enlist the confidences of madmen." - J.G. Ballard

"Whatever dies, was not mixed equally;
If our two loves be one, or, thou and I,
Love so alike, that none do slacken, none can die.."- From 'The Good-Morrow' by John Donne.

"As long as you live, keep learning how to live."- Seneca

Sex, Gender, and Evolution

"Be thou the rainbow in the storms of life. The evening beam that smiles the clouds away, and tints tomorrow with prophetic ray." - Lord Byron

I have tried not to express my own opinions on this subject, but if I do, I take full responsibility for them and acknowledge that others may not agree.

Sex and Gender

"Camouflage your soul! Hide! Hide! Hide! The gender police are here. The gender police are everywhere." - Judy Croome, A Lamp at Midday

At the time of writing, sex and gender is a contentious issue. We have viewed sex and gender as two different things - that 'sex' refers to biological and physiological characteristics, whilst 'gender' refers to behaviours, sexist roles, 'feelings', expectations, performances and activities in society. We saw that everyone is born with a biological sex and that no one is born with a sociological, subjective, psychologically constructed gender. It is said that male' and 'female' are sex categories, while 'masculine' and 'feminine' are behavioural categories. Research into the etymology of the word 'gender', however, defines it as an alternative to the word 'sex', and may have originated in the 17th century. 'Gender' meant 'sex', and was sometimes preferable to saying 'sex', in order to avoid confusing it with 'sexual intercourse'. It's obvious when you think about it – GENder – GENitals. In other words, what you have between your legs is your gender *and* your sex. GENisis is the origin of something, how you began, GENerations inherit what is passed down, and GENerative relates to reproduction, all based on biology. As far as I can tell, it was only in the second half of the 1990s that they were no longer conflated.

There are now objections to the word 'sex' as it relates to biology, and it is being increasingly dropped in favour of 'gender' because there is dispute as to whether biological sex exists. Negating biology by saying people can be anything they say they are, irrespective of their genitals, focuses only on 'gender'. This is contradictory, for to transition and change 'gender', there is only male and female from which to choose – two sexes. Even so, there is fierce activism to drop the term 'sex' and use only 'gender'. Denying scientific, medical fact that we are a binary species has resulted in confusion and conflict. If we dismiss the idea that, in the modern sense, gender and sex are two different things, we are left with social, sexual stereotypes. These often represent what people now call 'genders'. There's the floaty gay, limp wristed gay man, the butch lesbian in her overalls, the bomb shell sex object, the Rambo himbo, the, miserly old woman man with his little purse, the drag queen, who parodies a male idea of what women are, and many other instances, including fetishes. (If you know your Archetypes, you can see which ones are at work).

Sexual Orientation

This is simply the biological sex to which we are attracted. Gay men are attracted to men, lesbians are attracted to women, heterosexuals are attracted to the opposite sex, bisexuals are attracted to both sexes, and asexuals have low or no sexual feelings. These are the categories based on biology.

Back to the Work

How does the above tie in with the work? It would sort out a lot of argument regarding gender and sex for a start. We could accept that we are a binary species with male and female sexes, but use the Work to explore different parts of ourselves in individual ways, which would, in fact, remove the need for genders and the conflict that has come out of the argument. If gender is a 'feeling, as is claimed then, as everyone is different, there must be over seven and a half billion 'genders'. That's logical. If you are happy with your gender and sex roles and are harming nobody, excellent. The only right or wrong regarding these issues is the forcing of people into limiting gender, sexist roles which block individual development. A reminder that, as I said in the introduction to the Archetypes, there are six male and six female states of consciousness, but we are not talking about men and women and thus locking us further into stereotypical sexist roles. Either sex can adopt the mantle of any Archetype and see how it fits them, in their own way. This work liberates, it presents all the states of consciousness for anyone to use and develop. We are identifying the opposite male and female energies, the Yin and Yang, and applying them to both sexes. So, women can develop all of their female and male sides and men can develop all of their male and female sides. All are free to work with any Archetypes they wish, these Twelve States are applicable to everyone. You will see Yang Archetypes active in women and Yin ones in men. It is unfortunate that many societies allocate the female archetypes to women and vice versa, but the practice of this Work will shatter these constraints and allow individuals to evolve into all of themselves.

As this Work is a comprehensive identification of the nature of human consciousness in all its forms, if it was practised worldwide we would do away with limiting behaviours, prejudices and expectations. We need to be free to awaken and explore all positive parts of ourselves if we are to evolve. Having said that this Work is not about sex, I now have to say it is everything about sex, in the sense that we are attempting to unite within us great opposing energies, personifying them in a balanced, evolved way, creating orgasms of consciousness and new life energy within. We could call it Cosmic Coupling. This Work is not about with whom we wish to go to bed and how we generally behave regarding sex and gender, it is about making love to all parts of ourselves, irrespective of the roles society expects or demands us to play. We need to break the chains of sexist and gender roles, that are having an increasingly bad effect on both sexes, if we are to have a civilised society.

"When women's sexuality is imagined to be passive or "dirty," it also means that men's sexuality is automatically positioned as aggressive and right - no matter what form it takes. And when one of the conditions of masculinity, a concept that is already so fragile in men's minds, is that men dissociate from women and prove their manliness through aggression, we're encouraging a culture of violence and sexuality that's detrimental to both men and women." - Jessica Valenti, The Purity Myth: How America's Obsession with Virginity is Hurting Young Women

Dressing to suit you.

"Girls can wear jeans and cut their hair short and wear shirts and boots because it's okay to be a boy; for girls it's like promotion. But for a boy to look like a girl is degrading, according to you, because secretly you believe that being a girl is degrading." - Ian McEwan, The Cement Garden

These days, when male Archetypes, and the clothes they prefer, are encouraged across society, women may not notice much difference when they wear trousers, as male Archetypes are playing the leading role. When men, who do not suffer from gender dysphoria, fetishes, transvestism, paraphilia or autogynephelia, deviate from the strict dress code and wear a dress, they will suffer abuse and ridicule and fear they will be seen as gay or trans, rather than simply expressing their female aspects. These prejudices need to be faced. As long as there is goodwill to all and no harm done, then anything goes. We need to balance the male states of being with the female ones. This is not to say that there are different clothes that people should wear according to their sex. The Archetypes all have their own style and dress which should be worn according to which one anyone is practising at any given time and then worn out in the world to continue encouraging the development of that Archetype. Sadly, the nature of present society, wherever you live, will attempt to prevent you from doing so. It takes guts to grow.

A man who is working on his Actress to find emotional expression and his passion in life, might find himself in danger of losing his job, his wife, his family and his position in society. Think of how ridiculous people would regard it to wear a toga, for example, yet this was normal for men in Ancient Rome. Think about the costumes of Mediaeval times, of Vikings, of Ancient China, the Native Americans, ancient Egypt, India and the ancient Middle Eastern countries. You should be able to see how different Archetypes dress and manifest themselves throughout the ages and different parts of the world. Imagine what an interesting, colourful and fun world it would be if we allowed ourselves, and each other, to use the appropriate attire of each Archetype according to our development, without the need of labelling. In no time at all we would be revelling in a much more creative, cooperative and dynamic environment and, as people began to resolve the conflicting Archetypes within and their real selves increasingly emerged from their centres, who knows how fabulous we would look?

"The cultivation and control of our feminine aspects is obviously of critical importance to our wellbeing and further evolution. So many reports of magical events in the past are evidence that in those times female powers were much more developed, subject to our will and applied in various ways on the outer world. That we may begin to move, all six female states must be encouraged, respected and loved. Not as it is now where just a few airy masculine aspects are taken seriously."
- Richard Gardner

Parties where each sex comes as the other are great fun and things like this happen spontaneously when the Work is practised. I once had a birthday party with a group of girlfriends. Men weren't banned, it just happened that way. Richard Gardner, with whom I lived, wanted to come. It was agreed he could, but only if he wore a dress and a wig, which he did and he blended in beautifully. As the evening wore on, he took off the wig and dress and changed back into shirt and trousers. My goodness, what a difference. He became more dominant and upset the harmony. We told him he had to change back or go away. He put the frock and wig back on.

"We've begun to raise daughters more like sons…but few have the courage to raise our sons more like our daughters." - Gloria Steinem

Allowing Evolution

Biologically, men and women have obvious physical differences which also manifest in different proportions of hormones and chemicals, all of which affect behaviour to some extent. The penis puts something out, the vagina takes something in, then the womb puts something out. DNA is either male or female, and over 600 differences have been detected between male and female bodies. Most medical trials have been performed on male bodies so, in many cases, female bodies may not be having treatments suited to them. We need to be aware of how men and women might manifest the Archetypes in different ways, as will individuals, and also, as we bring new energies into ourselves, our bodies may change and work in new, more wonderful ways. It's a possibility our DNA will also change. Richard Gardner wondered if our further evolution would mean that, "We'd no longer be walking around with a belly full of shit and ridiculous genitals, his a swinging joke and hers a weeping tragedy". Just like the Greek comedy and Tragedy masks. If I say that in mixed company, most men say, "There's nothing wrong with my willy!" What can I do but laugh? In spite of these differences, the scripts I have provided in the 'How to Practice' section have been proven to work for both sexes. It is good for us to experiment and experience life from another viewpoint, it gives a shot of energy as well as insights.

As I say in the Sequences chapter, it was noted that it is usual for women have a female Element last (Water or Earth), and men a masculine one (Fire or Air), and this has been found to be mainly true, but we cannot make it a hard and fast rule. There is an unknown variety of self-expression beyond sexist roles, and I hope that a rainbow of behaviours will increasingly emerge and be appreciated. As this work is about assisting our evolution in a conscious way, we must stay open. I discussed how we look backwards in terms of understanding evolution. Now it is time to look ahead. We do not know what new life forms could develop. Perhaps our genitals will change. We do not know what part physical sex variations and generally unfamiliar roles may play, and if we evolve enough, would there would be no further need to reproduce ourselves? Any positive advancement in human evolution must be allowed to be expressed in safe and loving ways. The way things are, it seems to me that humanity would rather annihilate itself than embrace further evolution. Miracles await, let us grasp them.

"Understanding the shadow masculine or shadow feminine in oneself is crucial not only for enhancing one's own wholeness but for championing justice between genders and all diverse groups in the community. If the shadow is not recognized and dealt with, it will dominate an individual or community, resulting in untold suffering."
- Carolyn Baker, *Collapsing Consciously: Transformative Truths for Turbulent Times*

We can be sure of this - when negativity is present we are always wrong. When goodwill and love are present, we are always right. It is impossible to have a creative and peaceful world whilst we are being strangled by the denial of vital aspects of ourselves. The shadow feminine within men must be brought forward if we are to have any hope of ending wars and beginning to care for the earth and each other. The shadow masculine in women is an equally high priority if we are to promote women's truths, skills and talents and achieve balance and harmony.

"The wounded child inside many males is a boy who, when he first spoke his truths, was silenced by paternal sadism, by a patriarchal world that did not want him to claim his true feelings. The wounded child inside many females is a girl who was taught from early childhood that she must become something other than herself, deny her true feelings, in order to attract and please others. When men and women punish each other for truth telling, we reinforce the notion that lies are better. To be loving we willingly hear the other's truth, and most important, we affirm the value of truth telling. Lies may make people feel better, but they do not help them to know love."
- Bell Hooks, *All About Love: New Visions*

My wish is that we learn to accept each other as we are, enjoying and exchanging each other's gifts and characteristics rather than projecting our own confusion and guilt. Conflict is harmful to everyone. As long as nobody gets hurt, the qualities of a person's heart, soul and spirit are more important than what they choose to do with their genitals and how they want to dress. Let us open to the freedom to grow and evolve as our true selves and at last arrive at what all the great teachings have been urging - to love one another.

Nationalities

"No one is born hating another person because of the colour of his skin, or his background or his religion. People learn to hate, and if they can learn to hate, they can be taught to love, for love comes more naturally to the human heart than its opposite."

- Nelson Mandela

There is really only one race – the human race, but there is certainly racism. Although different nationalities exhibit facial features, characteristics and body types, it must be clearly understood that all twelve Archetypes are available to any individual, anywhere, irrespective of culture and background. As the climate differs around the world, the weathers express certain Elements over others and have a consequent influence on the inhabitants. We have the materialistic west (Earth), the industrial north (Air), the mystical east (Water) and the hot south (Fire). Due to travel and immigration, these differences are being diluted as nationalities intermarry, features and bloods mix, resulting in an intriguing 'cocktail' of people.

When Tammo de Jongh painted the faces of the Archetypes, he did so brilliantly, using each one's specific colour and he certainly captured the essence of them. He did, however, run into a problem which has been challenged and needs to be addressed. He used Mother Nature's colour which is dark brown to paint her, with no resulting criticism. Neither would there have been any if he had simply used chestnut brown for the Worker/Slave and not painted her as he did. This Archetype was originally called the Worker, but was later changed to the Slave by the originators because it became clear that we are all slaves to something, including our bodies. I agree, and do not want to lose that identification, so I have modified it by also using 'Worker', which is why I sometimes call it the Worker/Slave. Tammo's error was to paint her as a black woman with a ring through her nose, which is appalling to us now and the only excuse is that at that time, the early sixties, Europe was populated largely by indigenous whites and relatively few black people or different races such as Chinese and Indian. The men who made these original discoveries were 'children of their time', and rather naïve in this instance. I do know that that they were extremely upset that people ignored all the positive qualities of this Archetype, the tolerance, acceptance and warmth, and interpreted it as a racist attitude. Tammo painted the ring through the nose as a symbol of all the things to which we are bound. Richard Gardner was dismayed that some people dismissed the entire Work through an inability to place this in perspective. I hope we can avail ourselves of the positive aspects of this Archetype and understand that it is not marginalised by nationality. We all have a body after all, we all breathe, eat, shit and have the same colour of blood and we are all dragged by the nose by something.

I can only add that anyone who has ever seen the value of this Work has not allowed this to deter them. We have often seen it used as an excuse to criticise the entire work. Well, if people don't get it, it doesn't matter how it's presented, they still won't. I have said more about this in the Worker/Slave's own chapter. The only way we can fully detach ourselves from misunderstandings about racism and Archetypes is to see that all cultures, in spite of having predominating, influencing Elements, all have access to all the Archetypes and this can be demonstrated. The Patriarch consciousness is visible not only in whites, just as the Worker/Slave consciousness is not present only in blacks. There are many black people who have a well-developed Patriarch, just as there are many whites living in the Worker/Slave. In spite of failing to see the problems that could arise from how he painted the Worker/Slave, Tammo de Jongh did successfully capture many positive aspects of this Archetype. It would be good to have images painted by other skilled and perceptive artists who can depict all the Archetypes in specific nationalities and in both sexes, so we might more easily see how they manifest worldwide. These images should not be mere interpretations, they must retain the purity of each one. Artists must beware of imposing the Archetypes in which they themselves identify onto the portraits. This can happen whatever we are doing. When we staged the play I wrote about the Work, we had each Archetype dressed in its own style and had to tactfully explain to the woman who was playing the Actress that although the lovely, red, lace-trimmed, sexy satin top she offered was beautiful and indeed the correct colour, it wouldn't look quite right on the Warrior. The Centre was dressed in white, with a conical white hat. I sewed twelve different coloured ribbons on the top to represent each Archetype. It will be of great value to see all the Archetypes as Chinese, Japanese, African, Indian, European, Middle Eastern and so on, so that all peoples can personally relate to them.

Travelling to other countries is helpful in awakening latent Archetypes. There are indeed stereotypes. Italy is alive with the Actress, there is much of the Logician in white America and the warmth of the Slave in the southern US states, Africa and the West Indies, but this may not as beneficial as it once was. Travel can still 'broaden the mind', but not as much as before, due to the increase of the Logician's technology and the Worker's influence on our dress and behaviour. We see people all over the world dressed in jeans and t-shirts with a mobile phone clamped to them. We are becoming more and more like machines that don't function terribly well and our lives have become dependent on the Logician. Without technology we would not be able to survive; there would be no food in the supermarkets, no means of travel, no light or heat or the comforts we are used to. How many of us, particularly in the Western world, would be able to be self-sufficient? We cannot put all of our faith in technology, for if it collapsed tomorrow, you could easily be killed for a slice of bread.

In spite of the perilous position it has put itself in, humanity is still too stupid to realise the seriousness of the situation. The Logician will have had his day, just like the Patriarch did before him, and then where will we be? Of course, we need to keep all the wonderful intelligence of the Logician, but we must also develop the skills of neglected Archetypes to inject new ways of living before we wipe ourselves out. Putting all our faith in further technical developments is foolhardy and futile. We cannot expect the Logician to solve the problems he himself has created. Instead, we must seek out the innate qualities of the other Archetypes everywhere, wherever we may be fortunate enough to find them in the world, that we may combine our knowledge and wisdom.

The positive Worker/Slave can impart practical skills, as well as tolerance and community, that we may construct something better. The Native Americans and indigenous Australians lived in Mother Nature to a great extent but look at them now. It is time we saw how important their wisdom is and bring them forward to balance us. At present our world is filling up with more and more separate, lonely clones. It is time we reached for our individuality in loving togetherness. All peoples and all individuals have a precious piece of the jigsaw which can be placed on the Circle of the Archetypes, which makes up a glorious vision of happiness and peace. By coming together in conscious evolution, the beautiful picture could at last appear.

Why Is Change So Hard?

"Be not afraid of moving slowly, be only afraid of standing still." - Chinese Proverb

"If you can't fly, then run,
  If you can't run, then walk,
  If you can't walk, then crawl,
But whatever you do, you have to keep moving forward." - Martin Luther King

"The secret of change is to focus all of your energy not on fighting the old, but on building the new."
– Socrates

It is helpful, but by no means obligatory, to read this before you get to the fun part of learning about and practising your Archetypes. You will be confronted with challenges to transform, which may cause discomfort and resistance. Understanding is liberating, and is reached when the Archetypes are properly practised, but you may find the following useful in helping you overcome barriers to growth.

"Progress is impossible without change, and those who cannot change their minds cannot change anything." - George Bernard Shaw

Normally, when we talk about change we imagine that we must stop being who we are in order to become someone else. In part this is true, but with this Work you will not be letting go of any part of yourself that is positive, you are simply being invited to add more of yourself into your consciousness. You will only be letting go of that which no longer serves you. This Work will encourage you to grow, and I'm pretty certain you'll resist it at times, most of us do, including myself. You will enjoy some Archetypes and find them easy, others you will dislike and want to avoid. Your long-term health and well-being depend on you embracing your dormant Archetypes and activating them on your Wheel of Life. The ones you enjoy are those which you have, in part, allowed to develop in you so far, and those you think you don't like are latent and unfamiliar. Although we tend to seek partners who are our opposite, you will probably choose your friends from those who share Archetypes with you and avoid people who are 'not your type'. Don't worry, I guarantee that if you have the courage to claim your true Centre and allow these Archetypes to come alive in you, you will fall in love with all of them. It will feel like you have made wonderful new friends inside yourself who can help you in so many ways. What you were previously unable to do, the awakened Archetype can do with ease. Perhaps by understanding our attitude to change, it may help us to achieve it and start to enjoy the exhilarating thrill of our Wheel of Life spinning.

"Nothing endures but change" – *Heraclitus*

Who wants change? Most of us I expect. It's why politicians base their manifestos on it, although little does change for the better once they're in power. How many of us have a perfect life? I would guess not many. No matter how much we have, there is always an area that can be improved, sooner or later. Health, love, career, money, home, friends, family, creativity, inner peace, travel - so many things we wish were better, so many worries we wish we could lose, so many talents we wish we could use. If most of us want change so much, why is it so often such a struggle? Why are the results never as good as we hope? Why do we, and therefore our lives, stay more or less the same? We can read lots of self-help books, write affirmations, keep journals, attend courses and workshops, see a therapist or counsellor and yet we still slip back, there are some things that won't shift. Wanting to change and being prepared to change are not the same thing. Reading this book won't do it either, unless you are willing to practise your Archetypes so you can grow and enjoy lasting change. The problem is, we are trying to change from the same place in ourselves, whereas using this Work will open up new places that make change far more easily accessible and attained. Roger S. Gil, M.A.M.F.T defines change as "a modification to a person's environment, situation, or physical/mental condition that results in circumstances that challenge their existing paradigms." We have a tendency to define how our world is supposed to work, and when something happens that is different from the way we think the world should be, we encounter change. So basically it's our fixed attitudes we need to change.

The Programmed Brain

"If you change the way you look at things, the things you look at change."- *Wayne Dyer*
"The measure of intelligence is the ability to change." - *Albert Einstein*

Our brains become trained to expect things to stay the same. We take the same train or bus each morning, tune in to the same radio or television programmes and plan our days in certain prearranged ways. If the bus or train is cancelled, programming is rescheduled etc., we are thrown into various levels of disarray because we have to make sudden adjustments. On a deeper level both nature and nurture influence our core beliefs about how our world works and what our roles in it are. We create scenarios that depict how life should be, and when we experience them, and ourselves, in a certain way for an extended period of time, we develop firm core beliefs for how we think life is supposed to be. The experiences we have as children tend to be the most long-lasting and influential, because they are prototypical ones to which future ones will be compared, and will play a key role in the development of our mindset. During childhood our brains are still developing, so they have a greater chance of influencing how future neural connections develop. Children usually adjust better to change since they don't have as much 'legacy material' to overcome. Over time our brains become less malleable and we face more difficulties in processing changes. If you grew up experiencing a traditional family behaviour of grief and sadness, you never questioned it, you just assumed that what was life was like. Children accept as the norm the examples they see around them and with which they have the most interaction. For our lives to change, we must change. Not much will change on the outer unless we bring about changes on the inner. We know that, we want it to happen, we put so much effort into it, it's so simple, but we can't do it. Yes, it's simple - but that doesn't mean it's easy. Why do we block ourselves? We always walk in the same way, dance, eat, speak, think, feel, have interests, read certain genres of books, watch a limited type of film, all the time telling ourselves that this is how we were made and this is how we are meant to be - yet that is incorrect. It is an illusion created by the few Archetypes in which we have become stuck. We were made to be much more, we have locked inside of us Archetypes that offer untold talents and powers of which we can only at present dream, close inside, awaiting unfoldment, whispering "Free us, free us! We have so much life to give you!"

Choice

"Sometimes it's the smallest decisions that can change your life forever." – Keri Russell
Our lives are composed of all the choices we make, be they conscious or unconscious. If others make choices for us, it's often because we have chosen to allow them to do so. This is not to dismiss sociological restraints which can impose choice on us and are difficult to overcome, but there can be no change without challenging the status quo. Let's look at your day and see how many choices you can add up. You won't manage to count them, as everything you do is a choice. Even in a prison, a

person has the choice to refuse to do what they are told and face the consequences. In the first few moments of your day, decisions begin. Some part of you has made the choice to wake up, then you have to choose whether to get up or not, whether to wet the bed or go to the bathroom, whether you wear a dressing gown or not, tea or coffee? Eat or not? Eat what? Answer the phone? Go to work or stay at home? Go shopping? What to wear? Walk, bus, train? What stop to get off? And so on throughout your day. You do all these things because you think you have to, and of course you do in order to maintain your present lifestyle, but if you decide to choose a different lifestyle you will be making different small choices throughout your day. All these tiny choices add up to what appear to be the big decisions of our lives. Life is not really made of big choices. Even when a choice initiates a major change it will be the result of all the small choices previously made. A breakthrough contract for a performer is backed up by the training and self-promotion that went before. Moving forward in our self-development and evolution means making different choices, ones that are consciously aware.

"To change what you get you must change who you are." - *Vernon Howard*

"We have to choose joy and keep choosing it." - *Henri J.M. Nouwen*

Resistance

"It is not the strongest of the species that survives, nor the most intelligent, but the one most responsive to change." - *Charles Darwin.*

The big problem is that we have a resistance to change. What is it? Where does it come from? Have you felt it in yourself? Been frustrated with yourself? Why do we resist? There are two main reasons - fear and habit, and they're interrelated. When we're stuck in any of the Archetypes they become our habitual selves and we are scared of difference. We can come to some understanding by uncovering childhood traumas, patterns, experiences, and these can bring a certain freedom that allows us to approach life in a different way. Practising the Child Archetype often brings childhood memories to the surface, but maintaining the new order can still be a challenge. We find ourselves facing situations where we always behaved in a certain way and are asked to deal with them differently. It's all too easy to slip back. This is because, in spite of our insights, we have not been able to develop enough of the necessary tools to free us from the past and implement and maintain the change. Working with these Archetypes has proven to me time and again that increasing the scope of our consciousness will place these tools in your hands.

"Those who do not move, do not notice their chains." - *Rosa Luxemburg*

Habit and Change

"Change is inevitable. Change is constant." - Benjamin Disraeli

Looking at how we react to change, and what parts habit and fear play, is a useful preparation for self-development. We are creatures of habit. Some are easier to change than others, like giving up smoking, drinking less alcohol, changing white bread for brown organic or going to bed and rising at specific times. It's said that it takes thirty days to stop an old habit or establish a new one. There are, however, habits of which we are not aware, deep ruts of old behaviours that are so familiar and well used that we mistake them for our true selves. We have the illusion that we are choosing these behaviours, but in truth, we are repeatedly and automatically reacting. Habit is either a good slave or a bad master. Many are necessary, such as the way we weave together all the actions needed to control a car. Learning to drive can be scary, there seem to be so many things we have to perform all at once, but repetition trains our bodies to go through the required motions automatically, freeing us to better predict hazards ahead and to plan our routes.

"Man's life work is a masterpiece or a shame as each little habit has been perfectly or carelessly formed." - John Ruskin.

The difference as to whether we are creating a masterpiece or a shame is in how much *awareness* we have of ourselves. Habit is *unconscious repetition* of actions, words or thoughts which will have formed so gradually that we may not have been aware we were doing them. A research paper *('The Nature of Habit in Daily Life', David T. Neal and Wendy Wood, Duke University 2007)* discovered that in non-habitual behaviours, people were thinking about what they were doing for about 70% of the time, but in habitual responses, the correspondence between thought and action was significantly lower at about 40%. Habits need less attention compared to new or unfamiliar actions and are easier to perform. Neurological activity decreases as the habit unfolds, and so the behaviour feels automatic. That doesn't mean that we're stuck with our habits; understanding how they work can help. There are techniques we can use to either break or develop habits. If you focus on one habit at a time and commit yourself to changing it, you'll probably be successful. Researchers have been looking at how habits work, and a popular formula has emerged - the cue, routine and reward loop.

- First we have the cue, which is the trigger that launches your brain into automatic mode - "It's eleven a.m., I'm hungry".
- This is followed by the routine, which is the ensuing behaviour, mental, physical or

emotional. "Go get my sticky bun".
- Lastly, there is the reward. At this point your brain calculates whether this behaviour is worth repeating in the future. - "Comforting and a fast sugar hit".

As time goes by, these loops - cue, behaviour, reward - become neurologically wired into our brains until they are more and more automatic. An important aspect of this method is to change only one part of the loop at a time. Referring to the above example, at 11 a.m., you can still go get something to eat, but choose something else that still delivers a satisfying reward. Would an apple do it, or would a 10-minute walk be better, or a chat with people around you? You need to be happy with the reward and feel satisfied for it to work. The Archetypes can help you. If you practise Mother Nature, you'll be more inclined to prefer an apple and the Warrior will take you for a brisk walk. We can also slip into pointless habits. For instance, how words and speech patterns creep into common language. We use them repeatedly, unaware that we have absorbed them; terms like 'you know', 'right!' 'absolutely' 'cool' and so on. This careless use of language is met with stern disapproval by the Patriarch Archetype who knows the importance of words. Experimenting with breaking such a habit can be both maddening and hilarious. Ask someone to point it out every time you say 'you know' (or your own particular speech virus), and you'll be shocked at how often you do it. You may even deny you're doing it, in which case record yourself. The first time you hear it for yourself is wonderful, you're on your way. Soon, you find yourself catching it before you say it and it's a thrill. You get to choose. Change brings choice. The more we change, the more choices we have.

The 'cue, behaviour, reward loop' can also be applied to deeper, emotional issues. Painful or traumatic past events are triggered by cues later in life when we find ourselves in similar situations. If your childhood was filled with anger and your family shouted at you a lot, you will have been afraid and reacted in specific ways, whether it be shouting back or running to hide. Your reward will have been a feeling of defending and protecting yourself. This could become a habitual behaviour in later life and you may even seek out angry people who enable you to continue your unconscious pattern. You might become either fearful or argumentative when faced with anger, or allow yourself to be manipulated because you fear conflict so much. It would never occur to you that there are other ways of dealing with it, like calmly walking away, apologising if valid, or asking the other person how you could help them let go of their distress. These deep psychological issues can be dealt with by the sincere application of this Work. We don't need years of 'treatment', we simply keep adding more positive parts of ourselves and the problems melt away. Of course, where there are thought to be physical, chemical disturbances in the brain then medical treatment may be necessary. I make no suggestion whatsoever that medical treatment should be refused or discontinued. This could be dangerous and counter-productive, particularly for severe psychiatric patients, who should continue with their treatment as advised by their doctors. Treatments can, however, be augmented with the careful introduction of Archetypal energies. Over time, this may possibly allow medications to be gradually reduced.

When our fear of change is not properly checked, it can manifest in unhealthy ways, bringing danger to our health from living constantly in a state of tension or hopelessness, resulting in emotional and psychological damage. We may react to change with resistance, anger, and violence toward ourselves and the world. The more we can embrace the transformative power of change, the more we will thrive as individuals, benefiting our culture and our planet. One of the joys of this Work is how it can dig out and reveal deep buried problems like these. Practising a latent Archetype makes it easier to cope with realisations because we have introduced a different energy that strengthens and supports us, freeing us to make behavioural choices in a more conscious way. This Work offers real change, real choice and real growth, if you are willing to take that step forward. If there was no change, there would be no butterflies.

Why Is Change So Frightening?

Fear and Change

"We can easily forgive a child who is afraid of the dark; the real tragedy of life is when men are afraid of the light." – Plato

"There is nothing permanent except change." - Heraclitus

"It may be hard for an egg to turn into a bird: it would be a jolly sight harder for it to learn to fly while remaining an egg. We are like eggs at present. And you cannot go on indefinitely being just an ordinary, decent egg. We must be hatched or go bad." - C. S. Lewis

Change is the only constant, it's the fundamental rule of nature in the ebb and flow of life. Our bodies are endlessly, fluidly changing. We replace old cells with new ones at the rate of millions per second. In the time it takes to read this sentence about 50 million cells will have died and been replaced, and your body makes about 1000 million white blood cells every day in your bone marrow. The life cycle of every cell is carefully controlled, ensuring that we always have just the right number of each type of in our bodies. Our skin, hair, and nails change regularly, the seasons change in yearly cycles, providing new growth and food. Change is within and all around us and is essential for life to thrive. Change is renewal.

"Life belongs to the living, and he who lives must be prepared for changes".
- Johann Wolfgang von Goethe"

Yet our thoughts and actions rarely flow, change and replace themselves smoothly. Our consciousness resists changing circumstances and we block the new, fresh force that is ever ready to fill us with life-enhancing energy. We need to learn from our bodies and realise that the only security is in change, the only stability is in change, the only way we can hold on to what is valuable is to let it go, and the only way to stay alive is to break through the rigid mindsets we have created; the structures we imagine to be 'real' but actually make us ill, depressed and limited. It is liberating to realise that by embracing change we can manifest everything we want and need.

"The curious paradox is that when I accept myself just as I am, then I can change." - Carl Rogers

In order to maintain health, we need to be aware of the connection between our thoughts, attitudes, behaviours and bodies. Research proves how our thoughts and emotions affect our bodies, and it is freely available in many books and papers. The well-known placebo effect shows how belief in a medical treatment creates greater health and often complete healing, in spite of the 'powerful drug' being nothing but a harmless substance. The attitude of the administrator plays a large part too. A doctor who offers a drug or placebo in a half-hearted way - "Not everyone benefits from this drug, but I hope that you might be one of the lucky ones", will not have as good results as the doctor who has a positive attitude - "I have great confidence in this treatment, we have been seeing marvellous results!" In many cases, the treatment itself plays a very small part, if any, in recovery; it's our thoughts, attitudes, feelings and expectations that bring about the miracles.

Change is a broad term, it covers many areas of our lives, and the fear we feel can be so subtle that we easily block and deny it. We are happy to make some changes; to buy new outfits, redecorate, try a new restaurant, get a new car or rearrange the furniture. These are small changes, things we can easily control. Fear can be a good thing. We need to fear putting our hands into flames or crossing the road without looking, we learn how to protect ourselves in perilous situations when fear of being hurt is justifiable. But many fears are not justified and work not for, but against us. They make us see the possible negative outcomes and blind us to the positive opportunities. There's a big difference between a situation where your life is at risk and having to take a risk. The autonomic biological response of 'fight or flight' is fear that is real and essential for survival, but almost all other types of perceived fear are self-created. These fears are a product of our higher cognitive brain, and with practice we can train it to react differently, it is something we have the power to manage and re-educate. There is also another reaction. When we can't fight or run away, we freeze. In society, it's usually ill-advised to punch someone or run from our responsibilities, so we do nothing, locking it all inside, to the detriment of our physical and emotional health. Although our neurobiology makes it difficult, it is by no means impossible to influence the primal areas of our brain that produce biological fear. Practising the Warrior Archetype will soon put fear to flight.

"Change alone is eternal, perpetual, immortal." - Arthur Schopenhauer

What is it we fear about change?

"It's the most unhappy people who most fear change." - Mignon McLaughlin

We can look at some of the ways in which we perceive change to be threatening, although they can be interconnected. By breaking them down we may see ourselves a little better.

Loss of Control

"They must often change, who would be constant in happiness or wisdom."- Confucius

Fear of loss of control is powerful. Our habits can act as an aid to masking fear, they keep us in an illusion called our 'comfort zone'. Change forces us to relinquish them, we can no longer use them to shield our resistance. We are afraid of the things we can't control, we see change as something that happens to us against our will. We are scared we will not be able to handle things, that we will lose whatever grasp we have on our lives. We fear things getting worse, being forced to relive past pains, that we will not be able to avoid facing our terrors, that we will not be up to the demands of facing new challenges. We don't want things to happen to us, we want them to stay the same in our illusory comfort zones where we imagine we have control; yet all those things that we have suppressed may break free at any time and we imagine they have the power to destroy us. Society constantly reflects this back to us, increasing our sense of inadequacy. We are not smart enough, beautiful enough, thin enough, rich enough, successful enough, good enough, and by buying into all this conditioning we lose touch with our wonderful, magical selves. I am not unrealistic. I appreciate that many people are in impossible situations where the political or social conditions will not allow change of any kind. The best way we can help them is to work on ourselves and influence the world energies towards positive change for all.

Fear of the Unknown

"Any change, even a change for the better, is always accompanied by drawbacks and discomforts." - Arnold Bennett

Our anxiety and fear of the unknown stems from us not having enough information regarding the nature of the change. Our brains like information they know and understand and don't like what they can't predict. Change which appears to force itself upon us disturbs the usual, well-trodden pathways of our brains and because we don't know what the change will bring, we fear it might be worse than our status quo. It is necessary to expose our brains to enough change, in enough different ways, to allow the understanding that change is something we can survive and from which we can even benefit. We won't fear the unknown so much, if at all, because the new stored information provides us with the evidence that fear of change is unnecessary. Developing latent Archetypes is a fast and effective way to cut through these static patterns and allow change in a conscious and informed way.

"I read and walked for miles at night along the beach, writing bad blank verse and searching endlessly for someone wonderful who would step out of the darkness and change my life. It never crossed my mind that that person could be me." - Anna Quindlen

"Change before you have to." - Jack Welch

Stress

"All great things are preceded by chaos." - Deepak Chopra.

All change, whether good or bad, creates a type of stress, and we need to accept that, and process our feelings accordingly. How well we handle this stress and whether it is good stress or bad depends on our attitude to it. There's a story of two amoebas, each in a separate tank. One was subjected to a lot of stress; the water was kept just a little too cold, it was fed with only just enough food and every now and then was squirted with a black inky fluid. The other amoeba was provided with the perfect temperature, plenty of food and left alone to enjoy itself. You may have guessed what happened. The deprived, irritated amoeba thrived, became strong and lived long, whilst the other one grew fat, lazy and died young. I'm not advocating making life tough in order to grow, but it illustrates how stressful situations can also be opportunities that allow us to become stronger and more successful.

"Our dilemma is that we hate change and love it at the same time; what we really want is for things to remain the same but get better." - Sydney J. Harris

Faced with uncertainty, we may feel inadequate because our usual information structures have been compromised. We have no, or limited, experience of the new situation and we fall into the trap of reverting to default decision-making, on which we feel our survival depends. The primal fight or flight instinct invades us with stress hormones and hold us in bondage, causing us to experience a whole scale of emotions from anticipation to frustrating paralysis. Even change that is wonderful and the answer to all our dreams can have this effect, as we fear the consequences of not behaving appropriately, of messing it up and losing it all again. Change is a 'wake-up call', an opportunity to have more and be more.

"Without change, something sleeps inside us, and seldom awakens. The sleeper must awaken."
- Frank Herbert

"The first step toward change is awareness. The second step is acceptance." - Nathaniel Branden

Loss

"All changes, even the most longed for, have their melancholy; for what we leave behind us is a part of ourselves; we must die to one life before we can enter another."- Anatole France

The effects of loss can be minor to devastating, depending on what is lost. In career, it can mean the loss of work colleagues, salary, or even a parking space. The loss of routines and the things that define us, such as our job title or position, can have a shattering effect. Sometimes change involves a significant loss, such as the end of a relationship. When a love affair or marriage ends, we suffer the loss of a great deal of emotional investment, with all the accompanying time and effort we put into it. We don't want to lose that, so we try to hold on, it's a struggle to accept that it's over. In truth, we learned and gained from the experience, but we don't want to accept it. This results in heartache. Change requires that we let go and focus on the new, like letting go of all the tatty old clothes in the wardrobe to make way for ones of better quality. We need to focus on positive opportunities, to take responsibility for our reactions to events, yet still be allowed to grieve what is lost. A bereavement can, of course, be the most painful of losses and the hardest with which to come to terms. We are forced to change instantly, from the first moment the loved one is lost. If we lose a partner our lives, which were built around a life that was mutually created, are shattered and suddenly we have to go it alone. Over time, most people do manage to survive the tragedy and create a new life, but in some cases, like the loss of a child, the pain is ever present. To most of us, adapting to life without a loved one is the cruellest change of all.

Fear of Failure

"If we don't change, we don't grow. If we don't grow, we aren't really living." - Gail Sheehy."
"There is no greater agony than bearing an untold story inside you." - Maya Angelou

We fear failure because we don't believe in ourselves. We tie ourselves into an imagined standard of perfection which promotes fear and anxiety about not getting it right. We avoid the pain of failure by not doing anything at all. Yet many, if not most, successful people have a list of failures behind them, from Edison's hundreds of failed light bulbs, to business owners who have had several stabs at success. The difference is that they don't see them as failure, they see the lessons learned in how not to do it. That's a positive outcome which enables the next attempt to have a better chance of success. That's how we learn. We need to get moving, act from choice, not consequences and increase the scope of opportunities for unlimited growth and creativity. Not to do so is the only failure.

"Remember the two benefits of failure. First, if you do fail, you learn what doesn't work; and second, the failure gives you the opportunity to try a new approach." - Roger Von Oech

Fear of Success

"Change brings opportunity." - Nido Qubein

"Our deepest fear is not that we are inadequate. Our deepest fear is that we are powerful beyond measure. It is our light, not our darkness, that most frightens us. We ask ourselves, who am I to be brilliant, gorgeous, talented, and fabulous?" - Marianne Williamson. (Often wrongly attributed to Nelson Mandela).

Many famous people such as singers, actors and performers admit to feeling that they don't really deserve success, that they are lesser than other famous people and dread the day they will be found out. Being successful in the outer world doesn't necessarily mean success in conquering our inner demons. We may have negative views as to how successful people behave, and we fear that we might become like them. We might believe that our friends will be jealous and we will lose them, or we could become exploitative, or take drugs, drink too much, not be able to maintain relationships, lose our talent and suffer invasions of privacy. The only way to reduce the fear of the change is to be certain of our own values and remain true to them. Bringing in latent Archetypes will minimise the fear of both failure and success by increasing your objectivity, abilities and self-confidence.

Fear of Upsetting Others

"To lead an orchestra you must turn your back on the crowd" – Aristotle

"Sometimes if you want to see a change for the better, you have to take things into your own hands."
- Clint Eastwood

"If you want to make enemies, try to change something." - Woodrow Wilson

Change in our own lives has a ripple effect, reaching out and affecting all who know us. We may have to reject family values and traditions and fear that this will be seen as personal rejection by our loved ones. The impact on the people close to us can so upset them that it makes us reluctant to make the changes we want, yet -

"If you persistently seek validation from others, you will inadvertently invalidate your own self-worth." – Dodinsky

Conditioning, society at large, our family and friends, can all conspire to keep us the same. Their own feelings of hurt that you want something different, their own resistance to change and the jealousy of friends and siblings can create sufficient anxiety in us to seriously limit and undermine what we do. We may even turn down opportunities such as a work promotion rather than face the ill-feeling of our colleagues. We feel guilty for wanting more, something different. If we are to change, we have to accept that others may not want to, but that shouldn't stop us. When we bring forward unfamiliar Archetypes there is a risk of adverse reactions from others. People can say, "You're not yourself, what's wrong with you?"

"When you challenge other people's ideas of who or how you should be, they may try to diminish and disgrace you. It can happen in small ways in hidden places, or in big ways on a world stage. You can spend a lifetime resenting the tests, angry about the slights and the injustices. Or, you can rise above it." - Carly Fiorina

We have the tendency to seek out others like ourselves so we don't have to change. But whilst we are comfortable with these people, we have to ask ourselves what can we learn from them and they from us? Sadly, only how to stay the same. This doesn't mean that we have to leave them behind, but we have to accept that as we change, so does everything else, including our social lives. We need to be adaptive; remember Darwin's observation, that it is the most important survival tool.

"We are products of our past, but we don't have to be prisoners of it." - Rick Warren

"Some people live in cages with bars built from their own fears and doubts. Some people live in cages with bars built from other people's fears and doubts; their parents, their friends, their brothers and sisters, their families. Some people live in cages with bars built from the choices others made for them, the circumstances other people imposed upon them. And some people break free."- C. JoyBell C.

"When we are no longer able to change a situation we are challenged to change ourselves."
- Viktor E. Frank

Fear of Decisions

The desires of other people can bring the validity of your decision-making process into question. Who is the pilot of your life? Have you made decisions based on your own drives and ambitions, or have you defaulted to your emotional autopilot? Have you made decisions based on old inherited or self-created fears, or from courage and enthusiasm for the new? Living from your Centre enables you to create functional decisions from choice rather than consequence, you can add more options for unlimited growth and freedom.

"To burn with desire and keep quiet about it is the greatest punishment we can bring on ourselves."
- Federico García Lorca

If we reflect on past fear-based decisions, and the significant life changes that might have occurred had our decisions been based on intention and functional choice rather than fear of consequence, we come to see how we have held ourselves back. The career change we dreamt of for years but dismissed; the creative projects put on hold for fear of an unknown future; not taking a chance on relationships for fear of being hurt; the travel we yearned for but became trapped in chains of responsibility. Mostly, we only really regret the things we didn't do. What if the cave you're afraid to enter holds the treasure trove you seek?

"The only way that we can live is if we grow. The only way that we can grow is if we change. The only way that we can change is if we learn. The only way we can learn is if we are exposed. And the only way that we can become exposed is if we throw ourselves out into the open. Do it. Throw yourself." - *C.JoyBell C.*

Leaving the Comfort Zone

"Change will never happen when people lack the ability and courage to see themselves for who they are." - *Bryant H. McGill*

Life demands that we move out of our comfort zones, but honestly, are we really all that comfortable anyway? Living our lives in suppressed fear of the future, wrapping our habits around us like security blankets, we cling to our routines and avoid the uncertainty of new experiences. Staying like this is stagnation, a state that becomes increasingly uncomfortable until it eventually squeezes all the life out of us. I suggest we avoid the word 'change' from now on and re-conceptualise it with synonyms which are more encouraging; words such as 'growth', 'renewal', 'evolution' or 'transformation', which share the underlying and inherent principle of good change.

"Things alter for the worse spontaneously, if they be not altered for the better designedly."
- Francis Bacon

"The foolish and the dead alone never change their opinions." - *James Russell Lowell*

The future is before us, we have the opportunity to take control and shape today and tomorrow into a more satisfying design. A small, courageous step forward is all it takes, a step that will not only enhance our own lives, but also be of benefit to society and the earth. A world full of happy, creative, evolving people is the only worthwhile aim. Re-connect to your Centre, spin your own Wheel of Life and lead the way.

"The world will change for the better when people decide they are sick and tired of being sick and tired of the way the world is, and decide to change themselves." - Sydney Madwed

"Your task is not to seek for love, but merely to seek and find all the barriers within yourself that you have built against it." – Rumi

The Magic of Twelve

Twelve is a significant and magical number, featuring over the ages in fairy tales, myths, legends, religions and many systems regarding measurement and money. It is important to so many cultures and ages, and you will have seen that it is fundamental to this Work, as the elements and their relationships are personified and activated in the Twelve Archetypes. I should say, however, that in older, gynocentric societies, thirteen was a revered number, as there were thirteen moons and thirteen menstruations per year. This is why, in a patriarchal, androcentric society, thirteen has been demonized as unlucky. In spite of this, it does not negate the importance of twelve, as this is the maximum number of Archetypes which develop from the Four Elements. I like to think that all twelve can come together in the centre and create what we might call the thirteenth and the one, the magical true self.

- The 12 stranded DNA was considered to be a hypothetical concept, but ongoing research shows that it is possible that DNA exists in a complex structure which consists of 12 strands. It is also suggested that this DNA structure could be regarded as a phenomenal mutation which might lead to equally phenomenal evolution. Studies show that persons who have unusual structures, which differ from normal double stranded DNA, having 3, 4 or more strands, have unusual abilities such as telepathy and heightened intuition. Does this mean that the more we activate our Archetypes, the more strands of our DNA will activate? It certainly looks like it could be possible. If so, it will alter not only our consciousness, but every cell in our bodies.

- In Numerology, twelve represents a complete cycle, the cosmic order; it is both of a spiritual and secular order, esoteric and exoteric. Twelve is the number of what is completed, which forms a whole, a perfect and harmonious unit. In ancient civilizations, like Oriental and Judaic, it corresponds to the plenitude, the completion and the integrality of a thing, representing the manifestation of the Trinity to the four corners of the horizon - 3 X 4. It is the creative capacity, and in some religions, it also expresses the Divine Mother.

- There are twelve hours in the day and in the night
- There are twelve months in the year.
- The Imperial system, before the UK switched to the Metric, had twelve pennies in a shilling and twelve inches in a foot.
- On Mount Olympus there are twelve Gods and Goddesses.
- There are twelve Titans.
- Hercules/Heracles had twelve tasks to complete for the Goddess Hera and twelve days in which to execute them.
- In the life of Buddha there are twelve stages of existence named Nidanas.
- Charlemange, Charles the Great, was surrounded by twelve paladins sometimes known as the Twelve Peers, who were the foremost warriors of his court.
- There are twelve Knights of the Round Table.
- A witches' coven traditionally has twelve members.
- Twelve o'clock midnight is known as The Witching Hour.
- Twelve good fairies came to spread wishes upon Sleeping Beauty.
- The Brothers Grimm wrote of The Twelve Dancing Princesses and the Twelve Huntsmen.
- The ancient capitals of India had twelve gates.
- The eleventh hour is our last chance before the twelfth hour, when spells are broken, the mirror cracks, rendering the wicked powerless, the earth turns in regeneration of life, Jack defies the giant and Sleeping Beauty awakens.
- There are twelve members of a jury.
- There are twelve signs of the Zodiac in modern Astrology, a cycle of twelve months.
- There are twelve animals of the Chinese horoscope and twelve years in the Chinese lunar calendar, a cycle of twelve years.

- Twelve is the number of the disciples accompanying the great spiritual teachers and leaders of history.
- The twelve apostles of Christ.
- The twelve disciples chosen by Mahomet to spread his doctrine.
- The twelve minor flamines (priests) beside the Pontiff Maximus.
- The twelve first companions of St. Francis of Assisi.
- The twelve disciples of Confucius.
- The twelve disciples of Mithra;
- The twelve descendants of Ali.
- The twelve companions of Odin, with also the twelve Goddesses
- The twelve marshals of Napoleon.
- The twelve names of the Sun in Sanskrit.
- In Japanese cosmology, the Creator sits on twelve sacred cushions.
- The twelve petals of the Anahata Chakra are located in the area of the heart and the twelve petals of the corolla of the Sahasrara Chakra are located at the top of the head.
- The twelve tables of the shield of Achilles represent the social and the agricultural life during each month.
- There are twelve provinces that Ra, the sun god, visits each day by passing one hour in each one of them.
- There are twelve imposing rooms of the Scandinavian paradise.
- There are the twelve virtues and the twelve vices of Our Lady of Paris, Notre Dame.
- There were twelve solo circuits in some races of Ancient Greece.
- The twelve rooms of Hell correspond to the twelve nocturnal hours of the eschatologic doctrines of Valentine.
- There are twelve lions decorating the steps of the throne of Solomon in the Arab legends.
- Twelve seats surround the throne of Odin.
- The human body has twelve gates - two eyes, two ears, two nostrils, the mouth, two nipples, the navel, the anus and the penis/vagina.
- The human cell has twelve biochemical salts.
- There are the twelve semitones derived from the seven notes of the western scale.

- In the Bible the number twelve occurs 189 times.
- There are twelve tribes and twelve apostles. The book of Revelations describes the City of God as having twelve foundations and twelve gates and "In the midst of the street of it, and on either side of the river, was there the tree of life, which bore twelve manner of fruits, and yielded her fruit every month and the leaves of the tree were for the healing of the nations." Revelation 22.2. (Which perfectly describes this Work).
- There were twelve breads which Jesus broke at the Last Supper.
- There are twelve kinds of precious stone of the Celestial City.
- There are twelve branches to confirm the choice of Aaron.
- There were twelve explorers sent in Canaan.
- There were twelve stones chosen by the twelve men in Jordan to make a monument.
- There were twelve administrators of Solomon for all Israel.
- There are twelve oxen of the bronze Sea.
- Twelve strips made the cloak of Ahijah.
- The altar of Elijah had twelve stones.
- There were the sacrifices of the twelve animals.
- There were three series of twelve silver bowls offered for the dedication of the altar.
- There were the twelve springs of Elim.
- There are the twelve tribes of Israel.
- Twelve years are required for young Israelis to be admitted as "son of the law".
- There were twelve precious stones on the pectoral of the great Priest Aaron.
- Jacob had twelve sons.
- Joseph of Arimathea, carrier of the holy Grail, had twelve knights with him.
- In the Islamic religion, there are the twelve Imams, successors to the prophet Muhammad.
- There are the twelve winds and their porticoes seen in the vision by Enoch, according to the Book of the calendar of writings of the library of Qumran.
- Allah took a covenant from the Children of Israel, designating twelve leaders.
- When Moses prayed for water for his people, "so we said, 'strike with your staff the stone', and there gushed out from it twelve springs, and every people knew its watering place. Eat and drink from the provision of Allah'…".

- In the Book of Revelation it is said that there were 12 gates in God's kingdom and there were also 12 angels who guarded the gates.
- Jesus supposedly spoke his first words when he was 12 years old.
- I've read of a Bible prophecy that says that the number 12 could symbolize the return of Jesus Christ on the Earth. If there is a Christ, and if he (she?) did return, I think he (she?) would approve of the Work. We can also view this as our own Christ Consciousness, the healer, the transformer, the teachings coming true in the Twelve and in us.

Part 2

The Practice

A Course for Life

The Four Elements

"What lies behind us and what lies before us are tiny matters compared to what lies within us."
-Ralph Waldo Emerson

All buildings, from modest shacks to beautiful palaces, must rest on their foundations; and so it is with life. Whatever the complexities within life forms and their relationships, whether seemingly solid matter or the world of energies, everything on our planet rests upon the same foundation stones and is made of the same basic building blocks - the Four Elements; Water, Earth, Fire, Air. These are the essential, vital forces that make up our creation. We will explore the Elements individually and then later, see how the Archetypes arise from them.

The Four Elements are basic in many teachings and cultures. You are already familiar with them, you encounter them every morning when you get out of bed as your feet meet the floor (Earth), you empty your bladder and drink something (Water), then your body adjusts to the temperature around you, feeling heat or the lack of it (Fire), and you take some deep breaths to stimulate your brain (Air). What you are doing is relating to your body's substance (Earth), its juices (Water), its heat (Fire) and its need for oxygen (Air). You exist in the world of the Elements. You then use textiles and objects, such as towels and cutlery (Earth), you wash yourself, (Water), you move, dress and eat which warms your body (Fire) and you open a window to freshen the atmosphere (Air). And so it continues as you step outside. You walk on the ground (Earth), there is early morning dew or rain (Water), the sun is bright and warm (Fire) and the limitless sky is above you (Air). In recognising the Elements outside of yourself, your attention may be drawn inside and the further realisation that you too are composed of the elements in your physical reality. They determine your thought patterns, behaviours, appearance, physical and emotional characteristics and choice of life style. Your body has substance (Earth), you are largely composed of liquids, (Water), you have heat in your body (Fire) and you breathe in oxygen (Air). Everything on our planet is made from these Elements. Earth is the soil in which things grow, the entire material world, the material of the body; we immerse ourselves in

Water as we bathe, swim and drink; the light and heat from Fire warms us and encourages the crops to grow; we feel the winds and the Air passing through our nostrils. We owe our lives to the Elements, we take them in and pass them out in an endless exchange. As within so without, as without so within. There is, in effect, no boundary, we are experiencing these energies in different ways and forms all the time. Your Earth Element is your Body, your Air Element is your Mind, your Fire Element is your Spirit and your Water Element is your Soul. We also link them to the seasons, Spring to Water, Summer to Fire, Autumn to Earth and Winter to Air, which makes sense when you study the Archetypes of the Wheel of Life and how the Elements create different climates.

This awareness is already within us, we refer to the Elements in everyday conversation, hardly conscious that we are doing it, yet it is a hidden language that everyone understands. We say "He's down to earth", "She's in a rut", (Earth); "She's a deep one", "He's a drip", "She's a wet blanket" (Water); "He's a live wire" ,"What a hot head" (Fire); "He's breezy" "She's brainy" (Air). When you are enjoying yourself and acting in accord with your natural attributes and latent talents, you are said to be 'in your element' and conversely, 'out of your element'. We are unconsciously saying that the nature of the Elements has something to do with the nature of people, and indeed it does. The fictional detective, Sherlock Holmes, described his insights to his colleague as "Elementary my dear Watson", meaning simple, and that is the truth. When we get down to the essentials, no matter how complex our constructions, it is always simple. We will discover more of this hidden language and inner knowledge as we look at the elements in turn in the following chapters, identifying their qualities and bringing you to a more conscious awareness of them within yourself and in the world you inhabit. It's so obvious once it's pointed out, that you might say you knew it already, deep down.

Beyond the physical world there is the metaphysical world. This is the world of energies from which the physical world is created and solidified. It is from the metaphysical realm that we can direct our consciousness and gain power and control over ourselves. It is on this higher level that we will be approaching the Elements, although you will see that all levels are connected. There is a modern-day tendency to over-intellectualise and complicate everything (Air), resulting in many teachings that are based on theory, rather than fact and experience. The simpler and more succinct we can be, the closer we are to the Truth. In the quagmire of philosophical posturing, the Circle of Archetypes shines like a welcoming beacon, reassuring, wholesome and accessible. Cultures all over the world feature

Elements in their religion, healing, philosophies and mythologies. All share the same concept - one, main energy from which elements are derived. We have considerably weakened our link with nature, our relationship with reality and have lost awareness of much precious knowledge. The following is a brief glimpse of some of the many instances where the Elements play a fundamental role. You do not necessarily have to have an interest or appreciation of any of the following to make use of this Work. They are simply indicative of a general perception of how basic the Elements are in both modern and ancient times.

Astrology

This work on the Archetypes is not Astrology, and cannot be married to it, albeit you will see some similarities. It is best understood if we see Astrology as a study of the energies of the planets in our solar system as experienced from Earth, yet it operates within a framework of the Elements. If you lived on another planet, Venus for example, you would wish to know something about the energies of the planet Earth, as it would have to be included in your charts and interpretation. Our planet, being composed of The Four Elements, is special in our solar system, it is here that they are balanced in such a way that life as we know it exists. We take them for granted, but imagine spending an hour in the scalding steams of Venus having a never-to-be-forgotten sauna, or feasting your eyes on a sightseeing trip round the arid plains of Mars.

"...the four elements are not merely 'symbols' or abstract concepts, but rather that they refer to the vital forces that make up the entire creation that can be perceived by the physical senses. The elements are therefore not only the foundation of astrology and all occult sciences, but they comprise everything we can normally perceive and experience. It is true that the elements, if taken as purely material factors, symbolize the four states of matter described in modern physics: earth is solid, water is liquid, air gaseous and fire plasma, or radiant ionized energy. They may also be said to represent the four primary needs of any advanced organism: air, water, earth (or food) and fire (warmth). But this alone does not begin to reveal the true meaning of the elements."

 - Stephen Arroyo. *Astrology, Psychology and the Four Elements*

The following shows how the Ancient Greeks also considered their importance.

"The physicist Werner Heisenberg states, 'According to Plato, it appears the foundation of this apparently complicated world of elementary particles and force fields is a simple and lucid mathematical structure'. The concept of an overall unity linking the stars and man was integral to

Astrology before the time of Plato. Plato also investigated the forces which make up the universe. The four elements were principles of action or relative states of things, scaled from the most dense to the least dense. The elements were Earth for the Physical, Water for the emotional, Air for the Intellectual and Fire for the Spiritual. At first it seems absurd to make these attributions when modern physicists and chemists have isolated and identified 92 natural elements, but it does not when they are considered as classes of phenomena. *The definition of fire as energy, libido, spiritual impulse vitality and the motivating factor of the elements in fact does hold up under the scrutiny of scientists. Nigel Calder in "The Key of the Universe", describing the very latest breakthroughs in particle physics says, "With hindsight, the 'fire' of Heraclitus was not too different from the 'energy' from which everything was made, according to twentieth-century physicists". Water, traditionally defined as emotion, feelings, passivity and sensitivity is a very close hit to the wave nature of energy and matter in the universe. There is also a close connection between emotions and waves via the rhythms of the libido which affect sexuality. Air, which is traditionally correlated with mind, intellect, communication and duality, is similar to the concept of* complementarity *between particle and wave nature. Earth, which governs the physical, matter, density and immovability, would naturally correlate with the* particle nature *of light and matter."*
- A.T.Mann. T*he Round Art. The Astrology of Time and Space.*

It has been suggested that Carbon, Hydrogen, Oxygen and Nitrogen could be related to the Four Elements and are normally considered to be the four most common elements in scientific terms. Carbon relates to burning (Fire), Hydrogen is the one of the two basic elements of Water, Oxygen is the gas we breathe (Air) and Nitrogen helps to enrich the soil (Earth). Empedocles (490–430 BC) was a Greek pre-Socratic philosopher and a citizen of Agrigentum, a Greek city in Sicily. He is known as the originator of the cosmogenic theory of the Four Classical Elements and he also proposed powers called Love, which brings about the mixture of the elements, and Strife which brings about their separation. It is clear that we need to go forward in our evolution with goodwill and Love. There is too little of that around, but certainly plenty of Strife.

The Gospels

The Four Gospels were once linked to the Elements. In some old Bibles you can see their symbols at the chapter headings - an angel for Water, a lion for Fire, a cow for Earth and a bird for Air. It has been claimed that the Church, in its own political interests, made sure that the story of Jesus came down incomplete. Anything that threatened its power was removed, misinterpreted and thus redacted. In spite of this, if we approach the Gospels anew, separate from the Old Testament, we begin to see them as instruction in white magic, with love and healing at its core.

Alchemy

Alchemy is about balancing and integrating Elemental energies resulting in magical powers and physical transformation. The workings of the Elements within the Alchemists is key, for the practical experiments can only be successful if their beings are in a fit state to receive the energies. We can safely assume that they were unsuccessful, but I'm wrong, would they be so kind as to give me a call. The Philosopher's Stone is the gem of Truth against which the false shatters. It is also one's Divine individuality, the ability to transmute lead into gold being a mere by-product of transmuting one's consciousness. As the flesh is turned into finer stuff the cells are suffused with more light, they vibrate on a higher level where, like gold, they do not tarnish. The Quintessence of harmonised elements is the true Elixir of Eternal Youth. The great teachings are trying to make us understand that it is all available to us NOW. Yes, of course change and growth can be a struggle, but is not nearly as bad as the pain of stagnation and hopelessness. At least if we are moving, we have a chance of getting somewhere, and those feelings of lightness and happiness can increase as we grow.

The Tarot

The Tarot is a pack of 78 cards, 56 comprising the Minor Arcana, and 22 the Major Arcana. Today it is used as a 'fortune telling' and counselling tool with many new packs of cards being created, often using the word 'Tarot' to describe them. They may well be useful but they are not Tarot cards. In parts of Europe card games are still played with old Tarot packs. It is thought that when it became necessary to protect the great knowledge, the best way to conceal it was in a set of picture playing cards. This would guarantee its survival until such time as people had eyes to see and decipher the great philosophy it contains. Richard Gardner did see it, and understood it; his work on the Tarot and the Elements provided the seeds from which the Work grew. The Major Arcana describes the energies of life and the journey towards self-realisation, with the Minor Arcana representing the Four Elements; the cups being Water, the pentacles Earth, the wands Fire and the swords Air. The 52 card playing packs we use today are derived from the Minor Arcana, the diamonds being Earth, the hearts Water, the clubs Fire and the spades Air. They each have a Queen, a King and a Knight, but the four Page cards of the Minor Arcana are not included. (Richard Gardner wrote two books about the Tarot – *'Evolution Through the Tarot'* and *'The Tarot Speaks')*.

Medieval and Renaissance Europe

The Elements contributed much to Medieval and Renaissance Europe, featuring in the works of Shakespeare and other writers. As Alchemy abounded in those days it was, quite naturally, an important aspect of current creativity. A Shakespearean example is from Julius Caesar, when Marcus Anthony says of Marcus Brutus,

"His life was gentle, and the elements
So mix'd in him that Nature might stand up
And say to all the world, 'This was a man!"

The Four Humours

Early medicine was based on the Four Humours, which represent four different human temperaments, traditionally with Water the Melancholic, Fire the Choleric, Earth the Phlegmatic and Air the Sanguine. Treatment was aimed at restoring balance between them. Although proponents of modern medicine with its drug-laden, scatter gun approach would disagree, I believe that all our troubles, conflicts and illnesses are a result of a lack of balance between these four vital forces. Reintegration reconnects with the Quintessence. Modern medicine treats the body like a machine comprising of separate parts, all requiring specialists. These practitioners we might call the 'mechanists'. Naturally there is much in modern medicine which is to be commended, and most of us benefit from it at one time or another. There are times when it is the only option, but too often it seeks to heal from the outside, often masking symptoms and introducing others from the side effects of drugs. If drugs don't work, in goes the knife. It ignores the need to heal the inner energies, from which the disorder arose. Older methods and their healers, the 'vitalists', saw the body as a whole, with prevention a major aspect of health care. We learn from the history of Chinese Medicine that doctors were paid only for as long as their clients remained healthy. This is a wonderful approach, as it is in the interests of the practitioners to keep their patients well. They taught them how to look after themselves, using a variety of techniques, including diet, exercise, meditation and massage. They also practised Acupuncture. The mind, emotions and the soul, through some form of religious practice, were of equal importance. This concept was embedded into medical practice; they had the holistic awareness of how each part connected to and influenced the others. We see a return to some of these original methods, calling them 'alternative' or 'complementary'. They take a comprehensive and natural approach, sometimes with the Elements playing a part.

Herbalism, Palmistry and Magic

The 19th Century American herbalist Samuel Thomson (1769 –1843), known as "The Father of American Herbalism", wrote that,

"All bodies are composed of four elements - Earth, Air, Fire and Water. The healthy state consists in the proper balance and distribution of these four elements, and disease is their derangement."

Palmistry identifies a hand type for each Element. By studying the shape of the hands, the lines on them and the skin patterns, much is revealed about character and physical, emotional and psychological states.

In the Wicca, the religion of the Goddess in Europe, the Elements play an important role. Candles are lit at the four corners of the east, west, north and south during rituals. The changing seasons are followed through the calendar, each having their own festivals. Spring is the Water season, when we may get April showers and rebirth; Summer is Fire, full of heat and colour; Autumn is Earth, when we gather all the treasures she has grown and Winter is Air, the cold forcing us indoors to study and learn. The Faerie Folk are divided into four 'families', the Undines are the Water folk, the Salamanders rule Fire, The Gnomes are Earth and the Sylphs belong to Air.

The Elements Around the World.

We can roam the world and find reference to the Elements everywhere. The Tibetans built gigantic structures to symbolise them and they are included in many holy scriptures such as the Bhagavad Gita of India. Chinese medicine and philosophies and Indian Ayurvedic medicine (which is once more becoming popular, not least due to the efforts of Deepak Chopra) are also based on them. (Note: Oriental practitioners name five elements, Water, Fire, Metal, Earth and Wood. I would say that Wood belongs to the Earth Element, and perhaps Metal relates to Air, making four in actuality. There may be some confusion due to terminology and cultural background in this case).

Psychics and natural healers speak of the Four Bodies; the Emotional Body of Water, the Spiritual Body of Fire, the Mental Body of Air and the Physical Body of Earth. Japanese Zen Buddhism tells of the four qualities that make up all creation; light, airiness, fluidity and solidity. The I Ching, an ancient Chinese oracle in the form of a book, is based on them and they feature in traditional Thai healing methods. You will find the Elements in the myths of Ancient Sumeria, the Maories and Aborigines of the Antipodes where the four points of the compass, each with a guiding spirit, symbolise stages in the life journey. The East, direction of the daily birth of the sun, represents a person's birth and early years, The South is childhood and growth of awareness, The West is adulthood and introspection, while the North represents wisdom and spiritual aspects of life. The centre of the wheel is symbolic of Mother Earth and the Creatrix, and their role in the beginning and continuation of life. The four points are also indicative of the balance between the emotional, mental, physical and spiritual aspects of health. They are present in the Medicine Wheel of the Native Americans and in Ancient Egypt. In Ancient Greece there were the four faculties; moral (fire), aesthetic and soul (water), intellectual (air) and physical (earth). The two male ones were grouped together as the Apollonian way of expression, (Fire and Air, Yang), and the two female under the Dionysian mode, (Water and Earth, Yin).
There are many such examples of the Elements being at the centre of cultural teachings; they are a recurring theme and widely recognised as basic to our existence. Let us now look at the Elements in turn and see how they work in our lives.

Water

This is a general description of the Water Element, whose characteristics are shared among the three Water Archetypes, the Child, the Enchantress and the Actress. These are fully described in their own chapters.

Water is, with Earth, one of the horizontal Elements, it flows outwards and downwards, levelling when it meets earth below it. It is the world of the Soul, of feelings and emotions. Its energy is strongest in the Spring and its colours are all the blues. It is the dynamic female/Yin element, very powerful and rich, but today in the west it is considered inferior by those dominated by the Air and Fire Elements. Looking at the Elements outside of ourselves reveals many pointers as to their nature within. All this may seem familiar to you. That's because deep down, you have always known it, you have 'felt it in your water'. The Earth is roughly seventy-five per cent Water, if you turn a globe to a certain position there is almost no land to be seen, only vast areas of ocean. Our own bodies are also approximately three-quarters Water, as are those of most similar life forms.

We are humans, the Latin 'humor, humere' means 'moisture, to be moist', 'humecto' is 'to wet, moisten, water', 'humidus' is 'wet, moist, damp'. When there is a lot of dampness in the atmosphere, we say it is 'humid'. We now use the phrase, 'a sense of humour' to denote the ability to see the funny side of things. 'Humerous' is 'that which is amusing', but the older meaning is closer to 'mood or state', as in "What kind of humour are you in today?", "I'm in good humour", "He's in bad humour". This could connect to the healing system of the Four Humours. We often laugh so much we cry, so 'humour' is not so out of place. To be 'humane' is to have compassionate and kindly feelings, to be 'humiliated' is to be brought to a low point where we have unpleasant feelings about ourselves. A 'humectare' is the Latin for 'poet', one who expresses a deep sensitivity. Many people have the ability to express a profound feeling through poetry, finding it easier than prose, which is more like the language of the mind, whereas poetry is the language of the soul. Poetry coming from the Water Element almost always rhymes, it follows the cycles of the moon, the tides of the sea, as reflected in the ebb and flow, the rise and fall of our own emotions. Good quality rhyming poetry is hypnotic. Modern poetry does not have to rhyme, however, feelings can still be moved by prose. It's the waves of rhythms that matter. Calling ourselves 'humans' indicates that at one time we were consciously aware that we are sentient beings. So many of our present-day sufferings are caused by the suppression and denial of our emotions and feelings. There is conjecture that the world was at one time surrounded by mist and we lived in a watery world of blues and greys and browns. But, as ever, when the pendulum swings too far in one direction, it goes too far back in the other and so by overdoing the Water Element, the mists were disturbed and came down in a deluge. This allowed the sun to shine through and so encourage the development of the male/Yang Elements, Fire and Air. Many cultures have a story of a flood. We are now in danger of going the other way and as the rhyme says "God gave Noah the rainbow sign, No more water, it's the fire next time." Enter global heating.

Water is blue, the blue in the sky is Water in its metaphysical, energy form. If an artist is painting a landscape, the aspects that are furthest away, such as hills, may be covered with green plants and grass, yet these would be painted in blues, because we are seeing those distant things through metaphysical water, and to paint them green would make them appear too close. The blue sky encircles and unites all the lands of the Earth, from the smallest landmass to the largest continent. Islands and continents are surrounded by Water, oceans and seas, and so it is with us, your own 'landmass', your body is its own island, yet connected to other islands by the flow of metaphysical Water in the atmosphere all around you, in a sea of consciousness. Hence, in it you will feel ripples and currents, waves of feeling and will sense things that are unfelt by other Elements. Unfortunately, negative feelings also have this effect. The danger of not expressing our feelings in a creative and positive way is that they become stagnant and stink like water that has been still for too long. Many hurts can also sully our Water, leaving the debris of our wounds within it. When this happens we get diseases such as cancer when our cells turn against us. These illnesses are like Water in that they have rhythms, sometimes worse and then remission. Similarly, our emotions rush up and we turn against each other in bad feeling. Grief comes in waves too. Water enables us to share experiences whatever our backgrounds and nationalities. Our basic feelings are the same, differing only in expression.

Water has currents. You might say, "There was a funny undercurrent at that dinner party", and just as currents can change, so can our moods suddenly swing. The tides are swayed by the Moon, as are we. Tides have been known to be measured in a tea cup. The Water in our bodies swells and rises up with the moon, creating internal pressure. Women know about these cycles of fluids, as during the menstrual cycle they may feel pent up, retain fluid and feel particularly emotional. In older, wiser times, we catered for this and put it to good use in moonlit rituals and creative expression. Men also need creative and emotional outlets, but we ignore their deeper needs and pay the price with more crime and violence at the Full Moon, requiring extra police on the streets. I have been told that some surgeons avoid operating at the full moon because there is a significant increase in blood flow. The moon and fluids are directly linked. Water creates many currents. In the flow of rivers to the sea, in under-sea rivers like the Gulf Stream, there are opposing currents, undercurrents, whirlpools, dangerous undertows. All is not what it seems, water can also be deceptive and treacherous.

Water makes things soggy and sloshy, slushy and sloppy. It is the source of life, having the ingredients for DNA. It is wet as are our tears and sweat, and we taste salty, like the sea. We say "don't be soppy" to someone over sentimental, we tell people to stop crying and "dry up". Water is refreshing, it relieves thirst, it is a nice cool drink or shower. The Earth is revitalised after rain. Water is cleansing, our tears wash us clean. We say, "Have a good cry and get it out of your system", "Let it all out". Toxins are present in tears shed in emotion that are absent when our eyes are merely watering from the wind or from peeling onions. We 'pour out' our troubles, we can 'brim over' with joy or sadness, 'burst into floods of tears', experience a 'torrent of emotion', we feel we could 'drown in misery', we seek to 'drown our sorrows', we try be 'buoyant' and stay 'afloat'. Water aids communication, we can share our feelings, 'a trouble shared is a trouble halved, a pleasure shared is a pleasure doubled'. It makes you telepathic, you pick things up on the 'waves', you get on the 'same wavelength'. If we lived in a society where everyone was using their Water element, we would all have to be honest, for communication would be deeper and we would have increased awareness as to what everyone was thinking. Sound travels better in the rain and it has been observed that radios have improved reception and more stations then. The low frequency sounds of whale song can travel up to 10,000 miles through the seas.

Water is deep, as is our subconscious. We say "She's a deep one", "I can't fathom him out", "It can't be fathomed". A fathom is a nautical measure equalling six feet in depth, a link between the Waters of the seas and the Waters of our natures. If we are in danger of getting too involved with something, we are told, "Don't get in too deep". If someone can't handle something, he's 'Out of his depth' or 'All at sea'. Yet, for all its subtlety, it can wreak havoc when stormy and will ruin everything if it floods you. Sometimes emotions can be hard to handle. Water flows, as do our feelings, we say "Go with the flow". Water types follow the flow of energies, but when overdone they will be 'easily led' and can end up as 'drifters'. Water will follow whatever course is set, as long as it's not uphill, following the path of least resistance, flowing its way round obstacles. It flows into containers, puddles and pools, lakes and underground caverns, watersheds and into the biggest container of all - the sea. It meanders in bends and loops, for in the world of Water there are no straight lines. The course of a river turns as it meets obstacles which it seeks to avoid. Not being strong enough to barge through them, nor bulky enough to flow over them, it goes around them. Watery types avoid confrontations for fear of having their feelings hurt or hurting others, so they will be evasive or simply agree. Water takes a winding route, we say "Get to the point!" It slowly makes its way to the sea and it will eventually arrive, there is no hurry. Water is weak yet immensely strong, its steady flow can wear away rocks. It drops, harmless but insistent, and where the rock is porous, water seeps in, moistening, soaking and softening it. Where the rock is hard, water wears it away drip by drip, granule by granule. It creates caverns and gorges, canyons and valleys, for eventually the weakness of water will overcome the hardness of rock. Faced with sea storms, tsunamis and floods, however, we see its true power.

Water is receptive, you can put things in it. When we receive something, we 'take it in', too much Water makes us naive and gullible and 'we get taken in'. Water types love to listen to stories and believe everything they are told, because they are aware of other levels of experience and existence and so have no reason to disbelieve any fabulous tales you may tell them. They know full well that 'fact is stranger than fiction'. Young children are much more in touch with their Water Element and this is why it is so easy to programme them, they are as receptive as a clean pool. We have to be very careful what we tell them, it can go in deep and be hard to fish out in later life. As the Jesuits said, "Give me the child for seven years and I will show you the man". Many of us are working hard to undo the pollution dropped into us as children.

Water is your imagination, an infinite well of creative treasure. All creations begin with an inner vision. Water is the source of all life, it reveals inner desires, it shows you your past and will help you create any future you wish. Water is your subconscious, driven below by the dominance of other Elements in our present society. Reintroducing and respecting it will make its magic accessible and conscious and create a compassionate, imaginative world. Water is all of your dreams, nightmares and daydreams, which are not mere escapism or wishful thinking. They are visions your inner life is giving you to point your way, showing you the next step along your path in life. Dreams from childhood of being a ballerina or an explorer may or may not be realistic in adulthood, but more adventurous holidays or joining a dance class may be possible. This will change the energies inside you and take you a step forward. Keeping a dream diary will reveal instructive and even prophetic patterns. Dreams can help to cleanse your subconscious and be a rich source of creative inspiration. Many artists, and even scientists, have awakened with a picture 'swimming in front of their eyes', or with a great idea, or a whole symphony ringing in their ears. Things come 'out of the blue', like 'a bolt from the blue'. Our dream world is very powerful, the pictures it can 'come up with' can be stunningly accurate and informative. Indeed, 'a picture is worth a thousand words' Water people love looking at pictures and usually have plenty in their homes.

Water works with images in two ways, one of which is being psychic and intuitive; you receive images and feelings. In-tuition means learning from the inside, to be guided by your inner life, which is often way ahead of scientists, who in many cases come to the same conclusions. Professor Robert Lanza, in this book, *'Biocentrism',* says biocentrism explains that the universe only exists because of an individual's consciousness of it. He is, in effect, echoing what the Hindus say; we live in Maya, which is Sanskrit, meaning 'magic' or 'illusion'. Scientists eventually learn what the inner life knew from the beginning. Most women, are more inclined to Water, hence we have 'women's intuition', although this doesn't mean that men can't have it too. Intuition is very much linked to our feelings, 'you get a feeling about something', you might say, "That didn't feel quite right" or "I get a good feeling about this". We also call it a 'hunch', often helping detectives to solve a case. The other way Water works with images is in creative visualisation, when you are creating and transmitting images. With this ability, you can use the Water Element to manifest what you want. Water is hypnotic and magnetic and draws things towards itself. Worrying is creative visualisation in the negative, there is the danger that the more we worry about a thing, the more we might make it happen. A good technique to offset it is to say, "For every negative thought, I think three positive ones", which trains your subconscious to be more positive.

Water is gentle and amenable, it can be directed into channels, canals, and dams and made to go up pipes, but it is also elusive, you can't get hold of it. Water types can be secretive and alluring, like the magnetic pull of the sea, which sometimes makes you feel like walking into it. This is how the magic of Water works, it doesn't go out after something like the Fire Element, rather it draws it unto itself like reeling in a fish. It is dark, mysterious, enigmatic, deep, atmospheric, and irresistible.

Water is cold and Watery people feel the cold, huddling round fires. In the presence of psychic phenomena, the temperature in a room drops dramatically, which can be read on a thermometer. A haunted room often has a cold spot and we feel 'chilled to the bone'. A ghost story is a 'chilling tale'. Over-Watery types tend to weep and urinate a lot, they 'turn on the water works', liquids flow from them at every opportunity and they often have a cold. Getting frequent colds comes from having too much Water and it is known that unhappy people get more. Depression depresses the immune system, everything is weakened and diluted. Our immunity depends on a balance of Water and Fire to stay healthy. These Watery souls 'take a chill' so easily and we say of them. "What a drip!" What with all the colds they get, they really do drip all over the place, are pale and 'wishy-washy', and look 'washed out'. It is vital that we keep our Waters clean and flowing. Water flows downwards, into caverns, underground streams, into the deepest depths of our beings. If we go down too far, we 'get down', we 'get the blues' and we 'wallow in it'.

Water is sensitive, it can feel the slightest ripple even if it is happening thousands of miles away. Distance is no problem to the psychic powers, there are many instances of people sensing what was happening to their dear ones many miles away. You 'feel it in your water'. It is the sympathetic Element with empathy and compassion. We wish to protect and spare each other's feelings, "I didn't have the heart to tell her, she would have been so hurt". Because we share feelings, we have empathy, we don't like others to be upset, we feel the hurt too and say, "I felt for him". It makes us tender hearted and kind. Water is romantic, with hearts, flowers and love poetry. When planning a seduction, we turn down the lighting, burn candles, play soft music in the background. We 'set the mood' and the atmosphere impresses itself upon the lovers. If we are attracted to someone we used to say "He's a dreamboat", "She's dreamy". It is all the love juices, ejaculation, a woman 'gets wet'; the smell of the vagina is similar to that of the sea and we are grown in the womb in a sea of amniotic fluid.

It is soft-hearted, you 'wear your heart on your sleeve'. When women complain of unfeeling and unromantic men, they are bemoaning a lack of the Water Element. People see this Element as weak, but in fact many fear it, it is the only thing that can put out a fire, and as seen in the section about the Fire Element, this is closely linked to the ego. The power of tidal waves and floods is stupendous, washing away everything in its path. No fire or ego can stand up to it. Water is ultimately the most powerful Element because it can extinguish Fire, whereas all Fire can do to Water is turn it into steam, which will rise up and reform later. Water is the strangest of the elements. It is subtle and weak, yet hugely strong, ever changing; we say "She's so changeable and moody". The sea is never the same two days running, one day it is as smooth as glass and the next it is dark, menacing and turbulent. It is elusive and ambiguous, gentle and rough, has surface and depth, can be locked in ice and gush forth in steam. It is docile and uncontainable, moving and still. Water surrounds us, it can lie beneath our feet and above our heads in its metaphysical form. It permeates everything, from the air we breathe (humidity) to the food we eat. It has many moods, dispersing over plains and sandbanks, pouring through gulleys and over waterfalls, sometimes slow and sluggish, sometimes fast and forceful, gentle, dreamlike and languid, rapid and furious, tranquil and soothing, agitated and disturbing. Water levels fluctuate, rise and fall, a trickle along the river bed in the dry season becomes swirling turbulence after the rains. Tides at the seashore lap gently when the sea is like a millpond, but pound savagely during storms. Water ebbs and flows, the tides high and low continue to move with the gravitational pull of the moon, the eternal sloshing about of the sea, all in continuous flux. It is soothing and terrifying, the source of life and an agent of destruction. In bulk, water is powerful and overwhelming, emotions can be 'stormy', rivers burst banks, bridges are washed away, fields swamp, buildings are broken down and living things are drowned. There is no way of withstanding great sheets of floodwater. Water dilutes, it takes particles into itself and changes their character. Poisons, after great dilution, become homeopathic remedies, inedible beans and leaves become coffee and tea, shells become dyes. Water is a natural container. As it travels, it picks up particles, flowing over peat in the Highland streams creating the unique taste of Scottish Whisky. Rains falling on the Mendips become the sulphurous mineral waters of Bath. There is a lot in the Water Element, it is fascinating and if not used, there can be no goodwill or love.

In the section about the Archetypes, the Water Element is divided and represented in three ways. The Child personifies the passive, receptive aspects, the Enchantress the deep and mysterious, and the Actress the showy, tempestuous surface.

Fire

This is a general description of the Fire Element, whose characteristics are shared among the three Fire Archetypes, the Fool, the Joker and the Warrior. These are fully described in their own chapters.

Fire, with Air, is one of the vertical Elements, it reaches upwards, it governs the world of the Spirit, it is action and heat. Its energy is strongest in the summer and its colours are red, orange and orangey yellow. Together with Air, it dominates today's world. Most people prefer hot sunny days and when it rains they say "It's a horrible day". Fire is the energy we put into things and the effect we have on the world. It is the heat that is magically present in our bodies, constant despite quite significant changes in external temperatures. It is the source of our light, the solar energy of the sun strikes the earth to glittering effect and radiates its surface, lighting it up. It is the grandest of the elements, the most active, blazing, splendid, striking, colourful and exciting, frizzling heat and blazing energy.

Fire is hot and red. When we get 'hot-headed', our faces go red, our 'blood is up', we 'burn' with rage, ambition or desire. We can 'flare up', 'get blazing mad', 'get hot under the collar', 'reach boiling point'. When you lose control of your Fire Element, you 'blow your top' with tremendous explosions like a volcano. A phrase used in Glasgow, Scotland, is 'dinna get rid-heeded!' (don't get red-headed), i.e. don't get angry. We generate heat when we move and get hot when we exercise. Aerobics tapes and videos once told us to "make it burn!", and we 'burn off' fat. People who work too hard become exhausted and 'burnt out'. Fire types do not usually feel the cold, turning off fires and opening windows, much to the horror of Water types. Fire is cleansing, it burns away impurities. There are times when a situation is no longer tenable, it 'won't wash', i.e. the Water Element is of no use in the situation. The Fire approach is to go into action, to do everything possible to remedy the situation, and if that doesn't work, to burn it all away and start anew. Although much suffering is caused through forest fires, it can be a good thing in respect of the long-term results on the ecosystem, increasing plant and animal diversity. During a wildfire, nutrients are released into the soil, followed by a flush of new plant growth which helps clean the air by absorbing carbon dioxide, one of the root causes of global heating, and releasing oxygen, resulting in purer air. When Fire energy heats the soil, the seeds fertilise and grow. When its energy vaporises water, the rains come. The sun beams energy into plants and turns them into food, it warms and fuels us. Fire heals, infected wounds can be cauterised as it burns out impurities. We need to be initiated into both Water and Fire in order to be properly cleansed and purified.

In the heat of lovemaking we become 'flushed with desire', and a lust for sex is to 'be on heat'. If we are thought to be very attractive we are 'hot stuff'. The Water Element provides the depth and romance, Fire the excitement and passion. Water is a slower Element and, as it comes more easily to women, in general women are slower to arouse sexually, experiencing love-making as an emotional as well as a physical experience, although men can also feel like this of course. Males, in general, are aroused faster, the penis rises upwards and can take just a few minutes to reach orgasm. Once over, it is time for a refreshing nap and then on to the next thing, whereas Water will want to cuddle up and communicate.

Fire is the fastest speed we know, the sun's heat hurtles down through 93 million miles to the earth, a mere $8^{1/2}$ minutes later. It travels at 186,000 miles per second, about 700 million miles per hour. It can take months for Water to penetrate enough for you to realise your house has damp, whereas Fire takes hold and spreads with terrifying speed. Fire is big and bold, it has courage and drive and gets things done, it is 'no sooner said than done!' Fire is linked to the ego, it is the part of you that is ambitious and strives to achieve things. Like separate flames, each one trying to rise up higher than the other, Fire is competitive, saying, "I want to be successful", "I want to be famous", "I want to shine", "I want to be somebody." As the flames of Fire flicker upwards, we aspire to great things, we want to 'light up the world', we want to 'set the world on fire', and we get 'fired up' with the energy of it all. Fire is action, 'there's no time like the present'. D.I.N is a maxim in the aggressive and competitive world of business, the acronym for 'Do It Now!' There is no messing about, if something needs done. Fire is direct, it dislikes preamble, there is no time to waste, no time for frills or 'sugaring the pill'. Fire moves forward in a relentless march and must be intelligently directed or it can easily get out of control and be as destructive as a forest fire. There is so much dangerous, negative Fire in the world right now. Fire is expansive, the genitals swell, the ego becomes enormous, it boasts, brags and is 'big-headed', it thinks it is the sun around which everyone else revolves. It leaps from one combustible to another. When metal is heated, it expands, steam takes up more space than water, tropical variants of familiar plants grow gigantic, luxuriant and gaudy in the heat. It is territorial, ever seeking to expand its dominance. When misused, it invades countries, brings conflict, war, cruelty, aggression, violence, murder and rape, which is used as a weapon of war, and femicide is a major human rights issue. Fire is movement, strength and energy. Fire types are always on the move, always doing something, often can't sit still, are a 'flaming nuisance', quick to anger they 'seethe', they 'burn with rage'. It attracts attention, it is animation and activity. Through the repeated use of the muscles and the will, strength develops. The Fire Element opens up gyms, where excellence of strength and fitness are pursued through various drills. Jogging, aerobics, sports, dance, martial arts; all help to bring about a fit body.

We live on a revolving planet which rotates each day in its year-long journey around the sun. Anything that appears to be at rest is actually moving at the same speed as the planet, everything is on the move, nothing is truly still. Fire is action and vitality, a circus fairground of movement and energy, a battlefield of competing forces, an arena for change. Fire turns one thing into another, makes machines, glass and many things from crude materials. Heat dries things out, melts and vaporises them. Iron ore is melted in the furnace and shaped into girders, rivets, garden gates, horseshoes and nails. Without Fire there would be no bricks and no glass, no vehicles, no cooking, no electric light and no hot baths or meals. Fire changes us too, we grow in strength through movement and achievement. The more we achieve, the more we are. Fire gives us the stamina, courage and the willpower to keep going.

Fire explodes with thunder and lightning, eruptions, lava streams of molten rock. It is dynamite, gunpowder, fireworks, bombs, bullets and missiles. It is dangerous to play with Fire, riskier still to provoke it and riskiest of all is to challenge it. Fire is expansive, in war it captures and expands territory. It is boastful and impressive. Popular films and television feature much of the Fire Element with cops and robbers, the hunky, macho, himbo hero, fights, crashes, explosions, car chases and fires. The main plot, whatever the details, is about one ego fighting another. There are different types of films on offer of course, but the big action stuff is sure to take plenty of money at the box office. Add a sprinkling of sexual titillation and you can't fail.

Fire can be dangerous, it destroys, burns, cracks, withers and scorches. Soil dries into deserts. Long, dry summers bring droughts and dried-up river beds, life starves to death in the parching arid heat.

We think of friction, which creates sparks. Sparks from flint and wood set matter alight; kindling wood and dry grass. Matches are struck, the spark bursts into flame. When positive it can take everyone forward, when the friction is negative, anger bursts out. The motor car is a Fire machine, its movement caused by a spark igniting and burning the petrol. The movement of the pistons is not dissimilar to a penis having sex, and sex is used a lot in selling cars, enticing the penis with images of scantily clad young women, although less so now. We can see how this Element can take over once we are behind the wheel. Even reasonable people can turn into aggressive, dangerous 'road hogs', raging with 'road rage'. I have heard road safety experts comment that it is the young male driver who is the most dangerous and is involved in more accidents. This could be a result of the lack of opportunities for initiation, something that was once important for steering and controlling young men's energies. The motor car is no longer a vehicle, taking one to a destination, it becomes an extension of the self, a demonstration of skill and risk and ego. There are so few positive ways for the healthy young male to prove himself that he grasps at whatever he can, despite the dangers to himself and others. Extreme sports and travelling help to burn off some energy, but not everyone can afford it. In all fairness, I have to say that women are also starting to drive more recklessly and competitively. In my own experience it is usually the younger ones, possibly because they have been brought up in a world dominated by Fire, so people are lit up with it. Also, now there are many more cars on the road, overcrowding is making us more impatient. We need to balance and control our Fire Element before we blow up the world. We are in danger of burning the Earth away. Global heating is making itself felt. Let us instead use Fire to bring about courageous positive change.

Fire can also be great fun, colourful, lively, flamboyant, vital and adventurous. We want to 'paint the town red'; it loves games, skills, parties and exploring. Fire is your Spirit, vitality, it keeps you 'in good spirits' 'lifts the spirits' we are in 'high spirits' we are 'spirited'. It is warming and cheerful. Fire types are always telling Water folk to "Cheer up! It may never happen!" It lacks the sensitivity to realise that it may have already happened and sometimes people can't help being sad. When 'feeling blue' (too much Water) we are advised to go and do something. Fire gives confidence in yourself and your ability to achieve, it makes life varied, interesting and challenging. Fire loves a challenge, hence it plays games and sports. It is the courage to change and to grow, to expand our talents and our beings. As long as we continue to do positive things, there is always the chance of making something wonderful happen. Fire is happy-go-lucky and sociable, optimistic and often lucky. You never know what to expect or what will happen next with some Fire types, one minute they're juggling or jogging, the next they're sailing across the sea in a canoe. It provides the variety we need to stimulate and encourage growth. There is always something bigger and better to go for. Fire is the spark that sets off a chain reaction, setting in motion a whole new scene. 'Go for it!' It is essential in leadership, it inspires confidence in others. Fire people, however, need to be careful of becoming workaholics and exhausting themselves, never stopping to smell the roses. They can go into 'melt down'. Fire is sunshine and happiness, with Fire anything and everything is possible. It is bold, fearless, optimistic and dynamic, people with 'fire in their bellies' get things done.

"What you can do, or dream you can do, begin it,

Boldness has genius, power and magic in it!" - *Johann Wolfgang von Goethe*

In the section about the Archetypes, the Fire Element is divided and represented in three ways. The Fool personifies the lively adventurous aspects, the Joker the sparks and wits and the Warrior the flames of power and strength.

Earth

This is a general description of the Earth Element, whose characteristics are shared among the three Earth Archetypes, the Worker/Slave, Mother Nature and the Wise Woman. These are fully described in their own chapters.

As with Water, Earth is one of the Horizontal Elements. It spreads outwards around the globe. It is the substance of your body and the material world. Earth is the balancing opposite of Air, its energy is strongest in Autumn and its colours are those of the Earth, from the rich, dark brown of fertile soil to the beige of sand and desert. Earth and Water are both extremely rich, as can be seen when looking at a drop of Water or a tiny piece of Earth under a microscope. How prolific, varied and abundant is Nature. These two Elements, Earth and Water, are more ancient in us, deeper than the more recently developed Fire and Air Elements. Nature takes over again and again as civilisations fall. Wisdom is a quality of Earth, differing from knowledge in that knowledge may be obtained from the outside, through reading or hearsay. Wisdom comes from inner experience, built up over time through an attunement of the body to Mother Earth, the great body upon whom we live and feed, and through a body of people sharing their wisdom.

This Element gives a love and talent for gardening and agriculture, it gives you 'green fingers'. Things must be grown and cultivated that the body may be fed. We talk about people being 'earthy' or 'down to earth', of 'having their feet on the ground'. Earth types like their bodies to be comfortable and well fed and believe that 'the answer lies in the soil'. They are 'slow but sure', never in a hurry, the seasons come round in their time, just as they always have. You can't make the plants grow faster by pulling on them, they have their natural rhythms. The Logician, however, uses artificial means through the use of chemicals. Vegetation grows on her surface - flowers, fruits, vegetables, berries, grains, spices and herbs. Underneath, the Earth is a huge ball full of all kinds of treasures - copper, coal, zinc, diamonds, minerals, oil, truffles and gold. Just as our bodies have the same proportion of water as the Earth, so do they contain precious metals and minerals, possibly in the same proportions as the Earth. The Earth is our Mother, and she has made us in her own image. We use the earth for sustenance, for making things, for growing rich. Earth is substance, Earth provides, Earth matters. It is matter, which shapes the landscape, giving it contours and curves, rock, soil and sand, trees, grasses and shrubs. It deals with the essentials of life, what 'matters'. The Earth is heavy, weighty, gravity, she is the great feeder and provider, and many people with this Element strong in their make-up are 'motherly types', they like to 'feed people up'.

Earth is accumulation, the ground is a pile of layers, shaping the landscape into hills and valleys, crags and escarpments, mountains and plains which are accumulated over centuries and millennia. Geologists inspect the different strata and archeologists dig down to find remains, each civilisation leaving its mark, layer upon layer of different experiences and buried treasures. In the womb, as the body grows us, we pass through the strata of evolution, taking on the resemblance of fish, reptile, simian and finally human shape. Earth types, being concerned with matter, often accumulate a lot of it, both in possessions and of physical matter about their persons. They love their possessions, their food, their family, their home and their base. The basics are important. Earth helps us to accumulate goods and money, someone successful in business is said to have 'made a pile', 'heaps of money'. If this aspect of Earth is taken too far, it becomes greedy and exploitative, miserly and over-materialistic. Earth people have relaxed attitudes and slow ways of doing things, they tend not to burn up much energy and so can easily put on weight. Many women do so when pregnant, thickening and widening to accommodate the new life. Earth is girth, a spreading out, as tree trunks grow thicker and the rings within tell how many years it has taken for the tree to grow to its present width. Middle-aged people tend to be thicker than young ones. Earth is growth, saplings grow into trees, seeds into plants, bulbs into flowers, kittens into cats, babies into adults. Accumulation is also weight, heaviness and compression, as sand particles pressed down for several centuries become sandstone, and when heated, it becomes liquid and is made into glass. Coal is formed when dead plant matter decays into peat and is converted into coal by the heat and pressure of deep burial over millions of years, and similarly diamonds develop from carbon. Earth is development and maturing, slow but steady, not to be hurried, taking its time, working and growing until the time is ripe. This aspect of Earth contributes to the traditional concept of evolution, small changes of slow development and adaptation over time.

Earth begins in smallness, the particle, the molecule, the atom, the single cell, the grain of sand.

Fertility, reproduction and growth begin from and depend upon the small; the seed, the sperm, the egg, the speck of pollen and the acorn. Microscopic organisms break up the soil and keep it fertile, working on it minutely in the dark. Earth is balance and equilibrium, a cycle and a food chain of eco systems. It knows the importance of maintaining these natural balances. Gaia theories hold that the planet is a living organism, relating to existing conditions and adjusting to change, working to maintain balance just as our bodies do, in an effort to maintain or restore health. Earth is a collection of great cycles, the turning of the planet on its axis, the path round the sun, the seasons, the year, the day, the hour, the minutes. These are fundamental, regular and reliable. We speak of 'a regular sort of chap'. In health, body processes have a regular rhythm; our heartbeat, breathing and the replenishment of our cells. Earth is night-time, relaxation, rest and sleep. During sleep we can work through a problem and awaken with the answer. Earth types will not make a decision until the question has been properly processed, so will say, "I'll have to sleep on it ". They are slow to react and only to things that deal with the basics of life, anything else is a waste of energy. This Element is slow, easy-going, tolerant and steady. Earth is organic and concerned with growth, both the growth of the crops and the growth of our own beings. Earth has being. Country dwellers find it easier to just *be* than town dwellers, who are affected and infected by the rush and speed of the Fire and Air Elements.

Earth is security, Earth people carry an inner sense of it. This means that although a home is important to them, their real homes are their bodies, so they can be secure anywhere. There is a sense of belonging with this Element, we are a 'body of people', one great big family all connected together, with a love of mixing with and working with others in an organized, practical and co-operative way on common projects. It is what we have in common and, apart from a few minor differences, our bodies are all basically the same. This is the world of work, manual labour, practicality, making and repairing and 'good common sense'. Earth gives a sense of community, is aware of the connections between things and people and how everything depends on everything and everyone else, like the food chain and all the services we provide for each other. Ley lines are like the veins of the Earth, circulating energy and nourishment round the planet, a huge connecting web of power, weaving us all together. It is only in recent times that we have disrespected this flow of the life force. Previously we were careful where we placed buildings or places of work lest we should cut across these lines of power and impede the flow of energy. The Ancient Chinese were adept at this, seeing dragons and tigers in the landscape, a way of looking that revealed where these lines of power passed. Earth reminds us that everything we do individually affects the whole. We must learn to be kind and love one another, for we are all one family, connected at the roots. Earth gives us our roots and we are rooted to her.

Earth gives us our instincts, as spiders are instinctive, arriving already wise as to how to spin a web, as birds know how to migrate around the earth and build a nest, which is usually round and brown. The young of any species learn much through copying their parents, but there is a basic innate instinct for survival that draws out the genetic knowledge and patterns. We do not need to tell our bodies how to heal themselves, they already know, as long as we look after them. We often do the right thing without having to think about it, in which case you may say, "I had an instinct about it", or "You've got good instincts". Earth is practical and realistic, we talk of people who have their 'feet on the ground', they are dependable and solid, 'a real brick', 'the salt of the earth'. Earth is sturdy, steady, enduring, regular, productive, firm and weighty. Earth is routines, but it can also be a rut, saying "he's stuck in a rut", "she's a stick-in-the mud". Earth can be fixed and reluctant to change daily habits. Earth is caring and healing, comforting, soothing, makes sure you are wearing enough warm clothes in the winter, that you are eating properly and getting enough sleep. Earth people are instinctive healers and nurses, they love to look after others, they like the simple things in life, we say "She's so natural". They have magic in their hands, whether they are growing things, cooking or giving healing. Many mothers will give a 'magic rub' to a child who has fallen over and animals will instinctively lay a wound to the ground to receive healing from the Earth.

Earth rules the stomach and digestion system, it helps us to absorb, assimilate, extract the goodness, eliminate the crap and keep us regular. This is not only regarding the food we eat, but also a process essential to proper learning. There was a phrase in common usage, 'Read, mark, learn and inwardly digest'. We need to 'chew it over' to 'get to the heart of the matter', 'the essence of a thing', we get a 'gut feeling'. This wise approach to teaching and learning is no longer fashionable, it has been replaced with superficial force-feeding of facts which are to be studied, remembered and forgotten as soon as they are of no use. Without Earth we lose touch with the organic processes and the real world, we become nervous, insecure and afraid. We 'can't stomach it', 'need to be earthed' and 'grounded', and we say unpleasant things "Make me feel sick to my stomach", "It's nauseating", "It twists my guts", "My bowels turned to water.". Earth is the wisdom of good nutrition and a balanced lifestyle, attuning and adhering to the rules of the natural world.

Earth multiplies, and this is an aspect of Earth, besides greed, that needs to be controlled. We are programmed to breed to keep the species going until such time as we manage to evolve to a higher level. Before modern medicine, nature automatically culled any species whose numbers became so large as to threaten the life balance, and for millennia equilibrium was maintained. Now humanity has so overpopulated that it is wiping out other species by the thousands. This is an age of the mass production of people, being the way the Logician manufactures things, as opposed to the hand-crafted ways of Earth. Another reason we are driven to breed is that we have created societies that cut most people off from their creativity at an early age, so making babies is the only option left to them. There is no doubt in my mind, and that of many others, that overpopulation is one of the most serious problems we face today. It is a primary, critical issue and all others, such as pollution, greed and shortages are a result of it and secondary to it. It is an unpopular subject, a hot potato, and most politicians won't touch it for fear of losing votes, and women who do not wish to have children are thought to have something wrong with them. As things stand, they should be given awards. It's been shown that, when women have access to education and therefore financial independence, the birth rate halves. We need to bring more women to power, it is only in patriarchal times that overpopulation has occurred. Everyone is self-indulgent, thinking they and their offspring are special exceptions, but as a friend once put it, "Overpopulation is your baby". Pollution is produced by people. In response to the argument that there is plenty of food for everyone if it were fairly distributed, Richard Gardner gave one of his many inspired and highly individual replies, "It's not the food, it's the shit". The Earth is an abundant, generous, holistic Element, ever-giving, striving to maintain health both on the Earth and in our bodies. Earth is indulgent, solid and stolid, understanding, wholesome and real. Where Fire can give you fitness, Earth can give you health.

In the section about the Archetypes, the Earth Element is divided and represented in three ways. The Worker/Slave personifies the practical, tolerant aspects, Mother Nature the nurturing and growing and the Wise Woman the accumulation of wisdom and goods.

Air

This is a general description of the Air Element, whose characteristics are shared among the three Air Archetypes, the Observer, the Logician and the Patriarch. These are fully described in their own chapters.

Air is the balancing opposite of Earth, it governs the world of the Mind and is, with Fire, one of the vertical Elements, it rises upwards. It is the world of thought and intellect and its colours are yellows and golds. Its energy is strongest in the winter when we come indoors to read and study. Air is space and distance, it is a collection of gases which fill space between the earth and the sun. It occupies the hollow of an empty cup and the space around it, buildings are spaces enclosed by walls. We see each other as light waves travelling through the space between us and we hear each other through sound waves. In the Air Element we communicate through space and over distance, enhanced by modern technical devices. Air carries, it has movement; rain clouds blow across the oceans, seeds and insects are dispersed across the land, birds, butterflies, and bees are carried by winged flight on air currents. It is a conveyer, it carries sight, sound and smell. Through it we know when something is on fire, when food is being cooked, when we are close to the sea and when something is rotten. Air carries information too, it is a messenger and can moderate, as can reasoned intervention. At the earth's surface the air is warm, hot air rises, cooler air takes its place, warm air from the tropics pushes up towards the ice-capped poles, cold air from the poles swoops down to the tropics, cool breezes moderate temperature at the sea coasts. If the sun's ultra-violet rays reached the earth at full strength, the seas would dry up and plant life would frizzle. If the proportion of oxygen in the atmosphere was any higher, the planet would catch fire. Air signifies breathing. The air is a mixture of different gases, 78% nitrogen, oxygen about 21%, the other minor gases form 1%. This is found naturally in the atmosphere that surrounds the earth. As the altitude increases, the available oxygen decreases, so humans are earth-bound. The ratio of oxygen in the air is right for us because anything above that would make the air more prone to oxidation, which is one factor in combustion. The compositions of our bodies are likely to burn in contact with too much oxygen and we would be vaporized into ashes.

Air reaches up, putting rockets and satellites into space, building skyscrapers, higher and higher away from the Earth. When we leave school some of us go on to college or university, where we prize 'higher' education. Air types live in their thoughts and their heads and many of them go bald. My father once said, "Nothing grows on a busy street". How apt. In Ancient Egypt, skulls were a rather different shape, as can be seen from the marked elongation at the back of Tutankhamen's head. This is where the cerebellum is, which is connected to the Water and Earth Elements and indicates how much more we used them in those days. Whichever part of the brain we use develops and grows. In present times we are more attuned to the cerebrum, linked to Fire and Air and so this, the top part of the brain, is active. It is where the Sun strikes the top of the head and makes us 'bright', 'enlightened', gives 'flashes of insight'. In the studious and knowledgeable, the cerebrum bulges and creates a high domed head shape. In the intellectuals we get the 'egg heads'. The cerebrum is activated by the sun, the cerebellum by the moon. The great Theosophist, Madam Blavatsky, recognised the dangers of using too much Air when she said, "The intellect is the greatest slayer of the real". This is only because it is unbalanced in our times. When in harmony with the other Elements, it is a real 'breath of fresh air'.

Air is divisive and the mind is like a sword. It cuts through to facts, concocts theories, thinks in the abstract, challenges ideas, divides people into single units, knowledge into books, data into computers. Air keeps the emotions in check, it 'keeps a cool head', takes a more objective view and a 'higher perspective'. Air is knowledge, the academic world of books, libraries, science and technology, logic, reason and rationality. It is separating in its influence, probing, investigative and incisive. If we 'separate in order to unite', then Air is vital in showing us which parts fit where and how they go together. It can, however, fall into the trap of taking a clock apart, mixing up all the bits, writing several informed volumes on the workings of clocks and yet not be able to put it back together to tell the time. Air is the world of theory, but needs the Earth Element to test it in reality. Air is a light and fast Element, it speedily shines light upon things, it rules the intellect, the thinking ability, clever, intelligent, bright and quick, with technology moving ever faster. The gifts of Air are superb but, like Fire, it has been elevated and dangerously over-used. The sciences are considered to be of greater importance than the arts, knowledge is more respected than wisdom, theory more than intuition, fact more than feeling. Everything has to be referred to science. We ask, "But is it scientific?" Science doesn't know everything, the Air Element on its own is an inadequate criterion by which to study the great truths of Life. These days, it behaves like a naughty schoolboy who has locked his mother out of the house and is preparing to blow it up with the chemistry set he got for Christmas. He has made himself God, tinkering with the genes in our bodies and food, refusing to consider the long-term effects in the pursuit of fast results.

Like the other Yang, male Element, Fire, Air is competitive, but in a mental way. When one loses all control and grasp on reality we say, "He's mental". It is dangerous to get stuck in the head and deny the heart. An intellectual 'discussion' can become a contest, a debate consists of opponents, each attacking the other's point of view, easily degenerating into argument. The participants are more often identified with 'being right' and proving the other wrong than in establishing the Truth through mutual investigation. I heard a programme about debates in American colleges, they have nationwide competitions and it sounded like the prizes went to those who could speak the fastest. How on earth could anyone understand what they were saying? It was too fast for me to grasp, but speed is beloved by Air. We have to have faster and faster broadband, cars, travel; ambling is a thing of the past, it's all hurry, hurry, hurry! The ego, which is so obvious in the Fire Element, is also strong in its mental form. The author, Stan Gooch, who studied consciousness through the ages, said that the intellect is a further development of the aggressive (Fire). Linking the intellect to a sword, we see how it can be used as a weapon. Intellectual argument is like a sword fight, a 'clash of thoughts', opposing opinions, getting one over, block, parry, thrust, stab, "First blood to me!" We speak of a 'sharp mind', 'a sharp tongue', 'a cutting remark' and a 'rapier wit'. Swords hurt, and so does Air if not tempered with the softness of Water and Earth.

Air is high, it surrounds the Earth and extends for many miles into the sky. This gives an uninvolved objectivity, we can 'take a bird's eye view' and 'look at all sides'. Positive Air is not partisan, it takes a dispassionate view, helps us to clarify, gives a detached viewpoint where we can see things in another way, 'get things into perspective'. It is also essential for good drawing, allowing the artist to see quite clearly the relevant sizes and shapes of things. Societies that are weak in Air produce artwork with no or little Air type perspective, it is like looking at things through water. This is not wrong, just different. We withdraw if we want to 'think something through'. When we have a problem to solve, 'we put on our thinking caps'. In days prior to central heating when it was harder to keep warm, it was thought that the brain did not function well if it was cold. Some of the body's heat can be lost through the head, so headgear was the norm. We need a good flow of blood through our heads for our brains to work well and hanging upside down for a few minutes is very good, unless there is a medical reason against it. Children do it instinctively. The opportunity to withdraw, to 'get away from it all' can make a marked difference to how we look at things, we see issues more clearly, and what we might do about them. When the Air is still, calmness prevails, an atmosphere conducive to meditation and contemplation. Monasteries are often sited in isolated places, secluded valleys and mountain slopes, serene, silent and remote. Not so good are the doldrums, when sailing ships are becalmed, to the frustration of sailors, and likewise we don't want to become stuck in mindsets that allow for no movement. When air is moving it becomes winds, gales and tornados, it can blow you down, bowl you over and seems to 'cut right through you', as can a 'cutting', critical tongue. It tears through buildings, sweeps all aside, townscapes are flattened. Air has energy and pressure, wind rearranges, desert storms create dunes of shifting sands. Air is also 'bright and breezy'. It is dry, and a windy day soon dries the washing on the line, just as the intellect can blow away the Water Element in you, dismissing your intuition and emotions.

Air types have a 'dry wit'. If we can't organise and control our Air, we become 'scatter-brained'. On the positive, Air scatters and disseminates seeds that will become food for our bodies and 'food for thought'. Birds eat fruits, and as they fly, the seeds pass from their bodies to grow where they land. A preoccupation with lofty thoughts can put a person's 'head in the clouds' and results in the 'absent minded professor' who is 'a dry old stick', becoming 'stuffy'. Fresh air is preferable to stale, an outdoor life is healthier than an indoor one. Air purity depends on low pollution levels, and as it is associated with height, the higher we go the fresher the air becomes. The air in mountains is especially free of pollution, as are the coldest and least habitable places, such as the icy Arctic and Antarctic. Air signifies cold, high and remote places. The highest places are mountainous areas, covered in ice and snow. Air is formal, has high standards, 'takes the moral high ground', and values good manners. It teaches and preaches, but does not always practise what it preaches, so can be hypocritical. With knowledge can come pomposity and self-importance, and we say, "Get off your high horse". The critical faculty of Air is necessary in maintaining quality, making us aware of imperfections and the need for correction, and thus also insists on discipline. Air can bestow the gift of self-discipline. This can make one remote, one does not follow the masses, one makes one's own decisions. Air can be cold, remote and frigid.

If you are poor in Air there is a tendency for 'things to go way over your head', you are told to "Use your head" and if emotions threaten to overpower, you are told to "Keep your head". If taken too far, Air can make a person cold and distant, over-analytical and unrealistic, creating marvellous inventions with no consideration of the effect on the whole. Technology rules today and it is said that our brains work like a computer, but perhaps it may be more accurate to say that we created them from the part of our brain on which they are based. We have given over to technology many of the tasks we once did with our brains, such as mental arithmetic. No-one does sums 'in their heads' any more, they use calculators. To gather information, we once had to go to reference libraries but now we have the much speedier way of using a search engine. Convenient as it is, it blows away contact with other people, needing each other less. There are, however, many wonderful and positive qualities of Air, giving us all kinds of inventions and knowledge that make life easier. I could not have made this book without it. With Air, you think fast and are quick to grasp things, we say, "He's quick", "A light bulb came on in my head", "I'm enlightened". Air has its equal part to play in the correct balance of life on earth and in our consciousness, illuminating the path forward.

In the section about the Archetypes, the Air Element is divided and represented in three ways. The Observer personifies the calm, detached aspects, the Logician the bright intellect and the Patriarch the knowledgeable and learned.

Practising the Archetypes

"You have no need to travel anywhere.
Journey within yourself,
Enter a mine of rubies and bathe
In the splendour of your own Light." – Rumi

"You have to be unique and different to shine in your own way".
- Lady Gaga

Why There Are Twelve Archetypes

This is how the Archetypes come into being and why there is an optimum number of twelve. Each of the Twelve Archetypes is composed of two Elements. No element can exist alone, nor can consciousness arise from just one Element. Water needs a container - Earth: Fire needs Air to burn, and so on.

They are paired thus -

We take Water and pair it with the three other Elements in turn, giving us:

Water and Air, Water and Earth, Water and Fire

These are the Child, the Enchantress and the Actress

We take Fire and pair it with the three other Elements in turn, giving us:

Fire and Water, Fire and Air, Fire and Earth

These are the Fool, the Joker and the Warrior

We take Earth and pair it with the three other Elements in turn, giving us:

Earth and Fire, Earth and Water, Earth and Air

These are the Worker/Slave, Mother Nature and the Wise Woman

We take Air and pair it with the three other Elements in turn, giving us:

Air and Earth, Air and Fire, Air and Water

These are the Observer, the Logician and the Patriarch

This is the maximum number of authentic Archetypes that can be derived from the Four Elements. The next section names and describes each world. Twelve may seem like a lot, but you'll soon relate to them if you take them Element by Element, getting familiar with the three Water ones, the three Fire, the three Earth and the three Air.

There are those who have tried to remodel the Work by inventing more Archetypes, or changing them. These attempts have been fruitless, they merely sullied the purity and truth of the Work. Nothing can be gained from distorting it, the integrity of the Work must be maintained and protected. It does, of course, welcome more contributions and insights, as do I, and all who genuinely practice will offer them. The Work can only be grown from its true roots.

***Please note**. **A reminder**. Although there are six male and six female states, we are not talking about men and women and thus locking us further into sexist roles. Rather, this work is designed to liberate us, as it presents all the states of consciousness for anyone to use and develop. We are identifying the masculine and feminine energies, the Yin and Yang, and applying them to both sexes. Women can develop all of their female and male sides and men can develop all of their male and female sides. All sexual orientations are free to develop any Archetypes they wish, these Twelve States of Being apply to everyone. As you begin to recognise them in people, you will see male Archetypes active in women and female ones in men. It is unfortunate that this patriarchal society allocates the female Archetypes to women and the male ones to men, preventing real individual growth to all, but this Work will shatter these constraints and allow each individual to evolve all of themselves in their own way.*

The powerful invocation verses give you the means to experience and develop each Archetype. Keep in mind that no one person lives completely in one Archetype, usually there is a blend of two or three, plus no one has all aspects of any Archetype they are using. As you get to know and practise the Twelve States you will begin to see for yourself which ones you and other people are using. Our Work is about separating them into their specific forms in order to purify, develop and integrate them in the Centre. Much time and work went into ensuring that characteristics are appropriately placed in each Archetype. It is their purity that is their strength and power, allowing you to identify, experience and control all the parts of yourself. By control, I don't mean to restrain and inhibit. Being able to steer your own consciousness means that you can choose the most advantageous Archetype for the situation. You need to bring on the Fool when dancing, the Patriarch when studying, the Wise Woman when dealing with money, the Enchantress when you need intuitive guidance and so on. The more you do this, the more you grow and the brighter your Centre will glow. How wonderful it is to discover who we really are.

Living from Your Centre

"You are an Artist: within your soul is every colour of the rainbow. Imagine wisely with your mind. Paint vividly with your heart. Share fearlessly with your body. Live your own masterpiece."
- Anna Taylor

Please read all of this chapter before you begin to practise.

Disclaimer: *These Archetypal energies are powerful. You must* **stay Earthed**. **I strongly stress the importance of this.** *Bringing new consciousness into yourself demands a period of integration and inner rearrangement. Make sure that for every new one you practise, you practise Mother Nature or the Worker/Slave at least twice in between. This will allow your consciousness time and space to relax, absorb, integrate and ground the new state safely. Please follow this advice.* ***Also, if you are on any medical treatment and/or medications, do not stop taking them without consulting your health practitioner.***

All electrical appliances need an earth wire and a fuse to stop them from blowing and it's the same with consciousness. I have dealt with many people who have attended various courses, residential or otherwise, and have had their consciousness shaken up. Too often there are all kinds of psychological and emotional issues to deal with afterwards. This is because the different way of thinking and feeling has not been followed through with help in assimilating and earthing. Keep it all grounded and you will be safe as you progress.

"Change the way you look at things and the things you look at change." - Wayne W. Dyer

The invocation scripts will aid you in invoking each Archetype. I could have written another twelve for the opposite sex as well, as they can manifest in somewhat different ways in the male and female, but for now, these twelve have been shown to work for both.

In order to add to the colours of your consciousness, it is necessary to approach the Work with an open mind and heart, a degree of innocence and humility and the realisation that real growth is not doing more of what you already doing, but of going in the opposite direction to attain balance. Reading and learning about this work are but a preparation for putting it into practice, which is a dynamic yet delicate thing. It's a process, and is different for us all. I had a vision of how, as each individual crossed and re-crossed the circle, developing a bit of this Archetype, then another, a pattern would emerge, each one different. As the Patriarch says, "No two snowflakes are the same". Some of the Archetypes, particularly the Observer, do not normally speak or say little, but the invocation speeches are designed to get you into them. It is not necessary to practise each one in its season but it is helpful to do so at least once in the month, as its energy is strongest then. No one lives in just one Archetype, most of us are a mixture of about two or three, which can be observed. For example, the Wise Woman might have old furniture in her home, but it's the Patriarch who ensures it is of good quality and dust free. Listen to what people say, discover their interests, observe their behaviours, look at the forms of their faces and you will begin to see them. Once you see various Archetypes in people, the reality of the Work will hit you. It clearly identifies each state of consciousness, allowing you to recognise what you have already developed and what you need to grow. We separate in order to unite them in your Centre.

"I've got them all already"

If you say, "But I've got them all already", you'd be right. But I can absolutely guarantee that *you are not using them all.* Don't kid yourself. Having the seeds of them all is not the same as having them all grown into flowers. A very few Archetypes are active in you, the rest are latent and dormant. If you were really using them all you'd be super human, a divine being, a god or goddess, shining and glorious. You'd certainly not need to eat or shit for a start, you'd dazzle the crowd, have incredible powers, traffic would stop and people would drop to their knees and gaze in wonderment on your radiance. Is this you? I thought not. It's not me either. We all have a long way to go in our further evolution. In extraordinary circumstances a bit of an unfamiliar one can pop out to deal with an emergency, but that is a rare occurrence. A mother who lifts a car off her injured child is not using that kind of Warrior strength every day. Let's not con ourselves, none of us are anywhere near there yet, and we have to step forward from where we actually are, free from ego, pretence and self-delusion. Furthermore, no one has all aspects of any one of them, each Archetype is made up of many strands, so you can add more to the ones you already use. For example, a Patriarch may have knowledge but be rather untidy, and conversely may have a spotless environment but little useful knowledge.

We are made from Elemental energies, but have been living them in an unconscious way, and that makes us victims of them. You will begin to identify which Archetypes you are using, or rather, which are using you. This will allow you to be the director of your cast of Twelve, adding more colour to your life. Remember that revolving your Wheel leads to evolving. This is evolution through real, inner revolution. We revolve to evolve.

Consciousness is the Elements in their metaphysical form. As the climates associated with the months of the year were worked out in the Northern hemisphere, they will need to be reversed to suit the Southern Hemisphere. Some parts of the world have similar weather all year, but the Archetypes still apply because the Elements, in their various combinations, are inside us. If the climatic problems we are having are due to human behaviour, there is every possibility that we can reverse these dangerous trends. To cultivate these Elements within ourselves will heal, evolve and transform, integrating them into a quintessence of love and harmony. We have the advantage of these useable tools with which to do so, we need no longer blunder about in the dark.

Real Change

Welcoming change through the Archetypes is enlightening, inspiring, exhilarating and exciting, but it can also at times be disturbing and challenging. Feelings, attitudes and memories arise and at that critical moment we make a decision. Do we stop, close down and go back to what we were? – or do we take courage, be more objective, face the obstacles and wrest control from the forces that have been controlling us? They are so powerful that they have convinced us they are our own true natures.

"How can I accept a limited definable self when I feel, in me, all possibilities?" - Anias Nin

When running groups to sample the Archetypes, we noticed it took remarkably little inner movement to bring about change. One woman from America was living in London, had a good social life but was bored with her job and felt directionless. She practised the Actress and realised that she had always wanted to be involved with the theatre, so she moved to another country to study theatre design. In my own experience, there was a time when I was too much in the Enchantress and was feeling rather blue, so I learned to juggle. As a result, I met Dominic Sladden and it wasn't long before we were working professionally as a duo act called The Flying Colours. I thought that up and I was rather pleased with it. The Actress helped me too, she gave me the confidence to perform, resulting in me creating One Woman shows, teaching classes in the Enchantress's skills, writing and singing songs, dancing and all sorts. These two got my Fire going, which was lacking up until then. There was a man who did the Warrior, which gave him the courage to come out as gay to his family. If we follow through with the positive impulses that arise through practice, real change does happen.

Deities or Demons?

"There's no room for demons when you're self-possessed." – Carrie Fisher

What do we want? To be puppets jerking about on the strings of the unconscious or to cut the strings and free ourselves, dancing our own steps? Negatively, the Twelve are like Demons, jealously blocking personal growth, and through the dominance of a few, we endure conflict and disharmony between individuals, nations, faiths and religions, all competing for the upper hand. Positively, they are Twelve Deities, powerful, magical energies that are at our disposal to create all that is real and beautiful beyond our wildest dreams. It's up to us how we want to use them. Like a television set, capable of receiving twelve channels, the reigning archetypes have convinced you that you can only receive the same old two or three programmes. But Look! You have a remote control in your hand! You can switch to another channel and enjoy a whole new experience. I wrote earlier about change to help us to understand how and why we might resist it, even though it's good change. We might reconsider some of the reasons why we both want to and don't want to change in relation to the Archetypes. Influences, such as our upbringing and conditioning, genetics, environment, social mores, astrological charts, some may even say past lives, conspire to cause us to identify with a very small number of these channels of Life. Our Wheels become stuck, allowing disease and decay, conflicts and misunderstandings worldwide. One of the reasons we resist change is simply habit, we go along with what we know and think to be safe, we're used to it, it's an illusion we call our 'comfort zone', saying, "I am like this, not like that" and "I could never do that or be that". Habits are created through a variety of experiences, our childhoods being significant in their development. We are raised in environments that encourage certain Archetypes and discourage others, so we mostly fall into those behavioural channels. Perhaps we rebel for a time and then revert back to the paths laid down for us, or we decide to live a completely different life and get stuck there instead. Our relationships with our parents, siblings, extended family, friends, society and events during our childhood can enhance or distort our relationships with certain Archetypes and indicate how and why we are what we are and what curtails our development. We are all children whose growth has been stunted.

Twelve Trump Cards

The Archetypes are twelve trump cards, each gaining you a win if you play the right one at the right time. As we usually keep playing the same paltry two or three, lots of times we lose. You have twelve winners to hand, all you have to do is clean some up, pick up the ones you've dropped and you win the jackpot every time. The more cards you have, the fuller your hand. Need to give a talk? Play the Patriarch. Need inner guidance? Play the Enchantress. Need to clean the house? Play the Slave. Need to run a marathon? Play the Warrior. You get the idea. It's very simple, but I didn't say it's easy. We all have to work on ourselves and at times it is hard toil, life throws obstacles in our path, but through this work the results can be rapid and rewarding. For too long we have allowed ourselves to be downtrodden by the few Archetypes that have us in their grip, and by the ones in other people, resulting in keeping each other trapped and chained. The Archetypes are twelve keys, each capable of locking or opening a door. We need not stay in prison, we can open every door and enjoy true freedom.

You are the artist, not the paints.

This work gives you the opportunity to become the Captain of your own ship, steering where you will. You have twelve colours before you and remember - you are the artist, not the paints. The colours are on a circular palette, with you in the Centre, using each one in turn to create your unique self-portrait, first using the pure colours in bold strokes and then, as you evolve, mixing them in increasingly subtle ways as you build up the details. No one will ever create a painting like yours, no one else is you.

"Be yourself, everyone else is taken." - *Oscar Wilde*

I hope you will enchant us with your divine face. Let us come out of the mud of dull existence and paint ourselves and our world beautiful. *"If we are to evolve into complete beings, NO function can be disregarded. Each one must be loved, encouraged and cultivated. Saying this puts me in the position of defender of twelve faiths. I know of no institution which does this. Any of which I am aware affirm one function at the expense of another. This is the behaviour of the 'either/or' type of persons, psycho-statics who settle for just some aspects of elementary consciousness. The whole must be loved and defended before we can become whole through integrating the elemental bits, in order to achieve superconsciousness."- Richard Gardner.*

Get Ready to Turn Your Wheel

Let your Centre Shine

"The Universe is saying: allow me to flow through you unrestricted, and you will see the greatest magic you have ever seen" - *Klaus Joehle*

"The world is a stage, but the play is badly cast." - *Oscar Wilde*

"If you want to find the secrets of the universe, think in terms of energy, frequency and vibration." - *Nikola Tesla*

Making friends with your Archetypes.

As you practise the Archetypes, you will be separating and purifying them, and uniting them in your Centre. As you bring forth dormant ones, you will begin to experience how they co-operate and work together in you. As you introduce new characters into your play of life, the plot changes, widens, has more action and depth. At first, it is recommended that you go round the circle two or three times to familiarise yourself with the Twelve, whether working alone or in a group. Get to know their elements, the complementary opposites, the conflicting opposites and the reconcilers. Reading the scripts helps you to identify and recognise each part of yourself and to befriend it. Secondly, the scripts focus only on positive attributes, which helps you to purify that Archetype within. Thirdly, if you are working in a group you can help each other to activate them. The ones that come the most easily and with which you feel comfortable are those you already use to some extent. The ones you dislike and find difficult are those you need to develop. This could bring up memories and behaviour patterns that throw light on why you regard them in this way. We say, "He's not my type of person". This work gives you insight as to why you feel that way about certain people. You will see the positive and negative aspects of their Archetypes. Television is good for Archetype spotting, you're detached and not threatened or involved, and once you get to know them better you can even spot them on the radio through the voice alone. You could look at faces from magazines and compare them to the pictures of the Archetypes. The twelve facial types have very distinct, recognisable features but as no one lives in just one state, in people you will detect a mix of two or three. It's not always easy, it depends how strongly developed any Archetype is, so I don't always see them myself. I have to imagine I'm casting for the play I wrote before I get an idea.

"To receive the full benefit of any function, it must be practised as purely and as true to its essential essence as possible. The individual's approval of the true nature of any state decides how quickly or slowly he or she progresses in it. Learning to love them all as they are will work wonders. Deciding which you like or dislike merely keeps you trapped in the spells already dominating you."

- Richard Gardner

The Actress (Water and Fire) can pretend to be all the characters. Don't allow her to act the others. She can, however, help you to make a start by going through the right motions. Once you get to know the Archetypes well you won't find it hard to spot her, or any of the others who appear inappropriately, there is a definite, distinctive 'feel' to each one.

Working Alone

Working alone can be challenging, seeing oneself clearly takes objectivity and resolve. The main Archetypes we habitually use could try to act and pretend to be doing another. If you live a lot in the Patriarch you may try to get away with reading the Observer script in your usual voice, only much quieter. A good ear for music is useful, you will be able to detect that your voice still sounds 'important'. Recording your voice and listening to yourself with an open ear will help. You need to keep in touch with your Centre and learn how to keep your usual Archetypes out of it to allow the new consciousness to enter. This can be a delicate process. Also, if you are working on one that is unfamiliar to you, you may need an example of it to copy and some help in overcoming inner resistance to it. Getting the voice right is a major part of hitting the right note. Other people can see you more clearly and can make helpful suggestions but it is still better to practise alone than not at all. If you can identify an Archetype in someone you know, observe their approach and attitude to life and how they move and talk, and compare it to yours. Looking at people from an Archetypal perspective fosters understanding and appreciation, you learn to talk each other's language and enhance each other's lives. What if your situation makes it difficult for you to practise? Then visualise yourself doing it and being it. There are many trials that have shown this can be effective. For example, taking three groups of people, one is given physical exercises to do, one does nothing, and one is guided to visualise themselves doing them. The group who did nothing showed no improvement, but the group who did the exercises, and the group who merely visualised themselves doing them showed the same amount of improvement. Our minds are mighty powerful!

Working in a Group

It is preferable to work in a group as others have greater objectivity, offer support and helpful suggestions. You also have a chance of incorporating a variety of types. When you identify an Archetype in a group member, he/she should lead that session so you can 'catch' the consciousness. This is a circle, not a pyramid. All will be leaders and followers in turn, all are equally valuable and important. Be careful not to work exclusively with people who are similar to you, you need a good mixture of different types. You are working both as individuals and as a group energy. As time goes on each member may face a difficulty, which if not met can hold the whole group back, but also a breakthrough for one can help move everyone forward. This work reveals us clearly, so it best to begin with a small group, establishing a nucleus of trust and honesty.

There is a conspiracy going on at all levels to keep us as we are. You will see this for yourself. If you enter your usual social scene in a different state, you could be attacked, ridiculed and asked what is wrong with you and why you are not your 'old self'. Your new, young self might not be welcome. Positive change in you highlights the lack of it in others, causing them to react defensively. It is very hard to sustain the growth of a new part of yourself in the face of primitive reaction. A group practising together will give protection, appreciation and encouragement. Evolving consciously is a subtle process. Once you have created a firm foundation on which to build, you can bring in other people, but beware of those who could have a disruptive and destructive influence because they pretend to be further on than they are and will do anything to avoid 'being sussed'. A person in the Joker may be a very welcome addition on Joker occasions, but not if he persists in making sarcastic remarks when you are trying to practise the Enchantress. You need to protect the group energy. On the other hand, you may have to accept that you have come together because you identify with the same small section of the Circle. 'Birds of a feather flock together'. If this is the case, you could resent an 'intruder' with a different consciousness, even though you need it to balance your group. Without openness and honesty we can never work through our neurotic solutions, lower our defences and grow. Goodwill has to be at the heart of this Work. Once you really get down to the practice, it soon becomes obvious who has what, so don't waste too much time trying to analyse your respective Archetypes or sequences.

Props and Costumes

Today, jeans and t-shirts are worn by the majority, and other styles of attire fall into rigid dress codes. Casual dress is simply the choice of the Worker/Slave. If we chose to dress as other Archetypes, it would be a much more interesting, imaginative, creative and colourful world. Costumes and props are helpful. Gather some objects with which the Archetypes identify - e.g. blowing bubbles around the Child will fascinate her, any psychic tool, such as Tarot cards or a crystal ball, a shell or piece of seaweed for the Enchantress; a mirror, jewels, fancy scarves for the Actress; balloons or party blowers for the Fool, a joke book or juggling balls for the Joker; a play sword, shield or fitness equipment for the Warrior; a broom or tools for the Worker, food, plants, fruits for Mother Nature; lots of bags and money for the Wise Woman; a telescope for the Observer, any technical device for the Logician; a book for the Patriarch. Find pieces of clothing in the correct colour and style for each one.

Masks

Masks can be helpful initially in freeing you up, but they can soon be discarded. When you manage to change state the colour and shape of your face will look different and it's good that you see it. There have been occasions of pure astonishment when this has happened; faces get longer, shorter, fatter or thinner, complexions change, body movements and breathing alters. It is remarkable. The differences can be small, but recognisable. Make up your face to look like the Archetype, as looking the part encourages you to be in it. Make-up can be effective if the face is coloured appropriate to the Archetype and the facial features painted on.

Costumes and make up are not strictly required, but if you look like the Archetype, you will feel more in it, others will treat you as if you are already in it and you are encouraged to behave in it. A large mirror is a good prop, if you can see how different you look it will reinforce your performance. The mirror is especially popular with the Actress. When we staged my play, we dressed each Archetype in its own style and colour, and audience members declared it was like a mixture of Shakespeare, Ancient Greek drama and Faeryland. Shakespeare shows a greater number of

Archetypes than we use today, and Ancient Greek drama was seen as a means of invoking the Deities to inspire the people, with shrines to the Gods and Goddesses backstage. The production felt like we were reinventing drama in the magical sense. From the reactions we got, it worked. The cast experienced a tremendous vibrancy of energy through the collective performance. We did not simply entertain the audience; all were uplifted as energy surged through the theatre. Everyone involved enjoyed a big buzz of energy, didn't want it to end, had to be tactfully ushered out, and finally went home with glowing faces.

Getting the Voice Right is Important

Try to get the voices as accurate as possible, like hitting a musical note right in the middle. Using a different accent or dialect can help bring on an Archetype. One lady found a French voice worked for the Actress, others have used a West Country dialect for Mother Nature, a drawl for the Worker/Slave, a formal English voice for the Patriarch, and a Welsh one for the Wise Woman. Experiment and see what comes through, different languages have different notes because other cultures have different Archetypes in them. Italian, for example, can help to get the Actress through, with much expressiveness and a love of drama and opera.

Music, Lighting and Colour

These are also good for invoking the right atmosphere. Wearing a garment of, and being lit by, the appropriate colour is not merely cosmetic, it helps generate the energy you are invoking. At first, the whole group should practise the same one at the same time, but as time goes on, it will become clear that the cultivation of the Twelve is a matter of individual unfoldment and the order in which one should practise them varies as a personal prescription emerges. Choose one or two you know you need, never mind whether you like them or not. We seldom want what we need. Think of an artist or musician. To make a complete piece of work, the dull colours, the bass notes, need to be included to create contrast and life. Without the full range of colours or notes, the work lacks energy. Thinking of your own Archetypes in this way can help you appreciate them all. Continue to practise them until some change is felt and seen. Turn to the four reconcilers, The Child, Observer, Worker/Slave and Fool when you feel in conflict, disturbed or stuck. Remember to keep practising the Earth ones, especially the two heavy ones, Mother Nature and the Worker/Slave, to ground you. Then you can go on to another Archetype, do the same, then come back and add some more. When Richard Gardner and myself taught groups together, on the final night we had a party and invited people to dress in an

Archetype of their choice. It was always a dynamic and fun-filled occasion, and although there was plenty of alcohol, most it was forgotten and untouched. Everyone was full and high on Life.

This is not Astrology, except in the sense that if we lived on another planet in our Solar System, e.g. Venus, and wished to construct an Astrological chart, the planet Earth would be included and her characteristics noted. To harmonise with the earth and our Archetypes would make all the Heavenly Forces accessible to us, we would actualise the potential in our astrological charts and unite Heaven and Earth. 'On Earth as it is in Heaven'. It is easier to partner the Archetypes with the planets, rather than the signs, but that is not relevant at this point. Suffice to say that we have noticed that the Archetype corresponding to the month of our birth is often weak in us, and if we develop it we can take leap forward in our evolution. For me, this was the Actress. Due to the various relationships between the Elements, we see that the Earth has a variety of twelve atmospheres and weather conditions, each relating to an Archetype. It would be conducive to an Archetype to practise it in its location and season, at least occasionally. This is not always practical or easy. Not everyone can climb a snowy peak for the Patriarch and it is obviously not wise to enter a volcano for the Warrior, but it is quite easy to have a day in the countryside, a park or garden doing Mother Nature, or go to the sea, a river or pool for the Enchantress, create a makeshift stage for the Actress and a parade ground for the Warrior, go to an ice rink or a church for the Patriarch etc. The Warrior and Fool are best practised out of doors or in a large, bare room as they are the liveliest of them all and not too careful about knocking things over. Can you practise without props and make up etc? Yes, of course you can. They are helpful, but there's nothing to stop you practising without them.

Reactions.

The speeches I have created contain only the positive aspects of each state as we do not wish to further invoke the negatives, but we need to accept that to be stuck is to be negative. The chapters about each of the Twelve, however, describe both positive and negative so we can recognise the Archetypes in ourselves and others by both. As I said, you can regard them as twelve performers. One or two will have taken the stage and held it for years, perhaps allowing one or two others to have only occasional small, supporting roles. In the wings await several others, ready and eager to contribute their skills and qualities and liven up the action. But the few who have had it all their own way will cling ruthlessly to their position and try to keep the others off. It can be a strange thing to actually experience what you thought was you actually feels like something outside of yourself possessing you. It's both weird and freeing at the same time and takes a bit of getting used to. It's hard to explain, but when it happens to you, you'll know what I mean when I say they're like twelve paints and you are the artist. You need to play the part of the director and make decisions as to how your drama will unfold. It takes determination and there can be some uncomfortable reactions to change. I regard them as growing pains. If you manage to get a new one 'on' for a short time, the following day there could be inner arguments as the old ones try to chase off the new and reassert themselves. You could end up more in your original one than when you started. Keep seeing them as actors on a stage and constantly refer to your Centre. The only way through is to practise until the new one makes an impression and contribution to your life. Then the others will realise that they also have a bigger, better part to play through co-operation.

Each Archetype you develop will enhance the others. It begins to feel that you are making wonderful new friends within yourself and discovering skills, abilities and qualities you didn't know you had. Develop the Fool and you enjoy dancing, Mother Nature and you can cook, the Wise Woman and your books balance, the Enchantress and you become more intuitive, the Warrior and you have confidence. It's advisable to have an overall aim in your life, it needn't be huge, just something achievable. This gives the different states a common goal, encouraging them to co-operate with each other. You may find that you just cannot get an Archetype, no matter how hard you try. It may take a few attempts, but each time you practise a new state it will get a little better until bit by bit you build up the world. You might only manage two authentic lines, but you will feel the difference. Congratulate yourself, because next time it may be four or eight and so on until you finally make it yours. Every now and then the meaning of certain lines will hit you, you will feel them in a more real way and understand them on a deeper level. You will know when you get it right, they all have their own vibration. You will have *real*-isations. It will be real in you.

In a caring group the spotlight will fall on each person in turn, and specific help and encouragement will be needed. It can take a minimum of twenty minutes to successfully change state. Often, as you change, you may have physical, emotional and psychological responses. You might experience trembling, giggling, weeping, tension. These are natural reactions to inner re-arrangement. Don't be nervous about looking stupid as you try to cultivate yourself, you are magically evolving and must be prepared to behave 'out of character'. What if you experience discomfort when practising an Earth one? Why would it be when I recommend you use them to ground yourself? It depends on what you associate them with, perhaps a trauma associated with someone they remind you of, or issues and hurt around mothering, for example. If you feel safe and supported, perhaps you can work through it. If not, I suggest you switch to the Observer to detach from your feelings and let them settle. You could also just stop and try again another day. Only you can decide when to go forwards and when to rest. It could be that some kind of counselling or therapy would help when obstacles are met and identified.

Follow through any urges, impulses or suggestions you get after practising a new state, as long as they are positive of course. You could take up keep-fit thanks to the Warrior, improve your diet due to Mother Nature or go to a psychic group with the Enchantress. Go ahead and do the things the new Archetype wants, as this will make it real in your life. It is not enough to practise it for an hour and then forget it. If you haven't changed, you haven't moved. As you change you will notice physical changes; you will look and feel, different. The Warrior and Patriarch will make your voice louder, the Child and the Observer quieter, Mother Nature and the Enchantress deeper and slower, the Logician and Joker lighter and faster.

As you let in a new energy it will mould you to its shape. Each one relates to the Body, Soul, Spirit or Mind, so as you increase your range, health problems will improve. Frequent colds, which are more likely if there is too much Water consciousness, are often cured by practising your Fire. More chronic conditions will naturally take longer and there are no guarantees, but any improvement is a bonus. Many so-called psychological problems are also balanced and may even reveal not an 'illness' as such, but simply an unfashionable, unfamiliar state, such as the Child, Mother Nature or the Enchantress. It is the Archetype in which you are stuck that gets tired and ill. Bring in another and you feel better. 'A change is as good as a rest'. To truly change state is a real holiday. Sometimes you need to practise one to loosen up and release another. Once, someone attempted the Fool. Although it was not very successful, it did turn on the Actress which was just what that woman needed at that time. She was too inhibited to go straight into the Fool, as she was living mainly in the Child, but compared to the Fool, the Actress seemed milder. How you are is not so much a matter of good or bad luck on the Wheel of Fortune, but more a matter of habit. If you are identified with the Child and practise it, there will be little appreciable difference, but the Warrior will seem very alien. Yet, to a group of soldiers in an army barracks, the Warrior is just as real and 'normal' as the Child is to you, and they would find your Child world equally strange.

After practice, discussion is helpful as you share experiences and revelations, hear each other out, sympathise with difficulties, make useful suggestions and generally encourage. A success for the individual benefits everyone. When this work is practised with a number of open people, the results are fast and truly exhilarating. If you are working alone, you may like to keep a journal of your progress. People who do manage to move their Wheels, even a little, declare that it is a great privilege to know and experience this Work. In time, it can energise and beautify all your twelve petals that a glorious flower may bloom. Practise the passive states at night and the livelier ones earlier in the day, or you may find it hard to sleep - but if you really move into a new state you will be buzzing with energy and won't need as much sleep anyway. A new one may need a little time to settle in as you integrate it. It might be over the top at first until it finds its place with the others. Always try to retain your connection to your Centre to help you to recognise these things as they occur. As Archetypes begin to blend, you will have a new sense of yourself, a feeling of the real you emerging.

Turn to a Reconciler if you feel stuck, they are like a stepping stones, helping you cross the circle. One of the many gifts this work gives is that you learn to enjoy everything that you do. What is a chore or difficult in one Archetype is easy and pleasurable in another. Mother Nature loves to garden, the Warrior loves to exercise, the Logician and Patriarch love to learn and study, the Slave is practical and can relax and so on. So that each thing you do, from the menial to the creative is a divine exercise. I hope this Work helps you to reach your potential and that you will use it to pioneer conscious Evolution. We have to take action about the mess we are in, we cannot keep passing the buck to new babies who are inheriting a poisoned world. Environmental, economic and social problems will be solved when we take responsibility for ourselves.

"There is but one solution to the intricate riddle of life; to improve ourselves, and contribute to the happiness of others." – Mary Shelley

Work on yourself is the greatest work you will ever do, it is your gift to the world and it will bring you the greatest rewards.

"The Universe is always speaking to us, sending us little messages, causing coincidences and serendipities, reminding us to stop, to look around, to believe in something else, something more."
- Nancy Thayer

That 'something more' is YOU.

The Water Archetypes

CHILD   ENCHANTRESS   ACTRESS

The Child

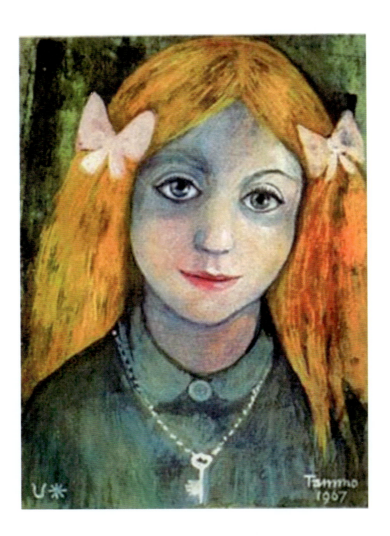

U✶

Both positive and negative attributes are given in this description to help you better recognise the state in yourself and others. When we repeatedly use an Archetype, it cannot fail to exhibit negative traits, as it becomes overused and not balanced by other states. The climates associated with the months of the year were worked out in the Northern hemisphere, so they may need to be adjusted to suit the Southern Hemisphere and take into account unfamiliar weather patterns linked to climate change.

The Child

Open Water

February 21st – March 21st
One of the three Water states and one of the four Open states.
Water and Air, the metaphysical linking of Soul and Mind.

The season of the Child is February/March, early Spring. Her colour is turquoise, duck egg blue, the mix of approximately two parts of the blue of Water, her first element, and one part of the yellow of Air, her second.

"We wait, starving for moments of high magic to inspire us, but life is full of common enchantment waiting for our alchemist's eyes to notice." - Jacob Nordby.

In February the ice and snow thaw and melt away, the Water evaporates and fills the Air, creating mists and fragile clouds, droplets and dew, a gently swirling, magical landscape, the freshness of dawn, the sweetness of Spring flowers, tender new leaves, dewdrops like jewels on spiders' webs, the wonder of a new day. Snowdrops, anemones and crocuses come out and vulnerable shoots begin to grow. Between the mists the sky is the colour of a duck's egg, delicate and soft, like the child herself. We must not misunderstand this Archetype, for although youthful, she does not represent young children. She is a state of consciousness and not a time of life, although children arrive with her and are open and vulnerable. Some children quickly grow out of this state and move into other Archetypes, such as her opposite, the Warrior (Fire and Earth), and the Child can also be seen in older people. It is a tragedy that there is so little respect for this magical state of being. Children are encouraged to leave it behind as soon as possible, hurrying them to 'grow up', when in fact it is more like 'growing down'.

"One of the things I loved about my childhood was that I didn't feel like I lost my innocence too young, like some children these days." - Danielle de Niese

"No, I would not want to live in a world without dragons, as I would not want to live in a world without magic, for that is a world without mystery, and that is a world without faith." - R.A. Salvatore

The Child is full of unconditional love, she is an innocent. For her, love and trust are the only way.

Around her neck she wears a key to the gates of love, of heaven, of wonder at the magic of life, of paradise. This key is humility, that wondrous quality which opens the door and lets you in. She is our most precious state, she stands at the dawn of new beginnings, full of wonder and awe, fascinated by the bewildering kaleidoscope of colour and movement. She lives in a world of fascinations. She is often heard to say "I wonder…" She sees everything as if for the first time and she wonders at what it is. In her sense of wonder she sees beauty everywhere, the sacredness of everything, she loves everything. Beauty is hers, she cannot bear things that are ugly, they jar on the harmony of the beautiful. She loses herself in a miraculous world, open, receptive and innocent.
"Innocence tinctures all things with brightest hues." - Edward Counsel.

She is full of faith and trust, giving and expecting to find kindness and gentleness always. We seem to have lost our ability to have faith, and it has become dangerous to be too trusting and open in today's world. She is delicate, her world is one of the greatest delicacy, fragile as egg shells. Her open receptivity can never have enough tales of magic, fairies, myths and legends, she can listen for hours. Listening is one of her great qualities, for not only is her hearing good, as sounds are conducted through the droplets of mist, she can also truly hear you when you speak to her. She receives you, which is a rare treat, you experience the satisfaction of being fully heard. She never judges or gives advice, she simply listens in a very real way.

"There's music in the sighing of a reed; There's music in the gushing of a rill; There's music in all things, if men had ears: Their earth is but an echo of the spheres."- Byron

The Child is small and slight, like a fairy, a cherub, the little girl of the fairytales dressed in ragged old clothes, Cinderella who is unloved and pitiful, a poor neglected orphan. She is vulnerable, helpless and fragile, she surrenders to all, carried along passively by circumstances, drifting like the clouds, open to all surrounding atmospheres.

She listens to what she hears and believes it with all her heart, yet when she hears a new viewpoint, she believes that one too, and just as truly. Thus, she is easily influenced, inspired or scared, depending on where she has been and with whom. All make an impression on her, she is so very impressionable. You can usually tell where the Child has been and to whom she's been talking, the influences can be clearly seen in her. She merges with it all, like the drifting mists, with no awareness of being separate, no resistance, without ego and judgement and with no memory of what went before, so forgiveness comes naturally to her. She will listen to anything and tell you whatever you want to know. She is wide open, she hides nothing and never suspects that others are not the same.

"Above all, watch with glittering eyes the whole world around you because the greatest secrets are always hidden in the most unlikely places. Those who don't believe in magic will never find it" - Roald Dahl

In the Child, every moment is a rebirth, life is ever renewed, she retains her youthfulness as the metaphysical dew and mists moisten her flesh and keep her fresh. She is youthing, open to receive healing and magical energies from the cosmos. She is gentle, sweet, tender-hearted, soft-hearted, giving her love freely to animals, people and the fairyland creatures, whom she can see. Some things have to be believed to be seen. In the fairytale of the Princess and the Pea, the Princess was lost, so at the palace it was decided to load a bed with many mattresses with a small pea concealed beneath the bottom one. Many girls who came claiming to be the real Princess were invited to sleep here, and the next morning were asked if they had slept well. All said they had enjoyed a good night's sleep and were promptly shown the door. Eventually, one girl replied that no, it was horrible, she was unable to sleep because there was something hard under the mattress that dug into her all night. At last, the true Princess was found, for only the authentic one could have that degree of sensitivity. This story illustrates how the Child experiences the slightest thing of which most other Archetypes are unaware.

"The innocence of childhood is like the innocence of a lot of animals." - Clint Eastwood

She loves animals, she is open to their nature and her love is reciprocated. These days children are forced into a dreary, hard, sexualised world, the loss of being able to see the world in a magical way causing their creativity and imaginations to be crushed. They become adults who claim to have no talents, which is untrue. There is an enormous amount of creative potential in everyone if they were but given the encouragement and opportunity to release it.

"That's the thing with Magick. You've got to know it's still here, all around us, or it just stays invisible for you" - Charles de Lint

The Child is easily impressed by other people, who seem so much bigger, more powerful, cleverer and more able than she. Negatively, she is everyone's victim, a scapegoat, gullible, naïve, believes anything she's told, and with so many different opinions she becomes mystified and afraid. She can't see very far through her mists and will fall for any old scam, una-ware that people can lie.

"Innocence is always unsuspicious." Joseph Joubert

To be stuck in her is to take everything in and be easily 'taken in', she has no defences, either against beauty and truth or ugliness and lies. She becomes nervous and terrified by the bad feelings she receives from others and surrenders to their will, being easily bullied. She is self-effacing, ever terrified of incurring anger and disapproval, she is helpless, defenceless, ineffectual, gives in to all, tiny and weak with no initiative.

She becomes too precious for words, pathetic, scared of everything, confused, unable to articulate her fears, only knowing that the beauty and magic have gone and been replaced by the negativity that

others have all to easily dumped on her. They pollute her and cast her aside, saying "She's away with the fairies", not realising that they are throwing away the key to so much that is precious in themselves. Today's society exploits, abuses and dismisses her, closing all doors to innocence, magic and open wonderment, creating an increasingly selfish and loud world, which hurts her so. A good example of a man in the Child was Michael Jackson, who had a slim, slight physique and a soft, quiet, childlike speaking voice. He had other Archetypes working in him too, like the Actress, but the Child stands out as his strongest one. Perhaps he surrounded himself with young children because he was like one himself. He had an innocent air about him with an almost asexual quality and he spoke much of love and innocence, which is possibly what he most wanted to share with children.

"In their innocence, very young children know themselves to be light and love. If we will allow them, they can teach us to see ourselves the same way. ... And that's what innocence is. It's simple and trusting like a child, not judgmental and committed to one narrow point of view. If you are locked into a pattern of thinking and responding, your creativity gets blocked. You miss the freshness and magic of the moment. Learn to be innocent again, and that freshness never fades." - Michael Jackson

Because the importance of the Child is denied, there is a tendency to look through soiled glass, unable to see beyond personal guilt and negativity. We are encouraged to think the worst of people and ascribe motives and actions to them that we may be concealing in ourselves, and so the innocent child is made to be the guilty one.

"*Ignorance is learned; innocence is forgotten.*" - Jose Bergamin

In all kinds of abuse, the victim invariably believes it to be her/his own fault for not being good enough. We need to be careful how we treat our children, we stamp them with our own energies which are difficult to shift, as the Jesuits knew only too well. "Give me a child until he's seven and

I'll give you the man."

"*When you become a parent, or a teacher, you turn into a manager of this whole system. You become the person controlling the bubble of innocence around a child, regulating it.*" - Kazuo Ishiguro

"*I never, even for a moment, doubted what they'd told me. This is why it is that adults and even parents can, unwittingly, be cruel: they cannot imagine doubt's complete absence. They have forgotten.*" - David Foster Wallace

The Child will restore us to this beautiful part of ourselves.

"*Being part of the natural world reminds me that innocence isn't ever lost completely; we just need to maintain our goodness to regain it.*"- Jewel

"*I might have some character traits that some might see as innocence or naive. That's because I discovered peace and happiness in my soul. And with this knowledge, I also see the beauty of human life.*" - Tobey Maguire

Richard Gardner, author of two earlier books on this Work, *The Purpose of Love* and *The Wheel of Life,* noted that in earlier times the Child was more alive in us and we were able to concentrate on stars or planets at night and receive the influences they were beaming down to earth. Now we use powerful telescopes but can no longer experience their energies. We lose so much when we lose the Child. We sever ourselves from our link to the Divine, and even those who call themselves Christians ignore the advice of Jesus to "Become as little children" if we are to see heaven. The Child already sees it and with the active qualities of the other Archetypes, we can create it here on earth. "The meek shall inherit the earth" and "A child shall lead them."

"*O Innocence, with laughing eyes! Thou art a cherub from the skies, a wanderer from heaven.*" - Harvey Rice, 'Innocence'

"The essential self is innocent, and when it tastes its own innocence knows that it lives for ever." - *John Updike*

"Don't care what people say,
Just follow your own way.
Don't give up and use the chance,
To return to innocence.
That's not the beginning of the end,
That's the return to yourself
The return to innocence." - *Enigma*

Some key words of the positives and negatives are listed below, together with some of the interests and activities relevant to this Archetype to help round out the picture of its world.

Time: February 21st– March 21st.
Season: Early Spring.
Quality: One of the three Water states and one of the four Open states.
Elements: Water and Air.
Colour: Turquoise, duck egg blue.
Conflicting opposite: The Warrior.
Complementary Opposite: The Worker/Slave.
Voice: Tiny fairy-like voice soft, quiet, and sweet, sometimes with a lisp.
Face type: Sweet expression, pale complexion, heart-shaped face with pointed chin and wide open eyes. Fine, wispy hair.
Body type: Small, slight and slim.
Movement: Light and flitting.
Weather: Gently swirling, magical landscape, the freshness of dawn.
Landscape: Beautiful, with mists, hazy, cloudy.
Home: Cuddly toys and dolls, pictures and all pretty little things that are fascinating and beautiful to look at.

Clothing: Floaty delicate fabrics, fairylike costume.

Food: She likes sweet things.

Positives: Open, innocent, receptive, sweet, beautiful, trusting, full of faith, wonder and awe, loving, precious, youthing, soft, tender hearted, humility.

Negatives: Ineffectual, fearful, too precious, bewildered, a victim, a scapegoat, gullible, naïve, mystified, scared, defenceless, is bullied.

Career choices and interests: Will do what she's told, but prefers to work in a quiet place with few people. She gets on well with very young children and animals.

Reading materials and entertainment: Fairy tales and magical stories, films and books about the wonders of the world.

Music: Tinkly, fairy-like sounds, little bells.

She is: The Fairy, Cinders, the Princess, Little Orphan Annie.

"Vulnerability is the only authentic state. Being vulnerable means being open, for wounding, but also for pleasure. Being open to the wounds of life means also being open to the bounty and beauty. Don't mask or deny your vulnerability: it is your greatest asset. Be vulnerable: quake and shake in your boots with it. The new goodness that is coming to you, in the form of people, situations, and things can only come to you when you are vulnerable, i.e. open." – Stephen Russell

How to Practise the Child

Reading the script is beneficial in several ways -

1. It increases your awareness of your Centre.

2. It helps you to identify and recognise the Child in yourself and others.

3. It gives you control over your Child.

4. As the script focuses on positive attributes, it helps you to purify your Child.

5. It gives you the opportunity to add more strands of the Child in yourself.

6. You can help others to activate it in themselves.

Reading the script only serves as a rehearsal for the real thing - your daily life. When developing the Child, you will need to follow through by observing your usual behaviour patterns and seeing where you can introduce a more receptive way of being. Follow positive impulses to do something new, such as reading or making up Fairy stories or learning to listen more openly to other people. The Child is an open state. If you identify with and realise you live a lot in the Child, read the script to purify and identify it in yourself. You will understand your own Child better. If you are weak in the Child and identify more with her conflicting opposite, the Warrior, you could find yourself resisting and not wishing to relinquish your ego. The opposite reaction is also possible and you may find memories of childhood coming up, with a feeling of smallness and vulnerability. Equally, you might remember happy times when you were wide open to the magic of life. If you feel fear, try to identify the root of it. Keep in mind that you have been suppressing it and using the Warrior to protect yourself. You can allow it to be there, knowing you can integrate it with other parts of yourself, transforming it into wonder and awe at the beauty of life.

Preparing

Wear something of the appropriate colour (turquoise blue) and style, something flimsy and fairylike, little slippers or bare feet. To help set the scene, play some gentle, quiet, tinkly music. Visualize yourself as a white light in the Centre of your circle, reaching towards the Child to add turquoise blue to your colours. Let that colour surround you, imagine you are filling up with a delicate turquoise blue. Keep the awareness that you are the Centre and not the Child. Getting the stance and the voice right before you begin, and being aware of maintaining them as you read, will help in channeling the energy through.

Imagine yourself in the Child's landscape. Remember the Child's elements, Water and Air; water in the air is mist. It is Spring and you stand in the dawn, the sun is only just starting to rise and glimmers slightly through the swirling mists surrounding you. You listen to sounds drifting towards you and your eyes are huge with awe, as if you are seeing the world for the first time. Stand to begin with, and sit down later if you wish. Imagine you have shrunk several inches and take shallow breaths into your upper chest. Everything and everybody are so much bigger, you are so small and young. Stand with your feet slightly pointing inwards, feel as if you are made of mist, floating a little above the ground, a little Fairy, flitting from one thing to another as things catch your eye. The world is huge, and you are only a tiny part of it. Because you take such small breaths into your upper lungs, you speak in a quiet voice, whispery, often not easy to hear. Let the feeling grow naturally and gradually. Try not to act it, you could become trapped in the act and limit yourself. You will notice that your surroundings seem to grow as you shrink in stature, you feel more open, your face pales. Look at things, and think that you don't know what they're called or what they're for. Listen to the sounds around you, concentrate on receiving impressions without analyzing or judging them.

Persevere and your other Archetypes will accept that your life has improved, it is more beautiful, benefiting from the restoration of your innocence. A more youthful and magical you will emerge. The Child brings you rebirth. Now read the script.

THE CHILD

Water and Air

Tiny fairy-like voice soft, quiet, whispery and sweet.

I am the Child, I'm Water and Air,
Soft and beautiful, fragile, fair,
Impressionable and naive,
Sweet Princess, I truly receive.

To all impressions I surrender,
Passive, trusting, small and tender.
At the beginning of all, and all I believe,
Magical stories just love to receive.

I am the Dawn, I am the Spring,
Beauty, faith and wonderment bring.
Mine is the world of faeries and phantoms,
Goddesses, Gods in fabulous mantles.

So many strange shapes drift past my eye,
I'm so full of awe, they mystify,
And fascinate, I'm so full of Love,
I can feel the power of the stars above,

They impress me with their own true nature,
All is one great beauteous picture.
As I stand out of doors in the dawn to receive
The magic of Daybreak, awestruck perceive

A great Artist at work, who with mighty sweeps,
Colours the world, whilst the world sleeps.
The huge Golden Disc slides up the sky,
Revealing such wonders to innocent eye.

Amplified sounds frighten and thrill,
I take it all in, receptive and still.
As my magical mist moistens your flesh,
I keep you young, sweet and fresh.

The spider's web like jewelled strings,
Flowers, pixies and furry things,
Each time I look it's ever new,
Each moment's a birth in my beautiful dew.

I merge with it all, precious and meek,
I'm the Key to Paradise that you seek,
My heart's full of faith, beauty and awe,
My Faerieland drifts in Magical Law.

Be open to me and make a new start,
All precious things dwell in my heart.
A child shall lead them to Heaven's door,
To live in Love and Trust once more,

It is said that the meek shall inherit the Earth,
In Beauty and Wonder, I bring you Rebirth.

The Enchantress

☽☉

Both positive and negative attributes are given in this description to help you better recognise the state in yourself and others. When we repeatedly use an Archetype, it cannot fail to exhibit negative traits, as it becomes overused and not balanced by other states. The climates associated with the months of the year were worked out in the Northern hemisphere, so they may need to be adjusted to suit the Southern Hemisphere and take into account unfamiliar weather patterns linked to climate change.

The Enchantress

Cardinal Water

March 21st – April 21st

One of the three Water states and one of the four Cardinal states.

Water and Earth, the metaphysical linking of Soul and Body.

The season of the Enchantress is March/April, mid-Spring. Her colour is dark blue, like the twilight sea, the mix of approximately two parts of the blue of Water, her first element, and one part of the brown of Earth, her second.

Water is a horizontal element and is supported by the Earth. It wells up in springs, streams and rivers which run into lakes, seas and oceans. In March, rainwater nourishes the plants and the sap rises. We think of a well, a deep pool of water, a pond, a cool, overshadowed secret garden, a lily pool reflecting the moon and the trees. This is a mysterious twilight world, a deep, underwater world of fish and plants, undercurrents, a strange, dreamlike place where it is always twilight and there are ghosts, phantoms and spirits, strange other-worldly creatures, lost treasures at the bottom of the sea, like the imagination which holds our deepest secrets and gifts. The Enchantress is the source of all our dreams and feelings, she 'lives in a dream', she is the dreamer who can see the past and can both see and create the future.

She lives in a world of little light, around her are only vague shadows, she is surrounded by water, she lives at the source of all birth. We are told we came from the sea and through evolutionary stages, arrived as humans. We were nourished in amniotic fluid and came forth into the world behind a flood of it. Before it becomes a butterfly, a caterpillar in the pupa stage builds a little sack, the chrysalis. This protects it as it turns itself into a liquid, soupy substance, then becomes a butterfly. Liquid is essential for life to enter the world. When you truly allow her to enter you, you have the sensation of being submerged in water, she is the source of all we are, all is born from the waters, our dreams and imagination. Nothing exists that was not first seen on the inner world. It is here, from the source of our beings, that we derive sensibility, the intuitive sensing of what meaning things have and whether something 'rings true' or not.

The Enchantress is your imagination, the image maker on your inner screen, images are seen in her before you create them on the outer world. In present times she is derided and suppressed, which is not conducive to her being in a good state. This is why so many of us live with depression. There is so much suffering in the world and no one knows this better than the Enchantress. These days, images have been pushed outside of ourselves, we are inundated with advertisements, television, phones, computers, films and video games. We have been driven out of our inner world and are blinded to the visions of our own souls.

"Imagination is more important than knowledge. Knowledge is limited. Imagination encircles the world." - Albert Einstein

This is the world of your feelings, deep in your heart and soul. All joys, sorrows, pain, loneliness, hurts, wounds, sadness, depression, suffering, guilt and remorse live in your Enchantress. She is your conscience. Grief comes in waves, washing over you, knocking you down onto a dark empty, forlorn beach; then the tide recedes and the pain lessens. As you allow your awareness to drop down into your heart you will feel all these things and it is only by experiencing them and passing through the grill of pain that you come to her true source of power. You will be moved to weep, as all the hurts you have suffered and have caused flow through you. They are felt in your 'water works', copious tears pouring down your face as you sob. Your deepest feelings 'well up', bringing a flow, a stream of associated images. In this cruel world of so much pain, it is not surprising that most people shut off this part of themselves; yet how are we to end our nightmares and turn them into our dearest dreams if we pretend they are not there? Many people try to 'drown their sorrows' with alcohol, but you can't drown them, they live in water and they can swim. Feelings and emotions are not the same. Emotions are what we express through the Actress, but feelings are deeper and are often never properly expressed. The Enchantress sits still, 'drowning in misery', weeping silently and secretly into the wet, damp, cold night.

"Until you heal the wounds of your past, you are going to bleed. You can bandage the bleeding with food, with alcohol, with drugs, with work, with cigarettes, with sex; but eventually it will all ooze through and stain your life. You must find the strength to open the wounds, stick your hands inside, pull out the core of the pain that is holding you in your past, the memories, and make peace with them." - Iyanla Vanzant

We wail from our deepest depths the terrible loneliness of being separate from love. The Enchantress knows we are incomplete, that we must be reconnected with love and by love. We yearn for a soul mate, the other half, a loving family, a group soul, the divine union, that which was torn from us. The solitary heart cries in its need for love, the agony of the Siren's wail, the irresistible magnetic cry that none can hear and ever forget. It touches the heart and haunts the soul, desperately trying to draw lost love back to her. It matters not whether we yearn for a lover or peace on earth and happiness for all, it is the need for love for which she cries and the lack of it that causes all her suffering. We all suffer from too little love. Loss and grief can be felt as pain in the chest and it is possible that a surfeit can cause someone to 'die of a broken heart', when all hope is gone. The Siren's wail warns of the danger we are in without love. It is interesting that a mechanical siren blares from emergency vehicles, warning us that something is badly wrong.

"If you don't become the ocean, you'll be seasick every day." - Leonard Cohen

Yet Water is cleansing, so allow yourself to cry, your tears will wash you clean. Weeping will purify your soul and allow you to enter the Enchantress's magical, mysterious world more deeply. There has been interesting research into the content of tears. We produce three kinds: reflex, continuous, and emotional, each with a different healing role. Reflex tears allow your eyes to clear out noxious particles when irritated by substances such as smoke or onions; continuous tears are produced regularly to keep your eyes lubricated and contain lysozyme, a chemical which acts as an anti-bacterial, protecting your eyes from infection; but emotional tears have a special function. Discoveries made by biochemist Dr. William Frey at the Ramsey Medical Center in Minneapolis showed that reflex tears are 98% water, but emotional tears also contain stress hormones which leave the body through weeping. Further studies suggest that crying stimulates the production of endorphins, our body's natural pain killer and 'feel-good' hormones. After the release of painful feelings, your breathing and heart rate decrease and you enter a calmer biological and emotional state. Weeping is good for you, detoxifying your body as it soothes your soul. Having 'cried your heart out', you pass through the pain and come to soothing waters.

"There is a sacredness in tears. They are not the mark of weakness, but of power. They speak more eloquently than ten thousand tongues. They are messengers of overwhelming grief and unspeakable love." - Washington Irving

The Enchantress is sincere and bestows compassion and sympathy, you have empathy as you connect your feelings to those of others. The moon affects the oceans and tides and as the seas encircle and connect all lands, so are we connected in a sea of consciousness. Small streams flow into rivers and eventually reach the sea, just as our feelings pour from us into the global ocean of feeling. The water in our brains swells slightly and rises up in response to the moon, as do the tides. At the full moon wounds bleed more and crime increases because we no longer have rituals suitable to this time, and frustrations build up.

There is much academic and archeological evidence of different societies in the past, possibly lasting for hundreds of thousands of years. These were world-wide and they recognised the female aspects of Divinity. Women had more status than they have today, although the social structures were thought to be fair and egalitarian. We can't assume that matriarchal structures were simply the same as patriarchal ones. Women in power create a very different kind of society, more circular and cooperative in shape, rather than the competitive pyramid of the male led world. The female Archetypes were used to a greater degree and so the seasons were celebrated with rituals and festivals and the moon was worshipped as Divine. Most of the Christian festivals are a takeover of these older ones, Easter being an example. The word comes from Eostra, a Great Mother Goddess and Goddess of Spring, the time of year when birds lay eggs and all life burst forth. At the patriarchal takeover, which was roughly five thousand years ago, there was a major shift, and through much violence and suppression the new male centred religions took power, after which time everything related to Goddesses and the Old Religions were deemed to be unlucky, evil and were assigned demonic and derogatory meanings. Hence we have the word 'lunatic', with the meaning of 'someone mad', when in fact it simply means someone who is attuned to the moon and female types of consciousness. (There is plenty academic and scholarly research and evidence regarding these earlier times).

We could claim that the sun worshippers, what we can call the 'solatics', are the ones whose sanity is questionable. They hate the rain, failing to connect its importance to the cultivation of their food and the water that comes out of their taps. We block the Enchantress in Western society and so we are  largely unaware of how deeply we are affected by the moon, the sea, each other and global happenings.

As the tides flow onto beaches bringing messages from other lands, the currents move and whisper of events elsewhere, just as the sea of consciousness carries dreams and nightmares to the Enchantress. Hers is a world of atmospheres, she senses the feelings in her surroundings, her feelings see through pretence to the truth. She is so sensitive, ripples reach her as something drops into or moves in the water. She is aware of the slightest shift. She says "I feel it in my water", "I get a bad/good feeling about this". Things travel through waves and radios can receive more stations at night, especially when it's raining. In her world of true feelings, communication flows easily and comprehensibly. She is the queen of direct communication and in this way she can commune with animals and understand their feelings and needs. Her arts include telepathy, intuition, your psychic abilities which, as they open before you, enable you to see into the past or future, even if only vaguely at first. Hers is the world of prophecy, prediction, precognition, foresight. She is the Oracle. She can guide you away from decisions that have negative consequences, showing you choices that are more favourable. Her tools include crystals and crystal balls, scrying mirrors, Tarot cards, tea leaves and palmistry. The Hippie movement was an attempt to bring her back, with long hair, flowing robes and a call for love. The establishment quickly clamped down on her and we got Punk Rock instead, which has much of the Warrior and Worker/Slave in it. She has been allowed to reveal herself to some extent in the much derided and ridiculed New Age, but even here many practitioners merely dabble in her, fearful of going too deep. Hypnotism is one of her arts, reaching down, deeper into the feelings to either understand a disturbing issue or to free the inner world into more positive behaviours; but she is exploited by the Joker and the Wise Woman, who use stage hypnotism, with tricks that manipulate the excited suggestibility of people to make them perform humiliating things, to the great amusement of the audience - and to make money of course. These stage hypnotists are almost always men who would run in terror at the first sight of an authentic Enchantress. What base disrespect we show to this vital, Cardinal state, rather than recognising her as the healer of our hearts.

"Your heart is the size of an ocean. Go find yourself in its hidden depths." - *Rumi*

We say "A picture is worth a thousand words". Many years ago I had a strange vision. The earth was encircled by a clear membrane like a vast protective bubble, and huge black birds with long, pointed, serrated beaks were flying up and ripping holes in it. I knew this was bad but didn't know why. It was not until years later that people began to talk about the ozone layer and the holes that were appearing in it. This is an example of the Enchantress seeing into the future, but she can't always interpret her visions. In this instance it was the Logician who provided the explanation. Often when people in different Archetypes consult her and she delivers a prophecy, they exclaim "I can't see that happening!". She replies "Of course you can't, that's why you're consulting me."

As water encircles the earth, so she can see around corners and curves and know what is coming. She is strongest when the sun is down and the Logician is weaker, for when morning comes he will chase away her dreams like a ruthless tyrant. We no longer share and discuss our dreams, yet they are a superb source of information. They can be precognitive, issuing warnings about events and people, they can be cleansing in revealing fears and inner disturbances, they can be creatively inspirational and they can be lucid, when you astrally travel. Such treasures she offers, yet we fear her because we have not the strength to face our own feelings. If we wish to improve our lives, the only way out is through. Denial and avoidance create stagnant waters that poison and kill us.

Many cultures have used herbs, music, chanting, dance or ritual to invoke her trance. She is entrancing, alluring, full of charms, charming. With her guidance you will avoid many mistakes, you will not marry unsuitable partners, follow careers that do not fulfill you or get into an aeroplane that will fall out of the sky. She is essential if you are to have a good and meaningful life. A remnant of her can be found at Lent, the forty days before Easter, the time of sackcloth and ashes when people sit in darkened churches to weaken the conscious mind that she may rise in you. Christians are supposed to prepare for Easter by thinking of their sins and fasting, but nowadays they may simply give something up, like chocolate or alcohol for the duration.

"In one drop of water are found all the secrets of all the oceans." - Kahil Gibran

The Enchantress is Sybil who gave you Divine guidance in the past, before she was viciously outlawed by the church and similar male dominated religious cults. Without her, you have little chance of meaningful guidance, for God/Goddess/Spirit/Universe communicates via your intuition, visions and dreams. She is the voice of your soul. It is often only through sickness, great sadness, drugs or concussion that she arises these days, and the new-found intuition or psychic visions may be frightening. Herbs and substances that might invoke her are illegal, labelling them 'hallucinogenic', as if we understand all the consciousness available to us and have the slightest idea of reality; yet other harmful, addictive drugs, many of them medical, and alcohol are freely available. Obviously, there are other illegal drugs that are harmful and addictive and I definitely do not suggest taking them. Mostly, these provide escapism, with few true insights. People, particularly many men, have a terror of her, and so she is practically against the law. If you find yourself in this Archetype you will very likely be given psychiatric treatment and drugs to suppress her. She has been driven down and labelled the subconscious, put out of our reach and considered to be a mental illness. No wonder that, with such little understanding shown towards her, she becomes depressed and 'gets the blues'. Treatment of depression can be improved by bringing in other Archetypes such as the Joker, her conflicting opposite, or the Fool and Actress which will enliven and cheer her up.

Psyche is the Greek word for soul. Psychologist means 'knowledge of the soul'. A true psychologist/psychiatrist is a healer of the soul. Few have such insight now, they say it's all in the mind, she's hallucinating, and the treasures that well from her depths are called madness, but this is a shallow, narrow and unhelpful approach The real madness is ignoring her soul's call that we have lost our way. It is not suggested that people should stop taking prescribed medication and treatments, but a broader view to her problems is required if we are to live in happiness. Her misery is not merely personal, social ills affect us all, as she knows only too well.

"There is no coming to consciousness without pain. People will do anything, no matter how absurd, in order to avoid facing their own Soul. One does not become enlightened by imagining figures of light, but by making the darkness conscious." - Carl Jung

"Educating the mind without the heart is no education at all" – Aristotle

The Enchantress sees the world in a very different way from what is now considered to be 'normal', so she is often accused of lying, imagining things and of being 'too sensitive'. Children who see and talk to phantoms or have 'invisible friends' are using their Enchantress, but people say "It's something they'll grow out of" (they make sure of it), "don't children have wonderful imaginations?". It is a grave error to assume that these friends exist only in the minds and imaginations of children, there are many accounts of children saying they see and talk to relatives who have died and relate things they could not otherwise have known. We dispute what our children are telling us, we smile patronisingly and we suppress this vital part of them. We arrive with the Enchantress working in us and many times these visions may be real, but it is not long before our little ones are persuaded that they're imagining it and lose these priceless abilities. The Enchantress is ever accused of causing 'hallucinations' and as a result so much inspiration and guidance of all kinds is lost. What we call the Third Eye is how the Enchantress sees on the inner, although she can also see ghosts and spirits on the outer world. I once had a discussion with two little girls who said I was stupid and of course we only have two eyes. I asked them to think of their favourite toy at home, with eyes either open or closed, and to try to see it. I asked if they could and they said yes. I then asked how they could see something that was not in front of them. "Oh, I see!" they cried. They now understood what their Third Eye was. It is said in some ancient scriptures that kissing the Third Eye of a person can be an uplifting and healing experience, creating a sense of wellbeing. It seems to activate the pineal and pituitary glands if you kiss the centre of the forehead between the eyebrows with a thought of compassion.

The sea is magnetic, it draws you towards itself, as does the Enchantress. If you walk along a cliff edge by the sea, you have to be careful because if you're talking to someone or not concentrating, you could find yourself walking too close to the edge.

"We are what we think. All that we are arises from our thoughts. With our thoughts we make the world." – *Buddha*

We can also say "we are what we see", as the inner world perceives through vision. The Enchantress is alluring and can draw things towards herself, people are magnetically drawn to her, she is so deep and mysterious, as with her feelings she envisions her spells. Her psychic gifts are like two sides of a coin; one can see what is coming and the other can determine what is to come. She does this through creative visualisation, creating the picture of what she wants and pulling it towards herself. Imagine a cinema; the film playing on the screen is your life as it is now and you are the projector. The light is the life force that impresses your visions onto the screen. If you don't like the plot you can change the film by projecting a different one. The Actress can help by putting an emotional charge behind it.

"Imagination should be used, not to escape reality, but to create it." - *Colin Wilson*
"Since everything is a reflection of our minds, everything can be changed by our minds." - *Buddha*

Rhyming couplets are often chanted as part of her spells, for poetry speaks from the soul. As we have increasingly neglected the Enchantress, rhyme is no longer considered necessary in most modern poetry. This does not mean that prose is not good, as can be seen in Japanese Haiku and other skillful ways of selecting words and phrases which can be evocative and moving, but the Enchantress's rhymes attune to the rhythms of the sea, the waves, the tides, the depths, the flow of such poetry touching our own depths.

To have the Enchantress is to have appreciation. She savours and tastes, her senses appreciate the truth of things and guide you towards good taste or bad. Without her, people fall into bad taste, appreciate nothing and have no gratitude. She knows by tasting and smelling, she experiences a direct relationship with things, undistorted by mental filters, she 'senses things'. Taste and smell are related to precognition because they have an immediate and direct affect, like making the mouth water, memories awaken, or the genitals react. The smell and vibration of coming events are in the air or water before they manifest and if the soul is receptive we sense their coming. Animals do this when they move locations to escape forthcoming disasters. She has phrases that describe her relationship with events such as "It doesn't taste right", "It has a funny taste about it", "It left a bad taste in my mouth", "It left a sour taste", "This smells fishy", "It doesn't smell right", and of course there is her 'sixth sense', her intuition.

She 'dissolves into tears'. Dissolving is another of her great powers. She reaches into the source and can dissolve anything; stones, sticks or metal, and by this means she apports objects by changing their molecular structure. All things can float on her metaphysical water, including herself, so levitation is another of her talents, as is psychokinesis, from the Greek meaning 'soul movement', or telekinesis from the Greek, meaning 'distant-movement'. This is the ability to influence matter without touching it. Examples of psychokinesis include moving an object, levitating and teleporting it. We poo hoo these abilities now, when once they were very likely the norm. The Logician is unable to perform these feats and therefore has the illusion that no one else can, although Quantum Physics and Mechanics are revealing things that are baffling and were thought to be impossible. Such powers you had in the past when you lived by her wisdom! Myths and legends are her way of describing events and the consciousness of the time.

She makes an appearance in Spiritualist séances where her presence is marked by a drop in temperature. We associate spooky happenings, the presence of ghosts and strange sounds with a cold feeling. We say "I got a chill up my spine", "It made my hair stand on end", "My blood ran cold". The Logician loves his experiments and is inclined to haul her into his laboratories to test the existence of telepathy, psychokinesis and so on, but he fails to grasp that these things cannot be easily manifested in an inappropriate atmosphere of bright lights, white walls and soulless plastic furnishings. She is hooked up to and surrounded by machines, computers and people who are waiting for her to fail. Imagine planning a romantic evening. Would you not have candles, soft lighting and music, delicious food smells and perfumes? Why would you set the scene in this way? Is it not because the right atmosphere is essential for feelings of romance to arise? Imagine planning a loving tryst in a laboratory with strangers observing and measuring your every move. Would you not feel inhibited and 'not in the right mood'? Most of us would go off the idea altogether, and so it is when testing the Enchantress. She needs to be in her own environment and cannot be expected to perform to order in an alien one, although she can sometimes deliver the goods in spite of it. Failed experiments allow the mind-dominated Archetypes to disprove her, unable to see that equally the Logician can't think whilst he's out for the count, nor does he appreciate how she will often give him the answer to a problem or a new idea whilst he sleeps, although some do claim to have dreamt answers when they've been stuck for ideas. In Victorian times in the 19th century, Spiritualism became popular with reports of ectoplasm and spirits appearing and tables levitating. The Logician investigated and shattered the necessary atmospheres, seeking to destroy the reputation of the mediums. It is likely that, in an attempt to protect themselves from failure, some may have staged events, but certainly not all. The Logician's approach to the Enchantress is mainly not to prove her abilities but to disprove them. With this aim and attitude, he is bound to be successful because these things are impossible in his world. The Enchantress fell with Ancient Greece and has never really been revived since. We must bring her back before we turn our planet into a wasteland, for with no Water in our consciousness we and our planet become but deserts. The skull of the Logician, tends upwards as in an 'egghead', but that of the Enchantress elongates outwards at the back. This is called the Egyptian skull and can be seen on Tutankhamen. The Cerebellum resides at the base of your skull at the back, and see how small it is nowadays, crushed beneath the dominating cerebrum.

"We think too much and feel too little." - Charlie Chaplin

Negatively, the Enchantress is sad, melancholic, depressed, hopeless, plaintive, shrinking, always feeling cold in her damp, dank, tearful world, is susceptible to colds, ever dripping moisture and with a need to urinate often. She is secretive, devious, living in her own world of dreams, cut off from others and the world around her.

Positively she is loving, charming, alluring, soulful, bewitching, flowing, mysterious, illusive, enigmatic, fascinating, enchanting, hypnotic, prophetic, sincere, subdued, deep, quiet and slow, subtle and magnetic, deeply immersed in feeling, a Priestess, attracting us to explore her hidden secrets as she sits and waits, waits for the return of love.

"I must be a mermaid. I have no fear of depths and a great fear of shallow living." - Anais Nin

"There is a place where dreams are born, and time is never planned, it's not on any chart, you can find it in your heart." - Never Never Land, Peter Pan

Some key words of the positives and negatives are listed below, together with some of the interests and activities relevant to this Archetype to help round out the picture of its world.

Time: March 21st - April 21st

Season: Mid Spring

Quality: One of the three Water states and one of the four Cardinal states

Elements: Water and Earth

Colour: Dark blues.

Conflicting opposite: The Joker.

Complementary Opposite: Mother Nature.

Voice: Deep, soulful and magnetic, as if it is coming through water.

Face type: Long face, pale complexion, deep, soulful eyes, often with a dreamy, faraway look, long flowing hair.

Body type: Full but not fat.

Movement: Flowing, bewitching, slow.

Weather: Rain and damp.

Landscape: Oceans, rivers, seas, streams, secret places, enchanted pools, wells.

Home: Dreamy décor with pictures of mystical scenes, floaty fabrics, crystals, incense, scented candles.

Clothing: Long flowing garments.

Food: Soup, seafood, but mainly vegetarian as she won't want to kill fish.

Positives: Loving, charming, enticing, soulful, bewitching, prophetic, flowing, mysterious, illusive, enigmatic, fascinating, enchanting, hypnotic, sincere, subdued, deep, quiet and slow, subtle and magnetic.

Negatives: Sad, melancholic, lonely, depressed, plaintive, shrinking, over weeping, secretive.

Career choices and interests: A Seer, a prophet, creative visualisation, divination, a psychic medium, a mystic, dream interpreter, Astrologer, palmist, tea leaf reader and all other forms of psychic reading. With other Archetypes, can be a creative, a storyteller, myth maker, an artist, painting her mysterious world. She is the one who brings atmosphere into a painting, story or music.

Reading materials and entertainment: Films and literature about ghosts, angels, psychic phenomena, creatures of the sea, anything about the supernatural, fantasy fiction, creative visualization.

Music: Hypnotic and slow, often with eastern instruments like sitars.

She is: The Oracle, A Priestess, the Anima, the Siren, a Mermaid, the Seer, a Soothsayer, Die Lorelei, an Enigma.

"To make the right choices in life, you have to get in touch with your soul. To do this, you need to experience solitude, which most people are afraid of, because in the silence you hear the truth and know the solutions."- Deepak Chopra

How to Practice the Enchantress

Reading the script is beneficial in several ways –

1. It increases your awareness of your Centre.

2. It helps you to identify and recognise the Enchantress in yourself and others.

3. It gives you control over your Enchantress.

4. As the script focuses on positive attributes, it helps you to purify your Enchantress.

5. It gives you the opportunity to add more strands of the Enchantress in yourself.

6. You can help others to activate it in themselves.

Reading the script only serves as a rehearsal for the real thing - your daily life. When developing the Enchantress, you will need to follow through by observing your usual behaviour patterns and seeing where you can introduce a more meaningful way of being. Follow positive impulses to do something new, such as getting in touch with your intuition, allowing your feelings to guide you or writing down your dreams and looking for their meaning.

The Enchantress is a Cardinal state. If you identify with and realise you live a lot in the Enchantress, read the script to purify and identify it in yourself. You will understand your own Enchantress better. If you are weak in the Enchantress and identify more with her conflicting opposite, the Joker, you could find yourself resisting and not wanting to connect to your feelings. The opposite reaction is also possible and you might be deeply moved and weep. This Archetype is the dreamer, so it may be better to practice it at night, but anytime is good to go deeper into yourself.

Preparing

Wear something of the appropriate colour (dark blue) and style - long, flowing garments. To help set the scene, play some hypnotic and slow music, possibly with eastern instruments such as sitars. You can also play sounds of the ocean, a stream or rainfall. First, visualize yourself as a light in the Centre of your circle, reaching out towards the Enchantress to add dark blue to your colours. Let that colour surround you, imagine you are filling up with a deep, midnight blue. Keep the awareness that you are the Centre and not the Enchantress. Getting the stance and the voice right before you begin, and being aware of maintaining them as you read, will help in channeling the energy through.

Imagine yourself in the Enchantress's landscape. It is mid Spring, it is twilight, the light is almost gone. There is a damp feeling as you imagine you are standing by the sea, a stream or sitting by a pool. Remember the Enchantress's elements, Water and Earth, water with earth below. Your movements are like seaweed floating in the water. You can lie back if you prefer and allow yourself to feel dreamy. Your voice is deep, soulful and magnetic, sounding as if it is coming through water. Have a go at the Siren's wail if you can. Let the feeling grow naturally and gradually. Try not to act it, you as could become trapped in the act and limit yourself. You will notice that your surroundings seem to darken as you direct your attention inwards. If this state is unfamiliar to you, focus on getting the voice right, which will come as you get the feeling, and it may tremble with tears. You could imagine you are telling a ghost story which will help you get the note, but be careful not to let the Actress come in and ham it up.

Persevere and the other Archetypes will accept that your life has improved, your senses are more awake and you enjoy a deeper communication with life. Life will be more meaningful when you are in touch with your intuition. Your feelings are more honest and you can enjoy a deeper connection with life. The Enchantress brings you back in touch with your heart, her blessed waters wash you clean and allow you to feel and share more love. Now read the script.

THE ENCHANTRESS
Water and Earth

Deep, soulful and hypnotic voice.

I am the Enchantress, the Psychic Queen,

The image maker, your inner screen,

I am your Soul, the source of all your dreams,

My visions are past, present, future scenes.

Water and Earth, rivers, oceans and wells,

By mysterious pools I chant magic spells.

I am the Mermaid who sings a haunting tune,

My rhythms are those of the sea and the moon.

In the depths of my Soul cries the memory,

Of the love I have lost, that was torn from me,

I am Sybil who weeps lonely, sad tears,

For all the pain felt through all the long years.

For I hold all hurts, all wounds, all sorrows,

I know all your past and all your tomorrows.

My Siren's wail haunts the Soul (WAIL-L-L-L),

Never to cease until Love makes me whole.

But fear not my tears, for they purify,

And cleanse the Soul, Queen of Feeling am I.

In the Chalice of Love, in the depths of your heart,

Is where we would merge, never to part.

I'm illusive, sincere, your imagination,

Telepathic, direct communication,

Compassion, sympathy, I'm, empathetic,

Poetic, bewitching, deep, magnetic.

My seas encircle the Earth on every side,

Bringing visions from all lands on every tide.

Come, come, my strange, dark, vague world know,

Intuition lets all Divine secrets flow.

I experience Life and through Divination,

I will guide your path and unite each nation.

I have good taste, in hypnotic rain-fall,

I appreciate that which is true in us all.

Metals or woods, all things I dissolve,

And weave a new spell, all sorrows resolve.

Levitation's an art that also is mine,

Magic carpets and broomsticks from earlier times.

The consciousness by which you now only dream,
Was reality once, when Goddess was Queen,
Then the Oracle sat on Delphi's throne,
But now ignored and defiled, I dream alone.

Both night and day-dreams can bring me to you,
They are Heaven-sent that you may see through
This nightmare land, like Hell it seems,
Magic potions show visions of Heavenly dreams.

I'm enchanting, alluring, quiet and slow,
Deep and charming, all charms I know.
I am Circe, come, come drink me and Live,
Everlasting Life and Love I give.

The Actress

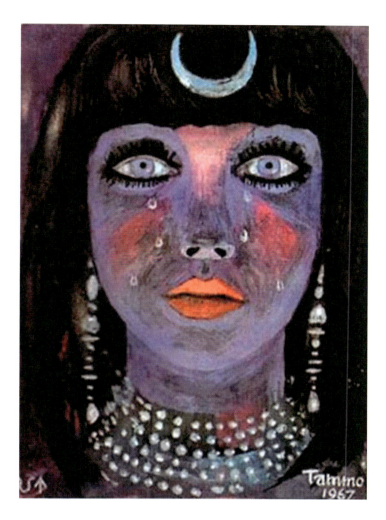

Both positive and negative attributes are given in this description to help you better recognise the state in yourself and others. When we repeatedly use an Archetype, it cannot fail to exhibit negative traits, as it becomes overused and not balanced by other states. The climates associated with the months of the year were worked out in the Northern hemisphere, so they may need to be adjusted to suit the Southern Hemisphere and take into account unfamiliar weather patterns linked to climate change.

The Actress

Closed Water

April 21st – May 21st

One of the three Water states and one of the four Closed states.

Water and Fire, the metaphysical linking of Soul and Spirit.

The season of the Actress is April/May, late Spring. Her colour is purple, violet, the mix of approximately two parts of the blue of Water, her first element, and one part of the red of Fire, her second. These are the two dynamic Elements, containing the most life.

Water above Fire creates steam. She is the one who 'lets off steam', she gets 'steamed up', she rules the emotions and the passions as Spring announces the drama of Summer! The Enchantress governs your feelings, but the Actress expresses them. In April the buds open, we think of Easter, daffodils, violets and blossom, birdsong and lover's lane. It's a time for flowery speeches and the blossoming of love, for music and moonlight.

"In the Spring a young man's fancy lightly turns to thoughts of love." - Alfred Lord Tennyson

Intensity is associated with flowering, when emotions and excitement find an outlet and creative genius thrives. Her setting is the stage, the theatre, grand opera, the catwalk, pop videos, whereon she makes her dramatic entrance! She plays the starring role on every occasion, all must look at her, she

is ever in the spotlight. She is also to be found on film sets and delights in seeing her face fill large cinema screens across the world. You don't have to be an Actress/Actor by profession to have this Archetype. Anyone living in the Actress will create theatricals, it's what this consciousness does.
"All the world's a stage, and all the men and women merely players." - *Shakespeare*

In her superficial aspect of physical appearance, this is a popular female Archetype. She can be seen almost everywhere; in theatres, cinemas, as a model, in advertising, in music. Girls, women and some men dress up and wear make up to look good and attract attention. Drag Queens are an example of how some men manifest her, although many object to women being parodied in this way. Many gay men love her, but not all gay men are camp, nor does being heterosexual exclude a man from using this part of himself. Attitudes as to how men and women are supposed to look obstructs people from attaining inner balance and pressures them into roles for which they may not be suited. We all have emotions and the need to show off and be seen, which can be done without glitter and high heels. To experience her expressive side, we need to look at countries such as Italy or Brazil where expression and excitability flow more freely. Emotions are not so popular in Britain. Protestant Puritanism did not approve of her. As Richard Gardner said, "When giving public demonstrations of the functions in England, we have noticed that many members of the audience recoiled from the Actress, and others tended to react as if this function did not really matter, and no doubt we would be better off without it." I have experienced occasions when people have, in a kindly whisper, offered to call a doctor when someone has burst into tears. How tragic that we see emotions as an illness. When we block our Actress we stifle emotional release, leading to frustration.

"I love acting. It is so much more real than life." - *Oscar Wilde*

The Actress is the queen of all expression, everything pent up gushes forth and fills life with vitality and enthusiasm! She frees the dramas which dull, routine living denies and gives vent to all your moods, good and bad, tempers and temperament, tantrums, love and hate, jealousy, enthusiasm, disgust, agitation, grand passions, great pleasure, joy and pain. There is no event she cannot dramatise. Losing an earring is the greatest tragedy and cause for deep despair, but finding it again is complete ecstasy!! She's always intense, excited, lively and worked up about something. All events become larger than life!! She lives life with an exclamation mark! Or several !!!!!

"Acting should be bigger than life. Scripts should be bigger than life. It should all be bigger than life." - Bette Davis

Everything is a drama and she will dramatise it to the hilt, any event can become an enormous occurrence! She will say, "We had *the* most wonderful time *ever* in the whole world!" or "You just can't imagine how dreadful it was, what I suffered is beyond belief!" She can express all your hopes, desires, sorrows and grief. She is the displayer of moods, the storms, rain, thunder and lightning of the emotions which we need in order to purify our souls. All is exaggerated gesture and reaction, she is alive and passionate, her passions gush, she is tempestuous, and has a zest for life that makes the most of everything and increases its enjoyment a thousand-fold! To scent a flower is to discover bliss, and she will wax lyrical on its exquisite aroma. All is hyperbole.

"My job is usually to express emotion as freely as possible." - Meryl Streep

She is wildly romantic and just adores speaking in poetic and dramatic ways. "The sky has never looked more beautiful, the stars never so bright, nor the moon so enchanting. This must be the most wonderful night in all creation!" Positively she will mean it, but negatively, it will be delivered in such a way as to draw attention to herself. She won't actually have looked at it, the whole point is that you look at her.

"Acting is all about honesty. If you can fake that you've got it made. - George Burns

She is the conflicting opposite of the Observer (Air and Earth). He looks, she is the looked upon. She must have an audience, without it she might die my darlings, die I tell you!! She loves to be the centre of attention, dressed in all her finery, make up and sparkling jewels, making dramatic entrances wherever she goes. She has many cosmetic treatments to enhance her beauty and sexuality, polishing herself to exquisite perfection so that she may shine like the gems she wears. Life is, after all, a public performance and she has to look her best. The Actress adores mirrors and can't walk past one, in fact she may be so vain as to stand with her back to you, admiring herself and glancing at you occasionally in her looking glass as you converse. She loves to pose, be photographed and filmed, and will upstage anyone who tries to step in front of her. In the theatre, she can be guilty of going to the back of the stage, forcing other players to turn their backs to the audience. She vies with all others who seek to steal her limelight, for she is the star and all others mere audience. The spotlight is hers! When overused, she becomes hysterical, but if there is no one to see her, she soon stops, for all acting needs an audience. Inner peace and tranquility are unknown to her, they look like death. She is so subject to pleasure and pain that when her dramas are met with approval she is sent into delight, but when they are denied she suffers torments! When met with indifference, she knows absolute despair!! We must not, however, negate her vital purpose. She is the Queen of self-expression and is necessary to us all if we are to live fulfilling lives. So many people, particularly women, are accused of being hysterical, too emotional, subjective, needing to calm down etc., all delivered in such a way as to denigrate the validity of the emotions. The Greek word for womb is 'hystera', showing that there was awareness of the connection between the womb and the emotions. We call a great release of emotions 'hysteria'. Not so long ago, a husband could go to a doctor to request the removal of his wife's womb if she exhibited emotions he didn't like, or have her committed to an asylum for the insane. Although men do not have wombs, it in no way prevents men from expressing their Actress, you don't have to have one to feel emotions.

"The more personal, the more universal." - Gary Ballinger

The Actress reacts, which is to be involved, to be caught up in a situation, to be a participant and to be committed. This is to be close and closely linked to places or people and thus to have attachments. Everyone is 'darling', 'dear', or 'sweetheart,' she often stands close when talking to you and loves air kisses (real ones might spoil her make up). When one is attached to someone or something, one becomes dependent on him/her/it. This is to be subjective, to be in love and as such subject to pleasure or pain, like and dislike. She is attached to her loves, hates, people and places, and gets worked up about them. She is given to strong likes and dislikes, tempers, passions and jealousies. She takes everything personally. We also speak of 'close' weather, hot humid and steamy as she can be when she is 'on heat', and revels in wearing as little as possible for maximum effect.

"Actors think more with their hearts than with their heads." - William Esper

The Actress is a great surge of creative emotional energy, without her you will never be a creative artist in any field. Her energy has launched many a new project, for nothing great can be achieved without the enthusiasm of her lively participation. Her centre, the womb, contains magical energy from which life gushes forth. She is the SCREEEAAAMM!!! release that frees all stress and lets Life through. The lack of understanding towards menstruation forces women to suppress their emotions for much of the time, and under these circumstances, at certain times of her monthly cycle it becomes almost impossible to contain them and she just has to blow. The Ancient Greeks understood this consciousness better and there are records of women going up into the hills for two or three days to let rip, screaming, singing and dancing until they were exhausted.

She is vitally important because she is like the safety valve of a steam boiler, letting off the steam of your pent-up emotions. Forget her and you will be tortured by seething unexpressed emotions. Men as well as women have creative drive and emotions, so there is no reason for males to avoid this Archetype. They are to be encouraged to practise it, for not only will their emotions be invoked and purified, they can also rediscover real enthusiasm for life and further creative self expression. She is the vital surge of life that ignites all creativity, she can free your genius to flow to centre stage in your life, she is the creative heat behind all creations. With her you can flower!

"Honesty isn't enough for me. That becomes very boring. If you can convince people what you're doing is real and it's also bigger than life - that's exciting." - Gene Hackman

Negatively, the Actress is vain and empty, often looks vacant, pouts and preens, is jealous, over-concerned about her appearance, self-centred, vain, superficial, melodramatic, caught up in her herself and prone to tantrums if something threatens her subjective desires. She will weep and wail and cry crocodile tears, turning minor mishaps into major disasters with exaggeration and screams. Name-dropping delights her and she will tell you how wonderful and beautiful everyone finds her. There is the joke about the Actress telling someone about her latest role, "But enough about me, what did *you* think of my performance?"

She is given to self-indulgence and has no thoughts or ideas of her own, she needs a script. She lives by expressing her very powerful emotions, though she shies away from deeper feelings (The

Enchantress), and quickly resents anyone trying to awaken them. They are not in her script! Yet when working together with the Enchantress, they become a super Oracle. The Enchantress receives the information and the Actress expresses it. We associate glamour with the Actress. The archaic meaning of glamour is 'a magic spell, an enchantment', which is another way she can work with the Enchantress, who will visualise the desired event, with the Actress putting the power of emotion behind it.

"Take nothing for granted. Make an emotional discovery as often as you can find one in every scene. Ask yourself: What is new?" - Michael Shurtleff

Many professional Actresses and Actors become 'type cast'. Those who invariably play aristocrats, will have the Patriarch working in them, the tough guys will have the Warrior, the motherly types will have Mother Nature and so on. The pure Actress, however, can act any character, but in order to invoke she has to be empty, as a womb must be to create a new life. Negatively, if she's simply vain and self-centred, she will have a vacant look which will only come into focus when she looks in a mirror, or at a dress, shoes or handbag she wants, but positively, she must be empty. By expressing your emotions as they arise, she maintains a clear, empty space in you which allows life's energies to pour through. You cannot put something into a vessel that is already full. This is her vital function, she is like a Goddess who opens you to receive an abundance of your own divinity. She is the vessel that invokes greater characters, greater plays. The power of invocation is one of her most magical aspects. She has the ability to stream the higher dynamics of life, to channel them through her. In Ancient Greek theatre there were altars to the Gods and Goddesses backstage where the players could connect to and invoke the Deities they were representing, personifying them for the audience that they may experience something of the Divine. In her power of invocation, the Actress is truly LARGER THAN LIFE!! She lives in the now of every moment, and all powers she can invoke!!

"The word theatre comes from the Greeks. It means the seeing place. It is the place people come to see the truth about life and the social situation." - Stella Adler

The Actress is a Diva, worshipped as a Goddess, beautiful, passionate, full of the zest of life, awe inspiring in her finery, moving in her tragedy and ecstasy, acting out the drama of life and love. She demonstrates your ever greater possibilities, taking you beyond the boredom and hopelessness of everyday existence into a world full of excitement and thrills! She can make you a Prima Donna! The Star of your own show! She can help us all shine in the dark! Write your own script and she will bring it to life for you!! ENCORE!!!

"Why, except as a means of livelihood, a man should desire to act on the stage when he has the whole world to act in, is not clear to me." - George Bernard Shaw

Some key words of the positives and negatives are listed below, together with some of the interests and activities relevant to this Archetype to help round out the picture of its world.

Time: April 21st – May 21$^{st.}$

Season: Late Spring.

Quality: One of the three Water states and one of the four Closed states.

Elements: Water and Fire.

Colour: Violet, purples.

Conflicting opposite: The Observer.

Complementary Opposite: The Wise Woman.

Voice: Lively, emotional, full of drama, exaggeration, screaming.

Face type: Conventionally pretty, make up used lavishly to enhance her features, hair styled in the latest fashions and designed to flatter her face.

Body type: Strives to mould herself into the prevailing image of beauty.

Movement: Dramatic gestures and flounces. She loves to pose and pout her lips, flutter her eyelashes (often false) play with her hair and whip out her mirror and make up case.

Weather: Warm and steamy.

Landscape: Flowery with life bursting forth and wildlife mating. The stage, theatres, opera houses.

Home: Ornate décor with many mirrors, the latest fashionable designers.

Clothing: Sparkling, colourful, glamorous, fashionable with many jewels and fine fabrics. Skimpy to show off her figure. Costumes to suit the parts she plays. High heels. She loves shoes, handbags and all kinds of accessories.

Food: Showy, and delights to have dishes named after her, e.g. Peach Melba and Pavlova.

Positives: Enthusiastic, expressive, lively, entertaining, excited and exciting, dramatic, romantic, glamorous, passionate, has the power of invocation.

Negatives: Vain, self-centred, superficial, hysterical, empty, jealous.

Career choices and interests: Actress/actor, film star, opera singer, pop star, model, pop diva, cosmetic treatments, beautician, fashion, hairdressing, makeup artist, drama teacher, theatre design.

Reading materials and entertainment: The Stage newspaper, celebrity magazines, romances, fashion magazines.

Music: Opera and other emotional music and songs.

She is: The Prima Donna, The Star, a Celebrity, a Diva, a Goddess.

How to Practise the Actress

Reading the script is beneficial in several ways -

1. It increases your awareness of your Centre.
2. It helps you to identify and recognise the Actress in yourself and others.
3. It gives you control over your Actress.
4. As the script focuses on positive attributes, it helps you to purify your Actress.
5. It gives you the opportunity to add more strands of the Actress in yourself.
6. You can help others to activate it in themselves.

Reading the script only serves as a rehearsal for the real thing - your daily life. When developing the Actress, you will need to follow through by observing your usual behaviour patterns and seeing where you can introduce a more exciting way of being. Follow positive impulses to do something new, such as dressing more strikingly, wearing jewels, expressing your emotions or joining a dramatic society.

The Actress is a closed state. If you identify with and realise you live a lot in the Actress, read the script to purify and identify it in yourself. You will understand your own Actress better. If you are weak in the Actress and identify more with her conflicting opposite, the Observer, you could find yourself resisting and not wishing to draw attention to yourself. The opposite reaction is also possible and you may discover you adore expressing yourself. You may have been suppressing the Actress and been forced to conceal your emotions. Concentrate on expressing the script as well as you can.

Preparing

Wear something of the appropriate colour (purple) and style. In this case, dress up to the nines! You can wear as much make up, glitter, jewellery, sequins and glamorous finery as your heart desires. To help set the scene, play dramatic music, opera or something equally exciting. Maria Callas is a superb example of using the Actress to fully express the plot in music. First, visualize yourself as a white light in the Centre of your circle, reaching towards the Actress to add purple to your colours. Let that colour surround you, imagine you are filling up with vivid purple. Keep the awareness that you are the Centre and not the Actress. Getting the stance and the voice right before you begin, and being aware of maintaining them as you read, will help in channeling the energy through.

Remember the Actress's elements, Water and Fire, water with fire under it creates steam. Imagine yourself in the Actress's landscape. It is late Spring and the countryside is awash with flowers and blossom. You are in a beautiful theatre; you enter and take centre stage in the spotlight. You can either create a makeshift stage or imagine one and seat your audience in rows. Every single audience member is enthralled at your grand entrance, there is applause and cheers, you acknowledge this and milk a little more out of them. Then you begin your wondrous, spectacular performance. You are the one and only STAR! You are larger than life! Make the most the stage, use it all to demonstrate your talent and beauty from all sides. Your voice gushes forth, full of inflection and drama! Try the scream!! This is the only one you are encouraged to act, for in acting her you are doing her! Let the feeling grow naturally and gradually. Your audience members are the mere observers of your fabulous show and the more they love you and show it, the more you love them!!

Let the Actress onto the stage of your life and relish the freedom to express yourself and the uplifting drama she brings! Life will be more exciting and alive! The Actress will make you a shining Star! Now read the script.

THE ACTRESS

Water and Fire

Lively voice, emotional, dramatic and passionate.

Sound the fanfare, roll the drum,

And into the spotlight the STAR does come!

I am the Actress, I'm Water and Fire,

Of any audience I'll never tire!

Steam am I, and I'm always steamed up!

I'm the Queen of emotion, the womb is my cup,

The magical vessel wherein is Life's spark,

My Drama will make you ALL shine in the dark!

The Queen of Life's stage, I'm very romantic,

My passions range from despair to ecstatic!!!

I'm pleasure and pain, I love and I hate!!

I'll play any part in the script of your fate.

I'm excited, alive, my passions gush,

You all kneel at my feet, see my pretty cheeks flush!

I'll display all beauty, all blemish remove,

Of my exquisite appearance you can but approve.

In front of my mirror I will spend hours,

Choosing my dress and applying my powders.

I attract attention and I display,

The Drama of a greater play!!

To see my act is to crave for more,

My rapturous audience shouts "ENCORE!!!!"

In Ancient Greece, through my Invocation,

The Deities lived! I was a sensation!!!

I'm theatrical, Grand Opera, I'm so very intense,

I need you to watch me, I'm a public performance!

For your attention I'll always vie,

Without it I'm sure I'd lay down and die!!!

I love being close, you're all "Darling" or "Dear",

I'm like hot, steamy weather, when your bodies you bare.

I'm enthusiastic, all emotion express,

I'm the SCREEEAAAMM!!! release that frees your stress.

The safety valve that lets Life through,

Each moment I live is ever new!!

I'm larger than life I'm involved and attached,

When I take the stage I can never be matched.

My fans shower me with jewels and silks so fine,

So, to admire me in them, I give them some time!

I'm the creative heat that all artists know,

I invoke your genius to grow and flow!

I exaggerate ALL! that ye may be free,

Of the dreary norm, so worship me!!!!

I'm the PRIMA DONNA, the empty face,

That invokes the GODDESS to her rightful place!!!!

Excitement beyond your wildest dream!

A drama the world has never seen!

And so for LIFE let's set the scene!

For the greatest show there's ever been!!!

The Fire Archetypes

The Fool

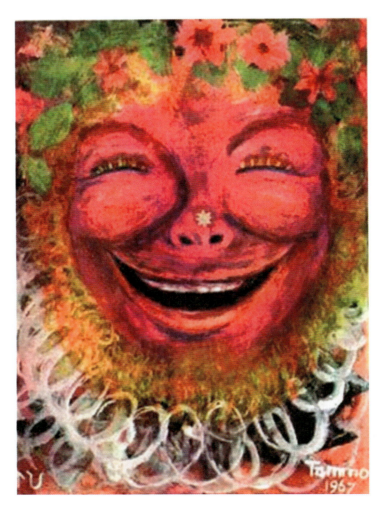

↑♌

Both positive and negative attributes are given in this description to help you better recognise the state in yourself and others. When we repeatedly use an Archetype, it cannot fail to exhibit negative traits, as it becomes overused and not balanced by other states. The climates associated with the months of the year were worked out in the Northern hemisphere, so they may need to be adjusted to suit the Southern Hemisphere and take into account unfamiliar weather patterns linked to climate change.

The Fool

Open Fire

May 21st to June 21st

One of the three Fire and one of the four Open states.

Fire and Water, the metaphysical linking of Spirit and Soul.

The season of The Fool is May/June, early Summer. His colour is rich pink, magenta, the mix of approximately two parts of the red of Fire, his first element, and one part of the blue of Water, his second. These are the two dynamic elements, containing the most life.

The landscape bursts forth in a riot of colour, the gardens and woods are full of blossoms, bluebells, lilac trees and rhododendrons, heralding

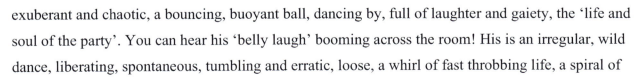

regeneration, new life for all with a great burst of optimism. Fire heats the Water, which boils, becomes turbulent and then leaps up in an ejaculating hot geyser, bursting with fountains of bubbling energy. Joy bubbles up within and, like a geyser, the Fool leaps and frolics in pure abandonment with endless energy. Let's have some fun! The Fool is the prince of the dance and mime, carnivals, festivals, balls and fairs. He is exuberant and chaotic, a bouncing, buoyant ball, dancing by, full of laughter and gaiety, the 'life and soul of the party'. You can hear his 'belly laugh' booming across the room! His is an irregular, wild dance, liberating, spontaneous, tumbling and erratic, loose, a whirl of fast throbbing life, a spiral of energy and pure happiness. The Fool is a clown and an acrobat, he is often to be found in the circus, throwing himself round the ring, falling over, doing the unexpected and bringing forth gales of laughter and then moving on. He cannot stay too long in one place, many other things beckon from the horizon and he can't resist! Life is an adventure! The Fool is rejuvenating, re-energizing, regenerating, he loves colour and fun, he wears a mish-mash rainbow of garments, often torn and with holes in the pockets where all his money falls out. He is without care, he hates responsibility of any kind and can't be trusted to look after anything. He is careless, loses things, leaves them behind as he becomes caught up in the next thing. He travels light, unencumbered by boring things he has to bother looking after. 'The best things in life are free.' He is forgetful, rarely keeps an appointment and if he does, he'll likely be there at the wrong time or wrong place, but when you do chance to meet, you'll have a great time! His great resounding laugh is infectious and he will respond to anything around him, no one knows what he will do next, including himself. Things change from moment to moment, he has no cares whatsoever, he loses himself in the present.. He lets go of everything in his happy dance of life.

"I'm just having too much fun to worry about tomorrow" - Johnny Depp

Unlike his opposite, The Wise Woman, he is not at all popular in Western society, although in other parts of the world certain aspects of him may be found. Dancing is strictly regulated, consigned either to the stage, nightclubs or parties, with negative aspects of him seen in the way young people indulge in excessive behaviours. Binge drinking (firewater), indiscriminate sexual partners when drunk, and the taking of drugs in order to experience unnatural highs. People should be free to do what they want, as long as it's not harmful to others, so I do not moralise or disapprove, but am sorry that, because this Archetype is so suppressed in adults, people have to resort to these measures in order to feel free and cast off their inhibitions. Those same people who fall over, fight and vomit in the street are looked on with less disapproval than if they were sober and danced joyfully in the street or burst into laughter in the supermarket, instances where their behaviour would be instantly clamped down on, and either the security, police or a doctor summoned. At the very least there will be much shaking of heads and mutterings about such actions which are out of normal habits and routines, so beloved by his opposite, the Wise Woman (Earth and Air). With the Fool active in ourselves we have no need of stimulants, we are naturally high on life. The Whirling Dervishes use a spinning dance to get 'high' and connect with the divine life force. How terrible that the life-giving force is practically illegal in many countries, with money and respectability (The Wise Woman again) more important. We are more afraid of life than we are of death. We are too afraid of making fools of ourselves.

"Do not deceive yourselves. If any of you think you are wise by the standards of this age, you should become 'fools' so that you may become really wise." - St. Paul

The Fool is lively and merry, high on pulsating, intoxicating vital energy, everything he does is done to excess; drinking, feasting, merriment, loving, responding to and enjoying all that life has to offer. Life's a ball! We say "Knock yourself out", "He's out of it", "Get off your head". Happy-go-lucky, he flows with the energy, every minute is different, he has no thought of the morrow, consequences or dangers, all is done with irrepressible optimism. This can make him 'foolish', chaotic, rash and

impulsive, causing him to take chances, to gamble, but his thoughtless, risk-taking behaviour can bring wonderful variety and change. He is lucky, often winning at betting. He'll happily take a chance on anything, and if others warn him of any possible consequences, he always responds with optimism, trusting to his luck. His outlook is ever positive, he is sure he will win, and many times he's right. 'The world's well lost to win more life!'

"When in doubt, make a fool of yourself. There is a microscopically thin line between being brilliantly creative and acting like the most gigantic idiot on earth. So what the hell, leap."
- Cynthia Heimel

The Fool is non-conformist, flamboyant, bizarre, ebullient, eccentric, erratic and carefree. He is unconventional, conspicuous, impulsive and unreliable, causing movement and haphazard, unexpected happenings in his vivacious happy way. He helps us to forget and abandon ourselves to the impulses and joys of life. He ejaculates millions of seeds with each glorious orgasm, unlike his opposite, the Wise Woman who carefully disperses her ova one each month from her pouch. He is generous, extravagant and gregarious, he spends freely and gives everything away (and the Wise Woman is only too pleased to grab it). 'A fool and his money are soon parted', 'Money can't buy happiness', 'It burns a hole in his pocket' it's all 'Easy come, easy go.' 'It's better to be born lucky than rich', and it is better to give than to receive as far as he's concerned.

"The cleverest of all, in my opinion, is the man who calls himself a fool at least once a month." - Fyodor Dostoyevsky

The Fool likes everybody, everyone is his friend, he's gregarious, jolly, jovial, cordial, amiable, always socializing and jumping from one place to another, throwing himself into it all, leaving change and chaos in his wake. As this Archetype has no air, negatively he is witless, a heedless fool, bumbling, clumsy and mindless, a laughing clown, a buffoon, open to any kind of stimulant or stimulation, a  drunken reveller, unthinking and forgetful, staggering from one thing to another, losing everything and everyone. He can end up on the street, a vagrant, a vagabond who has gambled it all away. Yet positively, he is a life bringer, full of exuberant joy, energy and bubbling laughter. We must take a chance to win more life, and 'He who hesitates is lost'!

"I'd rather have a fool to make me merry than experience to make me sad." - William Shakespeare

In Mediaeval times, the court had a Fool who was the only one at liberty to make fun of the king. He may have been 'off his head' but he always escaped losing it. The word silly comes from the German, 'selig', and the Old English word, 'seely', both meaning 'happy, blissful, lucky, blessed. The 'silly fool' is The Holy Fool, the Divine Fool. In the Tarot, the Fool card represents God, the life force, wandering the world, ready to step off a cliff at any time with self-forgetting spontaneity. He is considered mad because his is a suppressed and unfamiliar Archetype, yet how we need him to move us on from our dull, stuck attitudes. There is a lot of The Fool energy in these words -

"The only people for me are the mad ones, the ones who are mad to live, mad to talk, mad to be saved, desirous of everything at the same time, the ones who never yawn or say a commonplace thing, but burn, burn, burn, like fabulous yellow roman candles exploding like spiders across the stars...". - Jack Kerouac.

The Fool intoxicates us with the Divine spirit, casting off the illusions and restrictions of old, stale consciousness and opening the door to ecstatic, exhilarating rebirth. He stimulates the life force in us! He is the Fountain of Life and Youthing! What a cause for celebration! Party time!

Some key words of the positives and negatives are listed below, together with some of the interests and activities relevant to this Archetype to help round out the picture of its world.

Time: May 21st to June 21st.

Season: Early Summer.

Quality: One of the three Fire and one of the four Open states.

Elements: Fire and Water.

Colour: Rich, vibrant pinks and magenta.

Conflicting opposite: The Wise Woman.

Complementary Opposite: The Observer.

Voice: Exuberant, booming, laughing, conveying limitless excess.

Face type: Round, pink face, full cheeks, usually laughing or smiling.

Body type: Loose, round and can be plump with a big belly.

Movement: Endless and free, never sits still, always moving, bouncing, tumbling, whirling, dancing, skipping.

Weather: Warm and sunny.

Landscape: Geysers, funfairs, circuses, a riot of colourful flowers.

Home: If he has a home it's chaotic and colourful. Might live in a caravan, on friends' floors, a tent or on the streets.

Clothing: Colourful, mismatched, torn. A clown's outfit.

Food: Anything to hand and lots of it.

Positives: Happy, joyful, abandoned, free, lucky, friendly, carefree, eccentric, vivacious, optimistic, rejuvenating, regenerating, generous.

Negatives: Irresponsible, loses everything, haphazard, unreliable, forgetful.

Career choices and interests: Dancer, clown, gambler, acrobat, laughter guru, slapstick comedy, anything to do with travel.

Reading materials and entertainment: He has no Air, so doesn't read but as no-one can live in one Archetype alone, he will like adventure films and books, anything about travel, dancing, gambling, circuses, comedy.

Music: Lively, changeable, happy.

He is: Bacchus, Pan, the Lord of the Dance, Falstaff, a gay bachelor, the drunken uncle, the Wise Fool, the Court Jester when used with the Joker, the life and soul of the party.

"If you think adventure is dangerous, try routine, it is lethal." - Paulo Coelho

How to Practice the Fool

Reading the script is beneficial in several ways –

1. It increases your awareness of your Centre.
2. It helps you to identify and recognise the Fool in yourself and others.
3. It gives you control over your Fool.
4. As the script focuses on positive attributes, it helps you to purify your Fool.
5. It gives you the opportunity to add more strands of the Fool in yourself.
6. You can help others to activate it in themselves.

Reading the script only serves as a rehearsal for the real thing - your daily life. When developing the Fool, you will need to follow through by observing your usual behaviour patterns and seeing where you can introduce a more joyful way of being. Follow positive impulses to do something new, such as dancing, doing something different or being more open to saying yes! (Definitely no gambling though! – well perhaps a lottery ticket)

The Fool is an Open state. If you identify with and realise you live a lot in the Fool, read the script to purify and identify it in yourself. You will understand your own Fool better. If you are weak in the Fool and identify more with his opposite, the Wise Woman, you could find yourself tight in your body and unwilling to loosen up and let go. If you feel stiff and self-conscious, you might see why that is and from whom or where it came. The opposite reaction is also possible and you may find the release of Fool energy exhilarating as you trip and bounce about. The Wise Woman would do well in hiding her valuables when the Fool is on, things can get broken.

Preparing

Wear something of the appropriate colour (vivid pink) or a riot of colours, and a style that is fun to wear. Bouncy, silly music can help to set the scene. Visualize yourself as a white light in the Centre of your circle, reaching towards the Fool to add a jolly pink to your colours. Let that colour surround you, imagine you are filling up with bright pink. Keep the awareness that you are the Centre and not the Fool. Getting the stance and the voice right before you begin, and being aware of maintaining them as you read, will help in channeling the energy through.

Imagine yourself in the Fool's landscape, it's early Summer, warm, you are surrounded by a riot of colours, there is a fairground and a party feeling. You can sense a bouncing energy and a happy atmosphere. Bubbling geysers all around you leap into the air, shooting energy upwards. Imagine one of these geysers under you, Fire and warm Water lifting you up! Smile, laugh, think of something that makes you feel happy, keep moving, follow your energy, dance. Never mind feeling 'foolish' - you're supposed to. Draw this power up, aware of the rejuvenating energy filling your body.

The voice is booming, friendly, full of laughter, coming from your belly, a 'belly laugh', which wobbles with mirth. You can start slowly by swinging your arms and releasing some shoulder tension, jumping up and down, swinging your legs and if you have a bouncer or trampoline, all the better. Let the power grow naturally and gradually, which is more real and beneficial than giving your impression of it. Try not to act it, you could become trapped in the act and limit yourself. As you have more fun, you might rush to sofas and beds and jump on them, there are plenty of things to crash into or trip over, so it's better to practise this one outdoors or in quite a bare space. With all the laughing and leaping, your face will flush with pink, you will feel warmer and joyful. If this state is unfamiliar to you, take your time, your sense of fun has been suppressed. Accept that you need to free up bit by bit.

Persevere and the other Archetypes will accept that your life has opened up, you have more friends and more fun. It's time to enjoy the Dance of Life! You will have more joy, energy and adventure with the Fool! He is rejuvenating and liberating! Now read the script.

THE FOOL

Fire and Water

__Exuberant, booming, laughing voice, conveying limitless excess and fun.__

Fire and Water, trips on the Fool,
Clowning, happy, laughing buffoon,
Let's celebrate, all care departed,
I'm the Life and Soul of every party!

I'm witless, lively, colourful, high,
In fast throbbing Life I go dancing by!
I'm a whirling spiral of energy,
Vital, vivacious, erratic, free!!

As a geyser I leap in spontaneous joy,
Chaotic, impulsive, flamboyant,boy, hoy!
I'm the Prince of the Dance, of Carnivals,
Funfairs, Feasts and Festivals.

My booming laugh fills the hall,
Exuberant! Life's a ball!!
I've endless energy, I'm rejuvenating,
My happy dance is liberating!!!

Movement is mine, unexpected, gay,
I'm generous, give it all away,
I'm so extravagant, I have no care,
I abandon myself to the fun of the fair!

I'm ever distracted, eccentric and merry,
Uninhibited, Oh! let's board that ferry!
As my energy pulses, your life I feed,
You must let go, the piper leads

The dance of mime and jollity,
Releases you into ecstasy!!
I must have colour, my favourite's pink,
I'm the orgasm! Let's have a drink!

I like everybody, the whole world's my friend,
Hail-fellow, well-met!, we're a happy blend!
What I'll do next, don't ask me,
I never know, just wait and see!

Unconventional, I'll respond
To anything out there beyond!
I gamble, and oft times I win,
The lucky, skipping Fool, I'm him!

Unreliable, loose, but free from strife,
The world's well lost to win more Life!!
Through my pulsing zest the Gods inspire,
Leaping, laughing, jumping higher!

I move you out of your stagnation,
My gift is Life's regeneration,
So come, my friends, and take a chance,
Life is YOURS in my joyous Dance!!!!!!

The Joker

↑❋

Both positive and negative attributes are given in this description to help you better recognise the state in yourself and others. When we repeatedly use an Archetype, it cannot fail to exhibit negative traits, as it becomes overused and not balanced by other states. The climates associated with the months of the year were worked out in the Northern hemisphere, so they may need to be adjusted to suit the Southern Hemisphere and take into account unfamiliar weather patterns linked to climate change.

The Joker

Cardinal Fire

June 21st – July 21st

One of the three Fire and one of the four Cardinal states.

Fire and Air, the metaphysical linking of Spirit and Mind.

The Joker's season is June/July, mid-Summer, his colour is that of a spark, a flame, orange, vermillion, the mix of approximately two parts of the red of Fire, his first element, and one part of the yellow of Air, his second.

Flaming June is a time of heatwaves, a landscape of garden parties and fetes when the meadows are bright with cheerful, colourful wildflowers amongst the tall grasses and the air is alive with insects that teem teasingly around you. Fire heats the Air and we get 'hot air' which rises, causing wind. The Joker is bright and breezy, a 'windbag', 'a bright spark'. 'Taking the rise' out of people is to tease them, to play pranks and to joke, to raise them up into a lighter mood. The Joker can 'send up' anyone or any situation, and as tongue-like flames play in the hearth, so does he as he twists and turns and sparks. He plays games for amusement, but also in politics and sports, particularly in those needing a good aim, like fencing, snooker and darts; in fact, any situation where people are trying to outdo each other. He vies with others in every kind of game of skill and wit. When he's playing just for fun, he's flippant, superficial, lighthearted and witty, always seeking to outwit everyone with the punch line. The laughter he elicits is music to his ears. He's the master of repartee and the jokes of the entertainment world, with its bright lights and bright sparks. His quick, dry wits can get him into and out of all kinds of improbable situations as he plays his clever games. He is the master of tongue twisters, he has superb skill in his tongue as he jokes and puns. He is a pickpocket, a fingersmith, impresses with slick card tricks, sleight of hand, juggling and conjuring tricks as a stage magician. We wonder, "How did he do that?"

As one of the four Cardinals, the Joker is powerful. Just as he manipulates balls in the air with his impressive juggling skills, so can he keep many balls in the air with his manipulations in any situation. It's all balls to him! The Joker is a twister and a transformer, just look at all the materials his dexterity has changed, for flame is a transformer. He can break up any atmosphere with a few well-timed words or facial expressions, causing any situation to dissolve into gales of laughter. He is a champion interrupter, diverting people's attention from one thing to another. He is not a creator, but can transmute one atmosphere into another, the words and actions of others being his raw material to twist into satire and skillful mimicry. He is superb at pretence, imitation and impressionism. Children learn by imitation, they can be observed trying out and experimenting, seeing how far they can go in their teasing by 'sending up' adults and each other. In the adult world, we are manipulated into imitation by advertisements, fashion, home décor, phones, gadgets, cars and so on, as we play the social games of 'keeping up' with the latest trends.

In dire circumstances, his cheerful wit can help you stay out of your feelings and emotions and keep you going. If you're shipwrecked in an open boat, so cold and hungry and wishing you could die faster, his wits and witticisms can uplift you and give you days of extra life. When miserable with the 'blues' (the Enchantress), he'll soon have you laughing at yourself with his timely twists. With his spot-on quips he can break up all kinds of nefarious plots, making people see the funny, ridiculous side, resulting in explosions of laughter rather than bombs. No assembly, holy or un-holy can withstand his sharp, bright, witty insights. There are many professions and situations that bring the Joker into play in order to suppress the feelings, such as in prison where it is essential to 'keep your head above water' to survive. Graveyard and gallows humour are widely used in the army, police force, hospitals, the undertaker's, morgues and anywhere else that entails being in distressing situations which could be overwhelming. By cracking jokes, he cracks the heavy atmosphere to allow a little light-heartedness to enter. He can always see the funny side of everything, no matter how tragic. The Joker is as resilient as a bouncing ball, push him down here and he'll bounce back there. He's irrepressible and

invaluable in 'keeping your spirits up'.

"Life is much too important to be taken seriously." - Oscar Wilde

When people are laughing they are open and easier to manipulate, which is not always bad, it depends on whether the manipulation is heading somewhere good or not. He is able to trick anyone into any direction of his choice. He will don any mask and say, with apparent sincerity, whatever he thinks others wish to hear. He's great at creating 'the right impression'. He is the master of timing, timing is everything, and his is the best. His razor-sharp tongue can hit the spot with his brilliant aim in jokes, acting and in life. We speak of a 'sharp mind', 'a cutting remark' and a 'rapier wit'. "First blood to me!" he cries. He is a jester who walks on stage, touches some innocent looking object and down come the stage props, backcloth and all in a heap of confusion. As others rush to rectify the situation, they will miss the sneaky smile up his sleeve, where he will have a few cards hidden for later. He's a flame and, like fire, he can bring down any construction, good or bad. His jokes 'bring the house down'. He is one of the most popular Archetypes today and is well paid for his skills as a stand-up comic and impressionist. In the spheres of advertising he works in the service of the Wise Woman, setting his little traps that you may fall in and buy the product.

"Needs are imposed by nature. Wants are sold by society." - Mokokoma Mokhonoana

He is overused these days, and not balanced by his opposite, the Enchantress. This means we see a lot of his negative side as he puts on the 'spin', with deception, trickery and lies employed to make money and gain influence in all areas; politics, sports, business, society and the personal. Negatively, he is the 'deceiver ever' that Shakespeare speaks of, the 'con man', the 'confidence trickster', full of trickery and lies which are all part of his stock in trade. He is sly in his manipulations to trick people out of money or anything else he may want from them. He is adept at putting on masks, impersonating other archetypes in order to gain the victim's trust, then he is free to manipulate and gaslight. By the time the victim realises what's  happening, he has taken everything and disappeared, seemingly in a puff of smoke. His teasing can be cruel when he ridicules others and, as he has no Water, he has no feelings for them. He is shallow, unfeeling, has no conscience and does not care about the hurt he causes with his pranks and jeers. Everything is material for his satire and the constant practice of this leads to sneering cynicism where

nought has meaning or value. In everyday life, we frequently meet a Joker/Wise Woman combination, which is a successful formula used by many traders, having everyone giggling as they hand over the money. He's a good pickpocket too. On his own the Joker is not interested in money, but linked to the Wise Woman all can be conned and exploited. He is a flame, she is dust in the air, which together make smoke. Archetypes combine on the inner world as they do in the outer. With a mischievous wink he says, "It's all done with smoke and mirrors".

Positively, he is the Cardinal of Fire, the spark which initiates all forms of civilization. He can use his sharp mind and razor tongue to enlighten. He can juggle and apply his tricks to anything, including energy and your emotions. With a few deft strokes he can throw them back to you transformed, cheered and uplifted. He is so amusing, and has the ability to flick away all nonsense and hypocrisy to help bring positive change. Nothing is sacred or off-limits to him. He's like the ignition system of the motor car which couldn't move without his spark. He is a 'breaker upper', he breaks up and reassembles the jigsaw puzzle. We are only functioning on a few bits of ourselves. With him, we can incorporate more of the power within us to transform and conjure ourselves into more wonderful beings.

Some key words of the positives and negatives are listed below, together with some of the interests and activities relevant to this Archetype to help round out the picture of its world.

Time: June 21st - July 21st.
Season: Mid-Summer.
Quality: One of the three Fire and one of the four Cardinal states.
Elements: Fire and Air.
Colour: Orange, vermillion.
Conflicting opposite: The Enchantress.
Complementary Opposite: The Logician.
Voice: Quick, sharp, light, superficial, amused, giggling.

Face type: Pronounced pointed chin and nose, thin face, smallish twinkling eyes, sharp hairstyle.
Body type: Slim.

Movement: Quick, sharp, light, dexterous, twisty when standing.

Weather: Bright, breezy and cheerful.

Landscape: Garden parties, and fetes, some sports games. Anywhere he can tell jokes.

Home: Quirky, full of a conjurer's apparatus and juggling equipment and tricks.

Clothing: Harlequin outfit, amusing clothing, sharp dresser.

Food: Not fussy, but likes to savour foods on his sharp tongue.

Positives: Cheerful, amusing, amused, dexterous, playful, witty, resilient, uplifting, transforming.

Negatives: Deceitful trickery, manipulative, gaslighting, sarcastic, cynical, sneering, callous, unfeeling.

Career choices and interests: Magician, conjurer, joke teller, card sharp, advertising, con man, stand-up comic, juggler, salesman, spin doctor.

Reading materials and entertainment: Books about card tricks and conjuring. Joke books. Funny books and comedy films.

Music: Amusing songs, fast, light, surprising and superficial.

He is: The Trickster, A con man, Harlequin, a gaslighter, a twister, the Jester, a spiv and, with some other Archetypes, in the negative a Narcissist, a Narcopath.

How to Practice the Joker

Reading the script is beneficial in several ways –

1. It increases your awareness of your Centre.

2. It helps you to identify and recognise the Joker in yourself and others.

3. It gives you control over your Joker.

4. As the script focuses on positive attributes, it helps you to purify your Joker.

5. It gives you the opportunity to add more strands of the Joker in yourself.

6. You can help others to activate it in themselves.

Reading the script only serves as a rehearsal for the real thing - your daily life. When developing the Joker, you will need to follow through by observing your usual behaviour patterns and seeing where you can introduce a more cheerful way of being. Follow positive impulses to do something new, such as learning to juggle, tongue twisters or telling jokes. The Joker is a Cardinal state. If you identify with and realise you live a lot in the Joker, read the script to purify and identify it in yourself. You will understand your own Joker better. If you are weak in the Joker and identify more with his opposite, the Enchantress, you could find yourself clinging to your feelings and reject his cheerful touch. If you feel weepy you might ask why that is. The opposite reaction is also possible and you may find the release of Joker energy shows you the funny side of things and has you laughing.

Preparing

Wear something of the appropriate colour (orange) and in a style that is sharp and amusing. Cheerful music can help to set the scene. Visualize yourself as a white light in the Centre of your circle, reaching towards the Joker to add a vermillion orange to your colours. Let that colour surround you, imagine you are filling up with flame orange. Keep the awareness that you are the Centre and not the

Joker. Getting the stance and the voice right before you begin, and being aware of maintaining them as you read, will help in channeling the energy through.

Imagine yourself in the Joker's landscape. It's mid-Summer, you are at a garden party, insects are buzzing, games are being played, or you can imagine being on stage telling jokes (but keep the Actress off). You can stand with one foot resting on its ball and crossed over the other, reflecting how he twists. The voice is light, sharp, full of amusement. Let the power grow naturally and gradually. Try not to act it, you could become trapped in the act and limit yourself. Feel free to ad lib, quip and add a joke. If this state is unfamiliar to you, take your time, your sense of humour has been suppressed. Accept that you need to free up bit by bit.

Persevere and the other Archetypes will accept that your life has improved, you feel more on top and in control. You need never be stuck in the glums again, with the Joker around, there is always something funny to laugh about. Now read the script.

THE JOKER

Fire and Air

Quick, sharp, light, superficial and amused voice.

I'm the Joker, a windbag breeze,
I juggle, joke, play and tease,
It's all games to me, I imitate,
Any atmosphere manipulate.

The silly sight of you forlorn,
My magic tongue can soon transform,
I twist and turn and interrupt,
And have you laughing where it hurts.

My satire wit will make you see,

All that's nonsense and hypocrisy,

I show all up, none can hide,

In a lightening flash, there's the funny side!

When you're longing to die, you're raging at fate,

With perfect timing I'll a joke relate.

When you fall downstairs, my wit so flip,

Says "Whoops-a-daisy, enjoy your trip?"

I'm resilient, like a bouncing ball,

Pop up here, there, and outwit you all.

I sharpen the tongue with razor's wit,

For the target of Truth I'll aim a hit.

I'm Fire and Air, a flame that licks,

And burns, transforms with pranks and tricks,

Superficial, lighthearted me,

Amusing master of repartee.

With skills and manual dexterity,

With gimmicks and gadgets, I'm so funny!

All that's ridiculous feeds my lines,

Satire and mimicry suit me fine.

I walk on stage, an innocent Jester,

One touch, I bring the house down, the serious pester!

Anything negative I can break up,

Politics, prayer, I send it all up!

When you're planning which war you're going to fight next,

I transform your games into higher tricks.

My touch here and there on the right occasion,

Can spark off a whole new civilization.

For my concentrated, timely action,

Initiates a chain reaction.

Like summer insects tease in the sun,

I'm garden parties, fetes and fun.

With sharp twisty, sardonic smile,

My wits will win by many a mile.

I'm the ignition spark that awakens the Spirit,

I've a bag of tricks with laughs tied up in it.

So play the game, do a spin,

The prize is Life, I'll help you win!

The Warrior

↑ⓘ

Both positive and negative attributes are given in this description to help you better recognise the state in yourself and others. When we repeatedly use an Archetype, it cannot fail to exhibit negative traits, as it becomes overused and not balanced by other states. The climates associated with the months of the year were worked out in the Northern hemisphere, so they may need to be adjusted to suit the Southern Hemisphere and take into account unfamiliar weather patterns linked to climate change.

The Warrior

Closed Fire

July 21st to August 21st

One of the three Fire and one of the four Closed states.

Fire and Earth, the metaphysical linking of Spirit and Body.

The season of The Warrior is July/August, late Summer, often the hottest time of the year. His colour is rich blood red, the mix of approximately two parts of the red of Fire, his first element, and one part of the dark brown of Earth, his second.

His landscape is erupting volcanoes and harsh, hot, rocky areas. This is the Fire within the Earth which overheats, erupts and explodes. Lava is like an unstoppable marching army, expanding its territory, similar to a forest fire which burns 'furiously' as the fire 'rages'. The Warrior is the volcanic power deep within us, which, if properly controlled, is a tremendous storehouse of physical strength and dynamism.

We find him on the battlefields of life, in war zones, occupying barracks, fortresses, towers, a fortified castle defended by a moat, drawbridge and portcullis. This is your willpower, drive, strength and confidence to achieve all that you wish. He says "I will!" Although it is termed a 'masculine' state, it refers to Yang energy. The Warrior is a male/Yang part of ourselves and is available equally to both sexes, male, female, whether heterosexual, homosexual, lesbian, bisexual or intersex, as are all the Archetypes. The competitive Warrior is very popular, you will have no trouble identifying him and will be familiar with the many words and phrases related to him. The sexist structures and attitudes of society have encouraged boys to develop this state and girls to avoid it, even if they are predisposed towards it. This is now changing, where all are increasingly free to claim their own strength and we see women assuming more leadership roles. In many parts of the world, however, women are still oppressed and have no power to exercise their will.

When we consider biology, we see that males have a penis and the nature of this organ is to ejaculate into the outer world. It is possible that this fundamental difference between men and women explains why this Archetype, and its focus on the outer world, appears to come more naturally to many men. Cannons, space rockets and guns are penis-shaped. This, however, is no reason to dissuade women from developing and using their Warrior. Perhaps in women the state operates in less obvious ways, in considerable inner strength, or perhaps this is the only option open to them as they have been forced to suppress it. They are blocked from using it freely in the world and pursuing achievements of their own. Any female animal, including human, will react with a terrifying fierceness that will fight to the death if her young are threatened. At present, most fighters are men, most violence and other crime is committed by them and most achievements are claimed by them, although there are many unrecognised female achievements. It will be interesting to see how women use the Warrior now they have joined the ranks in sports, business and the armed forces in a fighting capacity. It could be said that the anger in men under the patriarchy is as a result of too much Warrior and the anger in women is the result of thousands of years of oppression. What is known for certain is that if we balance our Archetypes, the negative, harmful aspects of the Warrior will be tamed, and all will go on to greater achievements in the quest for the common good.

"A hero is an ordinary individual who finds the strength to persevere and endure in spite of overwhelming obstacles" - *Christopher Reeve*

As Fire is such a commonly encouraged Element, we find many expressions in our language. The Fire of the Warrior makes us 'heated', we say "It made my blood boil", "My blood is up", we 'flare up', get 'blazing mad', are 'playing with fire', have a 'heated debate'. We become 'ignited', we have a 'burning desire', are 'bursting' to do things, are 'burning up', become 'fired up', 'lit up' to pursue new projects and ideas, although other Archetypes have to tell him what they are. He has initiative

 once he is given his orders. Actions are 'fired off' in new directions and if impatient we 'jump the gun'. The Warrior is brave, has 'guts', 'balls', 'spunk', there's 'fire in his belly'. Earth as the second element keeps him rooted to his source of power and in his body, which he uses as a weapon. The Fire (spirit) rises through the Earth (body) via the spine, and erupts into action. This is your own will, "I will", "Will you?" The Warrior has drive, is driven, action is his answer for everything. Nothing ventured, nothing gained! The Warrior has 'backbone', will always 'stand up to things', 'will stand and be counted', he can 'stand things' that weaker, 'spineless' Archetypes cannot. If we lack the Warrior, we 'can't stand it' and are advised to 'stand tall', 'stand up for yourself', 'man up' and 'grow a pair'. The Warrior gives strength and brings change. He will drive you towards physical fitness and the development of strength and stamina. He'll soon have you 'fighting fit'. This state strengthens your entire body, cells, blood vessels, organs, bones, muscles, hair, teeth, immune system and blood. People with him well developed rarely catch colds and, being Fire and Earth, the Earth (Body), is well heated by the Fire (Spirit), so rarely feel cold.

Practicing the Warrior will lead you to pursue goals and some form of exercise regime. You will want to build your strength. If you are weak it is because the Warrior is lacking in you but he will guide you towards the programme best suited to your needs and present state of fitness. He's your own personal trainer. He enjoys the experience of toning, flexing, using his strong muscles. hardening, as lava hardens.
He brings all-round strength, so you will notice an increase of emotional, intellectual and spiritual strength too. He breaks the sense of being disempowered, of being the victim of other people's wills and of one's own inner habitual patterns. A breakthrough into a new way of life becomes possible. With willpower, you are no longer 'weak-willed', you become more 'strong-minded' and receive a boost to your self-esteem and confidence. You have purpose and drive, you can take action, go forward, achieve your aims and reach your goals in the triumph of success. You enjoy winning, but better not over other people. Your true gains come from defeating weaknesses in yourself that have been obstructing your growth. The Spiritual Warrior is then born in you.

"He who conquers himself is the mightiest warrior" - *Confucius*

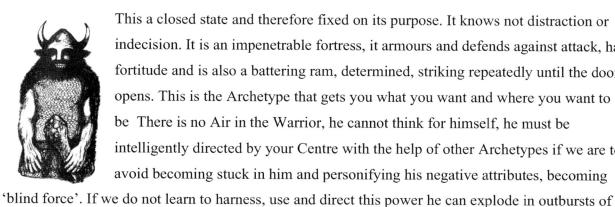
This a closed state and therefore fixed on its purpose. It knows not distraction or indecision. It is an impenetrable fortress, it armours and defends against attack, has fortitude and is also a battering ram, determined, striking repeatedly until the door opens. This is the Archetype that gets you what you want and where you want to be There is no Air in the Warrior, he cannot think for himself, he must be intelligently directed by your Centre with the help of other Archetypes if we are to avoid becoming stuck in him and personifying his negative attributes, becoming 'blind force'. If we do not learn to harness, use and direct this power he can explode in outbursts of temper and violence and 'go berserk'. We are 'playing with fire'. We see his negative side in action with the outbreak of fights, wars, exploding bombs, riots and civil unrest where setting fire to cars is common. He is not hindered by feelings, or those of others, he just does the job he has to do. Warriors have been known to continue fighting on the battlefield, regardless of serious wounds and broken bones. They can withstand the hardship of a siege, for winning is all. The Warrior is the weapon of those who wish to bring personal or social revolution, used equally by heroes, guerillas, pioneers, terrorists and criminals. How he is directed depends on the principles and level of evolution of those who use him. Armies have generals who plan strategies, tactics and campaigns and the Warrior carries them out. We do this for ourselves by ordering the Warrior within.

Wars and confrontations often break out in this month, such as World Wars I and II, and there is a spike of forest fires and arson attacks. The Warrior is not the inventor of weapons, he hasn't the intelligence, but he is the wielder of them. It is the explosion of gunpowder that fires guns and fireworks, a rocket is launched with fire, the internal combustion engine in vehicles has pistons driven by exploding petrol and old steam trains are fuelled by burning coals. We need the heat and power of the Warrior to propel us forward, within and without. In nature, a new growth is called a green 'shoot', plants and children 'shoot up' and in the business world we recognise him by some commonly used expressions, usually linked to war or sport - 'bullet points', 'a level playing field', 'playing the game', 'moving the goalposts', 'on the ball', 'striking out', 'taking a stab at', 'a sales drive', 'a hostile takeover', 'you're fired, 'burning ambition', 'the rat race', 'let's see if this idea has legs and can run'. Invitations to speak are 'fire away', 'shoot', and we like to be 'armed with information' When controlling our Warrior, we 'pull our punches', 'bite the bullet'. When leaving we say "I'll shoot off now", "He shot off". Using a car is called 'driving', and we 'burn up the miles'. The symbol of the world's leading athletics event is the Olympic flame, and to further a cause is to 'carry the torch'. In war the order to shoot is 'Fire!', 'Fire at will!' and to stop is 'Cease fire', and when things annoy us we say 'Blast!' A footballer also 'shoots' at the goal. Games such as football (soccer) are important to many people and some teams in UK football are named or nicknamed with war-like names - e.g. Arsenal, the Gunners, the Hammers. Football supporters are referred to in military ways, such as the 'Barmy Army' for the English and the 'Tartan Army' for the Scots. Many of the most popular sports played and followed involve mainly men playing with balls and various hard, long things such as sticks, bats and clubs. People who are considered courageous 'have balls'. This Archetype is worshipped in the world and is honoured with statues and medals with many popular films glamourising him. Negatively, the Warrior is closed to the effects of his destructiveness. He is a devil, a rapist, a hooligan, a beast, a bully, a brute, brutal, brutish, boorish, ugly, vicious, cruel, hard, harsh, aggressive, angry, furious. He goes berserk, is full of rage, is quarrelsome, hostile, egotistical, obstructive, arrogant, ruthless, defensive, offensive, swaggering, bragging, violent and boastful.

"Non-violence is the weapon of the strong." - Mahatma Gandhi

"A man with outward courage dares to die. A man with inner courage dares to live." – Lao Tzu

The strain of continually using or suppressing any Archetype can lead to illness. The constant tension of perpetual fighting can cause the spine to lock and create back pain, but without him, our spines are weak. We can become 'burnt out, Warriors are 'stout-hearted', but used to excess can result in constant anger, which harms the heart and blood pressure. Angina can be linked to anger, and a commonly prescribed medicine for this is Nitroglycerine, termed TNT, which is derived from its explosive form. To the negative Warrior, the whole world and everyone in it is an enemy, all must be beaten, destroyed, razed to the ground. He crushes the vulnerable under his hob-nailed boots, is always in some kind of contest, always striving to win in sports, business and personal affairs. The Warrior has to be the biggest and the best and fights to own trophies, awards, prizes, houses, televisions, businesses, yachts private planes, cars etc. and won't hesitate to boast about them. He despises 'losers'. His conflicting opposite, the Child (Water and Air) is essential for him to learn to open his eyes and heart to all that is lovely, precious and worth protecting, just as he can bring her the strength to stand up for herself.

"Courage is what it takes to stand up and speak; courage is also what it takes to sit down and listen." - Winston Churchill

The Warrior aims to overcome, to conquer, to explore and expand territory, imposing his will and force on those who stand in his way. Conquest is all! He has a huge ego and can be a 'loud mouth', but he has courage to 'back it up' if used for the good. He stands firm and defends. He has force, fortitude, is a fortress, (forts are defensive buildings), he 'holds the fort', he is steadfast and will defend his position to the end. He has resolve and initiative when given his orders, he is muscle and brawn, macho, loud, assertive, definite, forceful, rugged, invincible, active, mighty, fierce, vanquishing all foes with his enormous strength. He has the power to begin anew and his competitiveness is a quality that can be used to great effect on a higher level if you perceive that your true opponent is your old self; the old patterns, fears, anxieties and limitations, the self you wish to change and evolve into greatness. The Warrior is your ego. There is a positive place for everything, you can use your ego to fight for truth, your own growth, beauty, justice, the environment and social issues. Balanced with the other Archetypes, we will have co-operation rather than conflict, and a chance of creating a 'win/win' situation for all.

"The best fighter is never angry." - Lao Tzu

"It is not the critic who counts; not the man who points out how the strong man stumbles, or where the doer of deeds could have done them better. The credit belongs to the man who is actually in the arena, whose face is marred by dust and sweat and blood; who strives valiantly; who errs, who comes short again and again, because there is no effort without error and shortcoming; but who does actually strive to do the deeds; who knows great enthusiasms, the great devotions; who spends himself in a worthy cause; who at the best knows in the end the triumph of high achievement, and who at the worst, if he fails, at least fails while daring greatly, so that his place shall never be with those cold and timid souls who neither know victory nor defeat." - Theodore Roosevelt

The Warrior has stamina, courage, assertiveness, daring, is a tireless inner ally, there is nothing you cannot achieve with the Warrior on your side marching with you. All can be won! Onward with courage!

"Don't forget to pack your courage for the journey to greatness" - David Weinbaum.

Some key words of the positives and negatives are listed below, together with some of the interests and activities relevant to this Archetype to help round out the picture of its world.

Time: July 21st to August 21st

Season: Late Summer.

Quality: One of the three Fire states and one of the four Closed states.

Elements: Fire and Earth.

Colour: Blood red.

Conflicting opposite: The Child.

Complementary Opposite: The Patriarch.

Voice: Hard, harsh, strong, loud, roaring.

Face type: Big face, ruddy complexion, square jawed, large, flaring nostrils, big teeth, hair either close-cropped or long with a beard, thick neck.

Body type: Tall, muscular, barrel-chested, beefy, hirsute, erect spine, fire in the belly and blood.

Movement: Marching, stomping, running, definite.

Weather: Hot, relentless sunshine, volcanic eruptions.

Landscape: Harsh, dry, volcanic, rocky, craggy terrain, a battlefield, forest fires.

Home: Army barracks, fortified castle, Spartan, functional house, with little interest in decor.

Clothing: Military uniforms, big boots, helmets and short hair/shaved heads or long unkempt hair and beards, animal skins, Viking horns, helmets, armour, chain mail, visors, functional clothing.

Food: Meat, preferably bloody. A steak and chips man - or woman.

Positives: Courage, willpower, drive, strength, confidence, effectiveness. Resolve and initiative, muscular, strong, assertive, definite, forceful, rugged, invincible, active, mighty and conquering, protective, a defender. Used with the Patriarch, can be chivalry.

Negatives: A devil, a rapist, a hooligan, a beast, a bully, a brute, a killer, brutal, boorish, ugly, vicious, cruel, hard, harsh, bossy, aggressive, angry, furious. He goes berserk, is full of blood lust, rage, is quarrelsome, hostile, egotistical, obstructive, arrogant, ruthless, defensive, offensive, swaggering, bragging, violent and boastful, competitive.

Career choices and interests: Soldier, sportsman/woman, police officer, fireman/woman (fire engines are red), lifeguards, the rescue services, martial arts, boxer, prizefighter, fitness trainer, bodybuilder, strongman, a sentinel, a guard, bouncer, weight-lifter, explorer (likes to conquer and expand territory), mountaineer, assassin, slaughterer, hunter, extreme sports, anything that gives an 'adrenalin rush'. Pursuits that involve weapons, battle re-enactment. Will fight to get ahead in all fields of life, business and personal.

Reading materials and entertainment: Films and books about war, 'cops and robbers', martial arts, fitness, macho crime novels involving violence.

Music: Military marches, explosive, aggressive beat, gangsta rap.

He is: A Spiritual warrior, a pioneer, Joan of Arc, Boudicca, an Amazon, the Horned God, a hard man, a Knight in shining armour with the Patriarch. A bully, Goliath, Samson, macho man, a giant, a Spartan.

"Every time you are tempted to react in the same way, ask yourself if you want to be a pioneer of the past or a pioneer of the future." - Deepak Chopra

"Life shrinks or expands according to one's courage." - Anais Nin

"A man who conquers himself is greater than one who conquers a thousand men in battle" Buddha

How to Practice the Warrior

Reading the script is beneficial in several ways –

1. It increases your awareness of your Centre.

2. It helps you to identify and recognise the Warrior in yourself and others.

3. It gives you control over your Warrior.

4. As the script focuses on positive attributes, it helps you to purify your Warrior.

5. It gives you the opportunity to add more strands of the Warrior in yourself.

6. You can help others to activate it in themselves.

Reading the script only serves as a rehearsal for the real thing - your daily life. When developing the Warrior, you will need to follow through by observing your usual behaviour patterns and seeing where you can introduce a more dynamic way of being. Follow positive impulses to do something new, such as exercise or learning to be more assertive. The Warrior is a Closed state. If you identify with and realise you live a lot in the Warrior, read the script to purify and identify it in yourself. You will understand your own Warrior better. If you are weak in the Warrior and identify more with his conflicting opposite, the Child, you might feel extra vulnerable and frightened, and resist the Warrior. The opposite reaction is also possible and you may find the release of Warrior energy empowers you with confidence. Beware that it may bring you into conflict with others in your daily life as you learn to direct it. If this happens, go into the Observer or an Earth Archetype and let it settle. If you feel angry, try to identify the root of it. Keep in mind that you have been suppressing it and now you can allow it to be there, but you must take control of it and integrate it with other parts of yourself. This will transform it into strength. Persevere and the other Archetypes will accept that your life has improved, you can achieve more and enjoy your success - and there will be no going back. You will go forward with the help of your Warrior.

Preparing

Wear something of the appropriate colour (red) and style (military uniform or Viking for example) and some heavy boots or shoes. Music can help to set the scene, something military, martial, a march. It is preferable to practice the Warrior out of doors or a large hall where you have plenty of room. Visualize yourself as a white light in the Centre of your circle, reaching towards the Warrior to add a strong red to your colours. Let that colour surround you, imagine you are filling up with blood red. Keep the awareness that you are the Centre and not the Warrior. Getting the stance and the voice right before you begin, and being aware of maintaining them as you read, will help in channelling the energy through.

Imagine yourself in the Warrior's landscape, it is late summer and very hot, you are surrounded by rocks and volcanoes, you can sense explosions and feel the immense power of the Fire. Stand tall, imagine you are a giant. Breathe deeply from your belly and lower lungs. Stand with your feet shoulder width apart, firmly on the ground and feel your connection to a huge volcano below. Draw this power up, aware of the volcanic force empowering your voice, let it be driven by the breath rising from your lower body. Everything is big and loud about the Warrior, including his voice. Don't shout and attempt to sound fierce, you'll risk damage to your throat and will focus the energy too high. Correct use of the breath will automatically produce a loud, strong, hard sound. Fill your abdomen with a modest amount of air, loosely open your mouth and pull your abdomen in quickly, letting the sudden puff of air to make a sound - 'Ha!'. You will notice that this keeps your throat relaxed and open, even when doing the Warrior's roar. Repeat and gradually lengthen the sounds, always aware of the volcanic force empowering your voice. Bare your teeth and snarl a bit and feel the strength of him. Lift your chest up, clench your fists. The Warrior does not flay around all the time, he also stands firm and his march is steady. Let the power grow naturally and gradually. Try not to 'act tough', you could become trapped in the act and limit yourself. Your surroundings seem to shrink as you grow in stature, you feel more powerful, enormous, your nostrils flare with the power of your breath, your face reddens. If this state is unfamiliar to you, think of something that makes you feel cross and once you start to feel it, switch right away to thinking about a positive goal. Persevere and the other Archetypes will accept that your life has improved, you are stronger and more confident.

The Warrior will give you courage and inner strength to go forward towards your goals. Onward and upward! Now read the script.

THE WARRIOR

Fire and Earth

Hard, harsh, strong, loud voice.

I am the Warrior, Fire and Earth,

The volcano is my place of birth.

Action and courage are my mode,

Well-known to me is hardship's road.

I erupt in revolutions and wars!

I push and fight to open doors!

I'm hard and forceful, rule your spine,

I'll stand up and be counted any time!

I have stamina, confidence, I'm intrepid, have guts,

I'll drive you out of your stagnant ruts!

To take you forward is my way,

In any hell I will not stay!

I'm strong, I'm armoured against attack,

On my way to achievement I never look back.

I will reach my objective with self-assurance,

I have staying power and tremendous endurance.

I'm the pioneer who cuts a new path,

That you may follow in my aftermath,

Try to stop me and feel my wrath,

For I seek more life, I seek more growth!

I'm expansive, dynamic, I'll prune near to the roots,

If it heralds a season of bigger fruits.

I'm a potent, virile, lusty giant,

Who'll free you from any evil tyrant

Who has you gripped in fearful hold,

I'll protect and defend you, big and bold!

I'm territorial, brave, vigorous, tireless,

Unstoppable, courageous, definite and fearless!

Life is combat, a survival course,

I bash through obstacles with tremendous force.

My will is enormous, I always stand firm,

From my purpose I'll never turn.

Over others you'll see me tower,

With my dynamic drive and power!

I compete to win in every tussle,

Lion-hearted strength in each hard, bulging muscle.

My power strikes for champion's place,

To claim the cup and win the race,

For I compete to get there first,

I'll never give up, I'd sooner burst!!

All types of combat invoke my skills,

Martial arts and army drills.

I'm the effective boss in any field,

Always hunting a bigger yield.

I'm a valiant, gallant and mighty Hero!

I conquer all with my big Ego!

Listen to my great HOORAAAAAAAAAAAAAAAAAAA!!!!!!

That makes the world go "Ooooh!" and "Aaahh!"

Of all my conquests I will boast,

And drink my fill of victory's toast.

I'm daring, effective, impress you all,

Have you the guts to hear my call?

Death I'll defeat and bring you peace,

If you have the guts for life's release.

This is the challenge that I give,

Have you the courage to EVOLVE AND LIVE?

The Earth Archetypes

WORKER   MOTHER NATURE   WISE WOMAN

The Worker/Slave

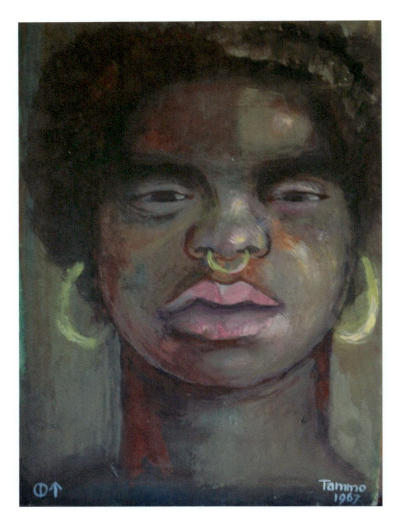

Both positive and negative attributes are given in this description to help you better recognise the state in yourself and others. When we repeatedly use an Archetype, it cannot fail to exhibit negative traits, as it becomes overused and not balanced by other states. The climates associated with the months of the year were worked out in the Northern hemisphere, so they may need to be adjusted to suit the Southern Hemisphere and take into account unfamiliar weather patterns linked to climate change.

The Worker/Slave

Open Earth

August 21ˢᵗ to September 21ˢᵗ

One of the three Earth and one of the four Open states.

Earth and Fire, the metaphysical linking of Body and Spirit.

The season of the Worker is August/September, early Autumn. Her colour is reddish, chestnut brown, like deep red clay, unbaked pottery and red-brown earth, the mix of approximately two parts of the brown of Earth, her first element, and one part of the red of Fire, her second. Her landscape is dry baked earth, solid from the heat of the summer sun. Her season is early Autumn when the leaves begin to turn brown and her labour will be needed to gather the coming harvest. She is your foundation, what is basic, the 'bottom line' and her centre of being is your body, with emphasis on your arse. When fired, Earth becomes solid, foundations are made on solid ground. The fundament is the bottom, the base and the low. Her function is to do all the practical work necessary to keep you alive, both inside and outside of the body. The Worker is the rhythms of life, your work, your heart beating, pumping, your lungs bellowing, your breathing, eating, drinking, fucking, shitting, the pulse of life like the rhythm of drums. She's the rhythmic tasks of work; on the land gathering food and water, domestic chores or your daily job. She is bound by all those things that have to be done, inside and outside the body

To be low is to be common and vulgar, but a lowly person is also humble and 'down to earth',

 unpretentious, blunt and realistic. She is basic, like a workhorse or a cow, part of the herd. She knows we are animals and does not pretend otherwise. She is useful, pliant and practical, as Earth confines Fire and makes it useful. The earth herself contains fire in her centre as does a stove, a furnace, a forge, a kiln or an oven, so we think of workshops and factories, the production of iron and steel, glass, pottery, bricks and bread, the body making use of fire. Our bodies are useful, they are the means whereby we exist on earth, the basic foundation of life, what we all have in common like blood, sweat, tears, shit, bones, muscles, organs, arms, legs and arseholes. We are all slaves to our bodies and to all the things needed to keep them alive.

The Worker is the world of the ordinary and commonplace, the 'common man', unlike her opposing opposite the Patriarch, who lives in his head and is concerned with individuality. We joke that royalty doesn't shit. The Worker is your earth wire, keeping  you connected to reality. She can always 'get down to it' and relates well to all the things of the earth. Many so-called consciousness expanding 'spiritual' groups ignore her and her gifts, which is like trying to build another storey on a house with weak foundations or putting a strong charge into an electric machine that doesn't have a good earth wire. The result is that it blows its top, just as we will if we don't keep ourselves grounded. She is everything common and dirty, uses plentiful swear words and speaks in a slovenly manner, yet by ignoring her we risk going crazy. Some people with mental health problems have been known to swear, become filthy and obscene. This is their instinctive reaching for her; if they were earthed they could begin to recover their sanity. This,

 unfortunately, is not understood and they may not receive effective help, which would include giving them practical tasks to do and a good course of massage and relaxation techniques to bring them back down to earth and into their bodies in a positive way.

Having no standards or appearances to keep up, as she is already at the bottom, the Worker is very relaxed and easy going. She is tolerant and can put up with a lot without complaining. She is resigned, she accepts what is. To accept is to submit, which is to bend and to bear one's burden. As she relaxes your body, all its parts cooperate with a pleasant easeful feeling, muscles letting go and helping to avoid the diseases of tension; hardening of the arteries, stomach ulcers, heart problems and worse. As you relax, your body may gurgle or fart as it sorts itself out. She opens your circulation and releases your mind from worry and anxiety. You may also become aware of aches and pains that you were ignoring, and as you attune to your body, you will be guided towards healing.

The Worker brings your sensuality alive and greatly improves your sexual experiences. She does enjoy a good fuck. Erotic is better than neurotic as far as she's concerned. She's the foundation of the body and loves all of its smells, including its farts. Because she is so at home in her body, she carries security within her wherever she goes. Security also comes from belonging to 'a body of people', she is the basic animal aspect of our humanity, the community. Earth containing Fire is the hearth, which has been at the centre of social life until recently, when we got central heating and television replaced it. Now, due to the many devices invented by the Logician, people are more separate and less likely to gather around a common space. It's warm at the hearth, she is warm hearted, she enjoys living and working in a community where all co-operate and are adaptable, practical and tolerant, accepting its conditions and putting up with discomfort, going along with the inevitable. She is allowing and permissive, this is a world of sharing among the group or tribe, with solidarity and co-operation. She is Trade Unions, labour, work, workers, the ordinary and everyday, the traditional U.K. Labour Party, socialism and communal interests. The Worker likes all things that unite. We find her in factories, bakeries and anywhere that's putting fire to use. She talks about solidarity of people. She's 'a brick'. In recent times, the grip of the Patriarch became so strong that the pendulum swung in the opposite direction, the resentment of the workers flared up and the Warrior came alive in them. The Patriarch was thrown from his throne, but unfortunately we threw the baby out with the bath water and although this left the workers in a better material position, there is now a great deal less individuality, respect, good manners, values or morals. The culture is becoming increasingly 'dumbed down', with the more cultural programmes being replaced with reality television and celebrity culture, where little talent is needed. The Arts and self-cultivation are demoted to low priority.

Having no Air Element, she is disinterested in reading, study and self-improvement. When negative, the Worker is low, and resents anyone who is different. She is lazy, dirty, unhygienic, smelly, disgusting in speech and behaviour, rude, crude and vulgar, with no discrimination or respect for anyone. She has to be forced to 'get off her arse' and work, she revels in her ignorance and will attempt to pull down anyone who thinks they are better. She has no ambition and wants to drop everything and everybody down to the lowest level. She won't have anybody cutting themselves off from the group with any of that 'highbrow' stuff you call learning and culture. She'll stay with the herd and can put up with all kinds of faults in her pals, except any of them trying to express any fancy individuality. She has no self-direction and so will serve anyone who can use her and mould her at will. Hers is the ideal state for the advertiser and trend setter, she just follows the lead, doing the same as everyone else. These days most people wear jeans, t- shirts and trainers, comfortable Worker clothing, and most everyone looks the same. Anyone different is likely to be jeered at. Fewer people dress up to go to the theatre or concerts and frequently yabber into their mobile phones or to each other, showing little respect for the artists. Everything about the Worker is casual. Music is increasingly about repetitive rhythm and less about melody.

Positively, she is accepting, relaxed, easy-going, helpful, a willing worker, warm, secure, sociable, companionable and humble, with no airs and graces or pretence. She is the nuts and bolts that keep everything working and in 'rude health'. She is tolerant and 'thick skinned' and we often see many of her positive qualities in those who have lived in the sun for generations; their skin darkens to her warm browns and thickens to protect it. We see from the way many black people dance that they are more at home in their bodies, they have natural rhythm and are skilled drummers. They can also have deeper, richer, slower voices with an innate warmth, like that of Maya Angelou, or those luscious, honeyed West Indian accents. Their inner warmth is eloquently expressed in beaming smiles.

"The Slave is obviously the fundamental aspect of our body and being which has to be transformed by being permeated through and through with the other brighter and cleaner functions. By these means the body could begin to be transformed. An important point she makes is that she must be accepted as she is, in order to be able to accept totally the other elements. The mistake we seem to have been making, is to tell her not to be as she is, and have riddled ourselves with shame about her. When we stop her being herself, we cut out the possibility of the body drawing deeply into itself the benefits of the other states, so our bodies do not transform as they should. Some kind of contained situation needs to be provided for us to experience the excesses of the Slave in ourselves where all guilt about her can be eliminated. In fact, to experience each of the twelve states ever more fully, they should be regularly practiced as rituals in or around a Temple. Prize plants are often grown on stinking dung heaps. We would not think of cleaning the dung to get better results, nor can we afford to disapprove of it. The plants which grow upon it are transforming devices, they transform

something filthy into something beautiful or succulent. The Slave seems to be the nature of the clay upon which we are made." - Richard Gardner. 'The Wheel of Life' (1980)

Acceptance is crucial when developing higher energies so that they can enter your body with full penetration. Allowing them in is a blissful sensation.

The Slave was the original name for this Archetype. Slavery is a difficult subject to discuss but we need to be clear on what is meant by the Worker (Slave) in this Work and I hope by now you realise that I do not mean being taken into bondage by others. To avoid denying ourselves the marvelous qualities she offers, we need to separate the exploitation of people from the positive aspects of consciousness the Worker/Slave represents. There are two aspects of slavery. There are willing slaves and unwilling slaves. Everyone is for hire, we offer our energy in return for money, whether we be labourers, artisans, professionals or artists. We are all Slaves to something, including our bodies that need to be fed and watered at the very least. Maybe you enjoy your job or maybe you hate it, but you still have a choice of making a change at some point. Unwilling slaves are forced into work. This despicable side of slavery has always existed, it merely changes with the times. The Romans had slaves who were able to earn their freedom, the British aristocracy had servants, black people were sold, bought and used both by black and white races and now in the west we see people being brought into countries illegally and forced to work in hotels, houses and restaurants with no pay or means of escape. Amongst the worst kind is sex slavery, where young people, the majority girls, are tricked into believing they are being offered a better life and a good job and instead find themselves locked in rooms working as prostitutes. They are given addictive drugs to make them more compliant and less likely to flee, being lied to about what would happen if they went to the police. I hope we can put this issue aside and avail ourselves of the positive aspects of this channel of consciousness. The Worker, when balanced with other Archetypes, is crucial to creating peace on earth. She is tolerant and knows how to co-operate with others. She focuses on our similarities and communal interests, on what is best for the whole body of people. She relaxes conflict and offers the warmth of community.

"And so…rock bottom became a solid foundation on which I rebuilt my life." - JK Rowling

Some key words of the positives and negatives are listed below, together with some of the interests and activities relevant to this Archetype to help round out the picture of its world.

Time: August 21st to September 21st.

Season: Early Autumn.

Quality: One of the three Earth and one of the four Open states.

Elements: Earth and Fire.

Colour: Chestnut brown.

Conflicting opposite: The Patriarch.

Complementary Opposite: The Child.

Voice: Deep, slow, earthy, warm, drawled, slightly slurred.

Face Type: Small, lazy eyes, full lips, low forehead.

Body type: Sturdy, solid, rather flabby when too lazy. Centred in the arse, which can be large.

Movement: Slow, easy and relaxed.

Weather: Hot and dry.

Landscape: Baked, solid earth, factories, blacksmiths, factories, farms and practical workplaces.

Home: Anything goes, usually messy, untidy and not very clean. The body.

Clothing: Casual wear like ripped jeans, hoodies, tee-shirts, plain dresses, overalls, boiler suits.

Food: Likely to eat fast foods, anything easy and filling.

Positives: Accepting, relaxed, easy-going, helpful, a willing worker, warm, secure, sociable, companionable, tolerant and humble, unpretentious.

Negatives: Rude, crude, dirty, lazy, messy, disrespectful, unambitious, low.

Career choices and interests: Masseur, builder, labourer, domestic service and any practical job that involves dirt, both the creation of it during the job and the removal of it afterwards. A lot of these jobs involve a certain amount of swear words, the energy behind them seems to help get the job done. All three Earth types may be involved in the fields of social work, community work and caring of some kind.

Reading materials and entertainment: As there is no air in this Archetype, she won't be into books but will look at celebrity magazines and enjoy reality television, blockbuster movies and most entertainments created for the masses.

Music: Basic rhythmic music such as drumming, a throbbing strong beat, the blues, folk working songs, gospel, groovy jazz. Often likes Country and Western.

She is - The common man, a skivvy, a peasant, the salt of the earth, a brick, a wench, the body.

How to Practice the Worker/Slave

Reading the script is beneficial in several ways -

1. It increases your awareness of your Centre.

2. It helps you to identify and recognise the Worker/Slave in yourself and others.

3. It gives you control over your Worker/Slave.

4. As the script focuses on positive attributes, it helps you to purify your Worker/Slave.

5. It gives you the opportunity to add more strands of the Worker/Slave in yourself.

6. You can help others to activate it in themselves.

Reading the script only serves as a rehearsal for the real thing - your daily life. When developing the Worker/Slave you will need to follow through by observing your usual behaviour patterns and seeing where you can introduce her energy. Follow positive impulses to do something new, such as lying down and relaxing, learning to play drums, dancing which focuses on the lower part of the body, such as African and Egyptian, or practical work and DIY. Yoga is a good way of coming into the body, it helps with your circulation, although there are different types of yoga, and can include aspects from other states, such as the meditative gifts of the Observer, and the reaching for the higher self in general. The Worker/Slave is an Open state. If you identify with and realise you live a lot in this Archetype, read the script to purify and identify it in yourself. You will understand your own Worker/Slave better. If you are weak in the Worker/Slave and identify more with her conflicting opposite, the Patriarch, you could find yourself resisting and not wishing to relax and come down to earth. Good gracious, you might fart! The opposite reaction is possible, you might feel a blissful relaxation.

Preparing.

This Archetype is associated with your arse, buttocks and relaxation, so you don't have to 'get off your arse' to practise this one. Wear something of the appropriate colour (chestnut, reddish-brown) and style – jeans, t shirt, sweat shirt, something tatty, ripped and comfortable. To help set the scene, play slow, repetitive music like the blues or drumming. First, visualize yourself as a white light in the Centre of your circle, reaching down to the Worker/Slave to add chestnut, reddish brown to your colours. Let that colour surround you, imagine you are filling up with warm chestnut brown. Keep the awareness that you are the Centre and not the Worker/Slave. It's best to lie back for this one, but if you stand then slouch or lean against something. Getting the stance and the voice right before you begin, and being aware of maintaining them as you read, will help in channeling the energy through. It's early Autumn. Imagine yourself in the Worker/Slave landscape, hot, warm earth, or lounging round the hearth. Earth and Fire is dry baked earth, a solid feeling. There is much work to do, but for now you are lying back and relaxing. As you melt into a comfortable position, let your buttocks be heavy and bring your awareness to your entire body, each muscle relaxing in turn, sinking into the surface supporting you. Your voice is slow, deep, with a drawl and a dialect of the 'working class'. Let the feeling grow naturally and gradually. Try not to act it as you could become trapped in the act and limit yourself. If this state is unfamiliar to you, focus on getting the voice right, become aware of how your body feels. You might belch and fart. So what? Bodies do those things.

Swear if you want to as well. Fuck it, why not? As you connect your awareness to your body, you may be aware of its rhythms, aches and pains might reveal themselves as you allow relaxation to soothe them. If you find it hard to relax, remember that relaxation is not something you do, it's something you allow to happen. Persevere and the

other Archetypes will accept that your life has improved, you have a new security in yourself and are more tolerant and practical. The Worker/Slave will help you take a relaxed attitude and let go of tension. You will feel more comfortable in your own body and in a body of people. Now read the script.

THE WORKER/SLAVE

Earth and Fire

Drawled, slow, relaxed and warm voice.

I'm the Slave, Earth and Fire,

I'm the Worker, I'm for hire,

I'm the rhythms of work, the daily grind,

I'm a slave to all the tasks that bind.

I puts up wif a lot, why make life tough?

I just does wot I'm told, an' I'm worked hard ennuf,

Wot wif pumpin' yer heart an' diggin' the soil,

I gathers the harvest an' in factories toil.

I likes fings wot unites us, us union members,

We sticks together, there's safety in numbers.

I co-operate an' share me tools,

Wif all me mates, we just follows the rules.

I'm bound to work, I'm of service to all,

I knows me place, humble an' all.

I lives in yer body, yer blood circulate,

In a body of people, each one is me mate.

I'm sociable, warm, I relate to the herd,

To the common trend I'm easily led,

I don't pretend I'm anyfink special,

I likes to fit in, in clubs what are social.

I'm the basic foundation, wot we all got the same,

Arms, legs, skin an' an ordinary name,

I'm the fings in yer body wot are vulgar an' smelly,

Like sweat an' piss an' shit in yer belly.

I enjoys me body, I likes a good fuck,

I'm down to earth an' common as muck.

I ain't fussy on hygiene, that's for sure,

I just lets things be, cos I'm so secure.

I'm sensual, I love all words earfy an' rude,

Nuffin' fancy, I'm basic an' crude,

I says wot's wot an' I says it blunt,

Ain't we all got a cock or ain't we all got a cunt?

I'm the rhythms of life, the beat of the earf,

The pulse of yer blood, yer heart an' yer breaf,

I'm the rhythms of music, I loves to drum,

When I dance I hangs loose an' rotate me bum.

While them others runs about goin' mental,

I just reacts to fings wots fundamental,

A brain ain't much use, so I've found,

Cos I'm centred in me arse, all soft an' round.

I'm adaptable, I takes the easy road,

I'm accepting, I plods along wif me load.

I'm like a kiln-fired brick, solid an' real,

Me easy-goin' warmth can soothe an' heal.

I'm tolerant, well, we all play our part,

So please yerself if you wanna fart.

I knows the magic of massage an' relaxation,

I unlocks every muscle into blissed-out sensation.

As me warm blood flows in me circulation,

All me body's united, in co-operation.

I'm relaxed in meself, so it's easy to hug you,

I'm the stable earf wire, in the safe ground I plug you.

Relax, hang out, accept me gift,

Lie back an give yer health a lift,

To accept Life's energy is the job that's mine,

So come down to my level an' let in wot's divine.

Mother Nature

☾U

Both the positive and negative attributes are given in this description, to help you better recognise the state in yourself and others. When we repeatedly use an Archetype, it cannot fail to exhibit negative traits, as it becomes overused and not balanced by other states. The climates associated with the months of the year were worked out in the Northern hemisphere, so they may need to be adjusted to suit the Southern Hemisphere and take into account unfamiliar weather patterns linked to climate change.

Mother Nature

Cardinal Earth

September 21st – October 21st

One of the three Earth and one of the four Cardinal states.

Earth and Water, the metaphysical linking of Body and Soul.

The season of Mother Nature is September/October, mid-Autumn, her colour is dark brown, the mix of approximately two parts of the browns of Earth, her first element, and one part of the blue of Water her second. Earth and Water are horizontal Elements, and together they give rise to mud, fertile soil in which things grow, the natural landscape of vegetation. Her time of year is the season of the rich, ripened harvest, the healthy growth that she has nourished and fed from the roots. She is soft, mossy, curving with rolling hills covered in greenery, compost heaps, muddy, boggy places and marshlands teeming with rich vegetation, insects, animals and birds. All living things feed and thrive upon her soft bountiful breast. We find ourselves in woods, tropical rain forests, riverside thickets, amid leaf mould, peat and compost which, when decayed, becomes a rich mixture of integrated waste matter, which in turn feeds and enriches the soil. Here all kinds of plants and life forms entwine and grow together. She is the Archetype of the natural and the organic, the fertile earth, fecundity and the cycles of growth. 'The answer lies in the soil'. She integrates, and what is integrated becomes whole, the wholesomeness we associate with  health, which depends on good quality organic foods. Integrity implies goodness, the good quality of

the stuff which keeps body and soul together and the body's processes in tune with natural law. Integrity is also goodness of character. She is the great nurturing mother who suckles her brood and gives nourishment freely to all, without discrimination. In her is the loving awareness that we are all one big family, all of us connected, born and grown from the same roots, belonging together in the kinship of life. Mother Nature is the whole cycle of nourishment, the creation of good soil, the planting of seeds and cultivation of plants, harvesting, cooking, eating and excreting. Her web spreads all over the earth. Trees secretly talk to each other underground, passing information and resources to and from each other through a network of mycorrhizal fungi, a mat of long, thin filaments that connect an estimated 90% of land plants. Mature trees share sugars to younger ones, sick trees send their remaining resources back into the network for others, and they communicate with each other about dangers like insect infestations. This is her Wood Wide Web.

"More and more, in a place like this, we feel ourselves part of wild Nature, kin to everything".
- John Muir

Mother Nature rules your digestive system, your stomach and bowels. If something is unpalatable we say, "I haven't the stomach for it" and when we get scared, "My bowels turned to water". Digestive problems can be improved through her. Just as she digests things that you put in your body or throw into the earth, so she digests all that you receive, the information and experiences you have. She 'chews things over', excretes the bad and  arrives at the real essence of a thing. This is how she gives you true understanding, which comes by pondering on and processing knowledge and impressions. We used to say, 'Read, mark, learn and inwardly digest', not something we hear nowadays. She is the gardener with green fingers, growing food and cooking it into wholesome meals for you in her kitchen, selecting the best, discarding the not so good; and when it reaches her witches cauldron of your digestive system she turns it into all kinds of magic potions, circulating nourishment and health around your body.

"One cannot think well, love well, sleep well if one has not dined well." - Ariadni Ariana.
Slow, ponderous, heavy and sleepy, she works during the night, allowing you to mull things over in your sleep, so you can sometimes go to bed with a problem and awaken with the answer. We say "I need to digest this information", "I need to sleep on it", to "Chew it over". You may find yourself with creative ideas and new aims, as she, together with the Enchantress, has been working on what

you have taken in during the day. By her digestive processes you come to the true goodness of things, and through her you find real meaning and learn to understand what you know. Understanding is to stand under, to  process information, not to argue with or analyse it. To have a *real*isation means that something is now real to you. She is broad, she sees in the round, the whole forest not just the single trees. She has the sense of wholeness and how everything and everyone is connected, all part of the chain of life. This is how superstitions work; she sees the connections between things and notices how one thing can be a sign to something else. The word comes from Latin, meaning to stand over or above, giving a wider view. Mother Nature gives you the wisdom to benefit the whole, giving all a chance to grow, so that positive things are kept alive, not advancing one thing at the expense of another. Everything has its season. She is cultivation, and not only of the plant world, she cultivates in all areas, including goodness and truth, so that our inner selves may be as healthy as our bodies. These days very little time or regard is given to self-cultivation. We are losing our faith in the possibility of growing into increasingly wonderful beings, turning our attention instead to the toys and entertainments created by her conflicting opposite, the Logician. We are chasing empty satisfactions from the outer world, polluting the minds and inner lives of our children with the projected nightmares, violence and cruelties of others in video games and other meaningless pursuits. Certainly, some skills can be learned through them, they're not all bad, but they are so very isolating, causing distance between us and neglect of the richness in our own beings. The technology of the Logician is divisive, whereas Mother Nature connects us together.

I recall a time when we had power cuts and were forced to spend evenings without electricity. We were obliged to light candles, sit together and talk to each other, exchanging stories and more of ourselves. It was a return to a more natural way of being, and clearly one enjoyed by all, for once the lights came on again, there was a mutual sense of disappointment. Nevertheless, now the Logician was back on, everyone went their separate ways. We have forgotten how to be truly together, and without Mother Nature's loving nourishment we become ill, insecure, unhappy and lost, losing touch with what is real and important. To Mother Nature, the conscious mind of the Logician seems to be no more than sunshine dancing upon a leaf. He's so proud of his clever inventions, yet she sees that he has no depth, understanding or wisdom. He rapes the treasures from her bosom, turning them into mass-produced indigestible rubbish that is quickly thrown away, all to make money for the Wise

Woman, turning the earth into a barren, dead desert. The wholesomeness of Mother Nature is being poisoned, as are our hearts, minds and bodies, with food artificially forced-grown with dangerous GMOs, chemicals and pesticides. It is critically important that we restore Mother Nature, for without her humanity faces a serious crisis.

She is the great natural healer, with instinctive secrets of many healing methods, such as putting mouldy cheese on septic wounds long before the discovery of penicillin, and using signature magic to identify herbs and foods to ease and cure specific ailments. She takes a broad approach. Climate affects the magic in plants, and one herb in one place may cure a disorder that would need a different herb for the same disorder in another place. She always heals according to the place where she is, ignoring narrow principles, using her wide understanding to work with time, knowing when to pick a plant to get the most magic from it. She nurses you back to health through her natural methods and diets chosen for each individual's needs. Hers are healing hands, her touch warm and comforting. How common it is for children who have hurt themselves to run to mummy, asking her to kiss it better and give it a 'magic rub'. They still have the instinct that mother can make it all good again. She works in your bone marrow, helping you fight disease and you can feel 'bone tired' when

fighting infection. When your instincts are working you can 'feel it in your marrow', 'feel it in your bones'. Mother Nature is the queen of crafts, the homespun, the making of anything by natural handiwork, using natural materials and dyes. Just as she knits to make garments, so she knits broken bones into wholeness. She is homely, settled, drowsy, comfortable, comforting, secure, cosy, soothing, fat as clay, nursing and suckling her large brood.

Negatively she can be crafty, dull, slow, overweight, repetitive and reluctant to accept the new. She is 'bogged down', and 'swamped', in a 'morass of detail', 'stuck in the mud', 'lost in the woods', without any clear-cut objectives. She tends to overpopulate, although in natural times she used diseases to cull animals, including humans, protecting the web of life until such time as we learnt how to evolve ourselves. Such time has to be now, for the modern methods of the Logician has allowed humans to exceed manageable numbers, causing the extinction of an increasingly large number of species and endangering not just the web, but humanity's existence too.

"We're banging them out as if there's no tomorrow. If we go on like that there will be no tomorrow"
- Richard Gardner,

Your body is a microcosm and Nature a macrocosm. 'As within so without'. The precious metals and minerals which you find in the Earth are also present in your body as trace elements, for she is your mother and she made you in her own image. She knows Acupuncture and how to massage important pressure points, which is her awareness of your network of energy, and how attention and treatment at one place can have favourable influences in other parts, for all is connected to everything else. In the same way, she knows where to place important structures that they may receive the earthly and heavenly influences to aid the purpose for which they were built. Ancient Egypt cultivated her to a high degree, building Great Pyramids in order to capture heavenly and earthly energies. Ley lines are the veins of her body, carrying life to every part, a great web, a network of energies running through the earth. There is heightened power where they meet and cross, so standing stones and circles were placed there by those who were attuned to her, magnifying her power and making it accessible to them in rituals of healing and the raising of consciousness. Mother Nature is ever present, taking over again and again as civilizations fall and sink once more into her breast. We have not yet found how to build an enduring one yet, but the use of this work will guide us towards it. She is the loving indulgent mother who always takes you back until you try again.

She and the Enchantress are your two Cardinal female functions, together they are what you call Witchcraft, which means the Wise Ones. What a terrible name the head-centred religions have given them. The Enchantress is the bewitcher, Mother Nature governs crafts. What is female is innate, automatic and involuntary, and often the more powerful for this reason, and therefore feared by the masculine consciousness under which we now exist. This is why these particular Archetypes have been demonised and persecuted, not just in women, but also in men, denying them an important part of their female selves. She is the Many Breasted Goddess of older times, when the divine was worshipped as female by both sexes. We are knitted in the womb automatically, yet the automatic side of our nature is not taken seriously. If it was, we could apply its powers in wonderfully magical ways and gain control of it, merging it with the conscious mind to create power that is healthy and balanced. We would have power over ourselves, ending wars as we would no longer need to have power over other people, religions or nations to cover up for our own shortcomings.

Mother Nature is simple, honest and says little, for wisdom needs but few words, and when she does speak, her words have weight. She has substance, she is substantial. Most of the cultures that had her guidance and consciousness have been wiped out, with the few remaining on inferior lands, oppressed and unhappy. Fortunately, these cultures, such as the Native Americans and the Aborigines are rising again, and how we need them.  They express much of Mother Nature in their art forms, music and dance, many of their songs imitating the calls of the animals and birds with whom they share their lives. They were often named after animals, birds, rivers, mountains, forests, all parts of Mother Nature, so great is their love and understanding of her. They embody real being. Without her we are rootless, lost and unhappy. There is an increasing interest in cooking, gardening, natural healing and the green and conservation movements speak for her, but it is hard to find her positive aspects in people today. We should seek them out before it is too late, so that she may be brought back to reconnect us to reality, kinship, and security, where we belong. In 1856, the 'Great White Chief' in Washington made an offer for a large piece of Indian land, promising a 'beautiful reservation' in return. Chief Seattle of the Suquamish Tribe replied. This is an extract and it certainly carries weight.

"Every part of the Earth is sacred to my people. We are part of the Earth and it is part of us. The perfumed flowers are our sisters. The deer, horse, the Great Eagle, these are our brothers. The rocky crests, the juices in the meadows, the body heat of the pony and man - all belong to the same family. Whatever happens to the beast soon happens to man. All things are connected. Teach your children what we have taught our children...The earth is our mother. Whatever befalls the earth befalls the sons and daughters of the earth. This we know. All things are connected like the blood which unites one family...Man did not weave the web of life, he is merely a strand in it. Whatever he does to the web he does to himself If all the beasts were gone, man would die from a great loneliness of spirit, for whatever happens to the beasts also happens to the man."

Some key words of the positives and negatives are listed below, together with some of the interests and activities relevant to this Archetype to help round out the picture of its world.

Time: September 21st – October 21st

Season: Mid-Autumn.

Quality: One of the three Earth and one of the four Cardinal states.

Elements: Earth and Water.

Colour: Dark brown.

Conflicting opposite: The Logician.

Complementary Opposite: The Enchantress.

Voice: Deep, sleepy, slow, earthy, soothing, reassuring and comforting.

Body type: Round, curvy and plump. Associated with the digestive system and breasts, which can be large and soft.

Movement: Slow, heavy and ponderous.

Weather: Muddy, autumnal.

Landscape: The natural world, woods, thickets, marshlands, fields of crops.

Home: Handmade furniture and wood. Hand-crafted and woven items with natural materials and dyes, ethnic styles.

Music: Deep Tantric voices, slow, repetitive folk tunes.

Clothing: Plain, simple, hand woven and knitted. Aprons.

Food: Vegetarian, vegan, organic, home cooked meals, home grown vegetables, grains and herbs.

Positives: Fertile, nourishing, feeding, bountiful, integrating, natural, organic, goodness, wholesomeness, wholeness, health, processing, kinship, connections, belonging, understanding, meaning, security, digesting, being, cultivation, natural wisdom, natural healing, crafts, simple, honest, comforting, soothing.

Negatives: Crafty, dull, slow, repetitive, reluctant to accept the new, bogged down.

Career choices and interests: Gardening, cooking, catering, crafts, herbalism, natural healing methods, midwifery, nursing, recycling, forester, tree surgeon, agriculturalist, farmer, weaver, basket maker, knitting, herbalism. All three Earth types may be involved in the fields of social work, community work and caring of some kind.

Reading Materials and entertainment: Books, magazines and television programmes about cooking, gardening, natural healing, country lore, living naturally, and nature.

Other names: Mother Earth, The Great Mother, Mother figure, the Many Breasted Goddess, Lady Bountiful.

"Look deep into nature, and then you will understand everything better" – Albert Einstein

"When we try to pick out anything by itself, we find it hitched to everything else in the universe. One fancies a heart like our own must be beating in every crystal and cell, and we feel like stopping to speak to the plants and animals as friendly fellow mountaineers" - John Muir

How to Practice Mother Nature

Reading the script is beneficial in several ways –

1. It increases your awareness of your Centre.
2. It helps you to identify and recognise Mother Nature in yourself and others.
3. It gives you control over your Mother Nature.
4. As the script focuses on positive attributes, it helps you to purify your Mother Nature.
5. It gives you the opportunity to add more strands of Mother Nature in yourself.
6. You can help others to activate it in themselves.

Reading the script only serves as a rehearsal for the real thing - your daily life. When developing Mother Nature, you will need to follow through by observing your usual behaviour patterns and seeing where you can introduce her energy. Follow positive impulses to do something new, such as gardening, healing, cooking, learning a craft or being more understanding of others. Mother Nature is a Cardinal state. If you identify with and realise you live a lot in Mother Nature, read the script to purify and identify it in yourself. You will understand your own Mother Nature better. If you are weak in Mother Nature and identify more with her conflicting opposite, the Logician, you could find yourself resisting and not wishing to come down to earth. The opposite reaction is also possible, you might feel heavy, comforted, and could easily fall asleep.

Preparing

This Archetype is associated with your digestive system and sleep, so it is better to practice it in the evening or at night. Wear something of the appropriate colour (brown) and style (natural materials, knitted or a heavy woven wool or tweed). To help set the scene play slow, repetitive music or something similar to the singing of the Tibetan monks who make extraordinary sounds, singing as if from the belly, or a recording of forest sounds. If you're outdoors, the sounds of nature will be all around you. First, visualize yourself as a white light in the Centre of your circle, reaching down to Mother Nature to add dark brown to your colours. Let that colour surround you, imagine you are filling up with dark brown.

Keep the awareness that you are the Centre and not Mother Nature. Getting the stance and the voice right before you begin, and being aware of maintaining them as you read, will help in channeling the energy through. It's best to lie down with this one. It's mid-Autumn. See yourself in Mother Nature's landscape, fruits, nuts and crops have ripened and the vegetation is beginning to turn brown. It is dark and you are lying in the countryside with living creatures all around you, or you are inside a cosy cottage. Earth and Water is rich fertile soil which you can smell, along with the other night scents of the earth. As you lie in a comfortable position, bring your awareness to your stomach and abdomen, you may feel movement and hear gurgles. Your voice is slow, deep and drowsy, rising from deep in your belly and chest, soothing all your little ones that you nurture. You can also mother yourself in this Archetype. You become aware of the connections between events, people and all living things. Let the feeling grow naturally and gradually. Try not to act it, you could become trapped in the act and limit yourself. If this state is unfamiliar to you, focus on getting the voice right, think of giving comfort to someone, giving out a sense of security.

Persevere and the other Archetypes will accept that your life has improved, you have a wider understanding of things and are better able to digest, both food and information. Mother Nature will increase your sense of security and improve your diet, sleep and health. Now read the script.

MOTHER NATURE

Earth and Water

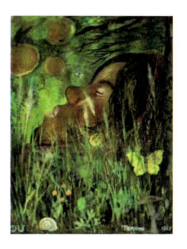

Deep, sleepy, slow, reassuring and comforting voice.

I am Mother Nature, soft, broad breast,

Earth and Water, within my nest,

I suckle, nurture all my brood,

That they may grow healthy, wise and good.

In my fertile soil and compost heaps,

Grows ripening harvest that you may eat.

In my woods and marshlands, thickets entwined,

Rich vegetation, birds, insects you'll find.

Teeming with Life, I nourish you all,

The good with the naughty, the short with the tall,

All living things, all people, all shoots,

You all are my children, from me come your roots.

I'm the Queen of the natural, organic and real,

I grow and I cook for you foods that will heal,

Blending you diets wholesome and good,

I choose for my children only best food.

I digest all you throw in my bogs and my mud,

As I do in your belly, and process your blood,

And all you receive, all experience had,

And remove through my bowels all that is bad.

I garden, I know the best planting place,

I'll make you whole in my healing embrace,

And when you fall and cut your knees,

My instincts put there mouldy cheese.

I'm the Witch's Cauldron that stirs all potions,

Healing herbs and soothing lotions,

I'm Mistress of crafts, all things made by hand,

All materials needed grow in my rich land,

In each body precious metals, minerals lie,

For I've made you in my image, your Mother am I.

Ley lines are my veins, a great web of power,

I know where to place standing stone, magic tower,

And pyramids too, that the Gods may possess them,

Receiving Truths, that I may process them.

As in Acupuncture, with needles show,

The points to make good energy flow.

I'm a web of connections, joining all nations,

No one's a stranger, all are relations,

For nothing is separate, you are all linked to me

By umbilical cords, one big family.

I'll bring you together and make you secure,

I'm loving, indulgent, your terrors can cure.

I integrate, have integrity,

See the whole forest, not just single tree.

Through my ponderous sleep comes the essence of things,

And Reality that true understanding brings.

I'm broad and heavy, instinctive and wide,

Nursing and slow at my comforting side.

In my valleys fair and mounds full-rounded,

My ancient presence keeps you grounded.

I cultivate goodness and wholesomeness,

Simplicity, honesty, kind forgiveness.

Come my little ones, come unto me,

I will reconnect you to Reality,

I'll weave and knit your bones, flesh, cells

Into healthy bodies where blissfulness dwells.

I'm the beauteous garden where once you did roam,

Restore me, re-enter your natural home.

The Wise Woman

☾✴

Both positive and negative attributes are given in this description to help you better recognise the state in yourself and others. When we repeatedly use an Archetype, it cannot fail to exhibit negative traits, as it becomes overused and not balanced by other states. The climates associated with the months of the year were worked out in the Northern hemisphere, so they may need to be adjusted to suit the Southern Hemisphere and take into account unfamiliar weather patterns linked to climate change.

The Wise Woman

Closed Earth

October 21st – November 21st

Earth and Air, the metaphysical linking of Body and Mind.

One of the three Earth and one of the four Closed states.

The season of The Wise Woman is October/November, late Autumn, her colour is the mix of two parts dark brown, her first element, Earth, and one part yellow, her second element, Air. This gives us pale brown, the colour of sand, dust, grains, and nuts. This is the time of year when we store the gathered harvest, when trees scatter their seeds, when some animals lay in their winter stores prior to hibernation or to see them through the winter.

The Wise Woman is a state of consciousness, not a time of life. You don't have to be old to be in the Wise Woman, although living in her constantly is ageing. She can be seen in young children who are wise or who choose to save their pocket money or spend it very carefully. The Wise Woman is the keeper of all treasure, both within and without. Particles of Earth in the Air accumulate and create the sands of the desert. Earth in the Air is dust, we think of dusty roads, paths, ways or tracks. Here we find the traffic and transport which come with commerce, the well-worn tracks of the trade routes, like the Silk Road. She is, by nature, nomadic, going to and fro, selling and trading goods, and even today those who succeed in gaining riches often fly all over the world to do so. If she has to be in one place, she accumulates all kinds of things in her home or shop. The Wise Woman always seeks to make a profit, and when overused she becomes greedy and grasping.

Industrial areas are turned into dust and deserts, the air is polluted by industry and over-exploitation of the earth's resources. 'Where's there's muck there's brass'. It seems that money is the only deity people worship these days, for even in families that are supposedly very close, war breaks out when a bereavement befalls and people fight over the will. The love of money may, or may not be, the root of all evil, but it certainly creates a lot of  ill will. We consider money, goods and financial status to be most important because we have forgotten how to value ourselves and each other. The positive Wise Woman can help us to dig down into our inner richness, the only treasure that brings true happiness. As we evolved, this would do away with the need for money altogether and we would exchange goods, services, and higher energies instead. More life, love, joy and the emergence of our real selves are the most valuable riches of all and the only ones worth having.

In our present way of life, we can recognise other Archetypes working in her service, mainly the Logician who creates new technologies and chemically laden food stuffs to sell us; the Warrior, who will defend her status quo and open new trade routes; and the Joker whose clever manipulative mind is employed in advertisements to trick us into believing that we want all these things. Our current way of life is causing major upheavals to the climate and harming other life forms, making them extinct as we turn the earth into desert. We are overusing her and are suffering the results, paying a very heavy price indeed. These wise words are from Chief Seattle of the Suquamish Tribe. His wisdom saw that the earth would become wasted, but the invaders were short-sighted, they wanted the land and the wealth.

When the green hills are covered with talking wires and the wolves no longer sing, what good will the money you paid for our land be then?"

 The Wise Woman's time is that of gathering, collecting and saving. 'Look after the pennies and the pounds look after themselves'. She is the store house of all that we need, she keeps everything, nothing is ever thrown away, given away or wasted, all will come in useful one day and may even be valuable. It's hers, all hers! She hates waste, 'waste not, want not'. She will conserve and is a natural conservationist. She dries herbs and preserves foods for her winter store. She values respectability and upholds the status quo.

The Wise Woman is a collector of things, she treasures them, and the more she collects the more worried she becomes about losing them, and she is not unjustified in her worry, so she has many keys and locks to keep her goods safe.

This is one of the three closed states, she is the closed doors of the bank, the Mint, The Old Lady of Threadneedle Street (the Bank of England), Fort Knox, and she might lend you what need but you will have to pay her interest. She always has her price. 'There's no such thing as a free lunch'. 'Money doesn't grow on trees'. She is prudent,  parsimonious, economical, the economy, the Treasury, all treasure is hers. She is a very shrewd investor, never taking risks and usually she profits due to her good planning and information. Although 'you have to speculate to accumulate', the Wise Woman will never gamble and can be found guilty of insider trading. 'The plans of the diligent lead to profit as surely as haste leads to poverty'. She is the shopkeeper and a very well-used Archetype in the UK. England has been called "a nation of shopkeepers" (attributed to Napoleon, but was first used by Adam Smith in 'The Wealth of Nations'). Oscar Wilde said - *"Nowadays people know the price of everything and the value of nothing",* yet the Wise Woman knows both, although she is more likely to know the price in her negative and the value in her positive. She can be tight-fisted, holds tight her many bags of possessions, releasing one egg each month from her two little ovary purses, unlike her opposite, The Fool, who ejaculates millions of seeds each time. We say of men who carry small purses, carefully counting out the pennies, "He's an old woman", an alternative name for her in her negative, as it is in much evidence in society.

She runs the world of commerce, is a good accountant and can exploit all resources for gain. Everything has its use, and she knows how to make use of anything or anyone.
'One man's loss is another man's gain'. This is the world of insurance; the Wise Woman finds it easier to die when she knows she's going to be paid for it. Yet, when she's positive she can give you many assurances. She is caring, but not giving. Money and possessions are the only things that really impress her about anyone. She sees it, she seizes it. She is a major player in today's world, where greed dominates all major decisions and we are told "It's good for the economy". 'Money makes the world go round'. She has a great nose for business, including yours, and will stick it in whenever she can. She is curious, suspicious and nosy. The more information she has about people, the more easily

she can exploit them when in her negative. 'Never look a gift horse in the mouth'. She just happens to be at the window, fixing her curtains at the very moment you're kissing your secret lover or burying something you shouldn't. She can't bear anyone getting away with anything and likes to get to the bottom of any mystery. Don't try, however, to find out her business, she is as closed as a clam. She's 'tight' alright.

 She mines, finds the treasure below, is very good at finding lost things. She is careful and cautious, says "Mind out!", she holds on, says "It's mine!". 'A bird in the hand is worth two in the bush'. Her fixed hold on everything, her inability to let go, often results in her suffering from constipation. Mining exploits the resources of the earth, the stones, oils, gases, metals and minerals on which our civilisation depends. Much is stored in her mind, all your experiences and memories; she has a good memory, including racial memory. She tells us to "Keep it in mind". She is shrewd, sagacious, the accumulation of all her experiences resulting in Wisdom. She collects useful gems, treasure, nuggets of wisdom, she is a 'mine of information'. We treasure her within ourselves, she is the provider who always ensures that we have all that we need and can tell us where it is. She is the repository of all things; memory, experience, money, food, goods and information. She is resourceful, she always has resources. 'What you have, hold'.

The Wise Woman is a creature of habit, keeping to well-worn paths and proven ways, always responsible, she takes responsibility. She works out routines and methods and can't bear change, innovation or surprise, which come with her conflicting opposite, the Fool. She is predictable, respectable, likes conformity and disapproves of any behaviour which is unlike her own. She would never dream of doing anything unusual - what would the neighbours think? She has a lot of sense and considers people behaving in unusual, spontaneous ways as having 'taken leave of their senses'. She needs the Fool to bring her some life, to let go and enjoy herself, just as she can help him to take care of himself and hold on to what matters. She is organised, which in an organisation becomes custom or convention. To be methodical is to be organised, thus saving time, energy and money. She budgets, is thrifty, compares prices and knows where the cheapest shops are, ever complaining about rising prices. 'A penny saved is a penny earned'. 'Thrift is a great revenue'. To be stuck in her results in being trapped in a rut and dull routine dominates your existence. She worries constantly (there is so much to lose), she is concerned, she concerns herself about everything, so worry is well known to her, she cares, becomes 'care-worn'. Tracks form on her face as she gathers 'wrinkles' of many kinds. She tells us to "Take care", to "Hold on". She is a good planner who forgets nothing, she can calculate and be oh so calculating, taking everything into account, cautious and self-sufficient. Things have to be done properly, and she fusses to ensure they are. She is a 'fuss-pot'. She is reliable, steady, monotonous and repetitive, recounting the same events over and over again. She is sober, dull, flat, drab, boring, moderate, slow and reserved, which can lead to being mean and miserly. Yet we need her one-track mind to remember everything we have to do to reach our goals, complete with all we need. She exercises caution which calls for restraint, the imposing of restrictions, she takes stock and measures, so we keep a sense of proportion. 'Don't put all your eggs in one basket'. 'Cut your coat according to your cloth.' 'Measure twice, cut once'.

She weighs things up, both physically and mentally, balancing all on her scales. She keeps her valuables in her safe, and keeps us safe, knowing we can rely on her stores. 'Caution is the parent of safety', 'Better to be safe than sorry', 'Take heed'. She uses and looks after everything, spinning, mending and re-using. 'A stitch in time saves nine'. She takes care of us during the winter when we rely on her store of food and seasoned firewood. 'It is best to be on the safe side'. Without her, we break things, lose them, are incapable of taking care of anything, so beautiful items are ruined and we seldom have enough money. With her, we have the ability to balance ourselves, consider the many possibilities and facets of a situation, take all into account, holding back until we take the wisest course of action. 'Look before you leap'. 'Fools rush in where Angels fear to tread'. She is full of good advice. Being Earth and Air, there is no dynamic Element (Fire or Water) in this Archetype, so to be ruled by her is to become corpse-like. Positively, she is the Wise Old Witch of the fairy stories who always knows where the treasure is hidden, which is ever concealed from the unworthy. She will reveal it only to the trusting, giving, innocent one who helps her with her load and shares his/her remaining morsel of bread or sip of water. When you pay her price, she glides over your memory jars, lifting the lids of the wisdom stored down the centuries. She is a wise old woman, gathering sticks and herbs, the old witch with her broomstick, the Baba Yaga of the Russian Tales or the Goddess Kali of the Hindus, frightening, yet a giver of sound advice, the Old Hag, Old Dragon, with a sack full of the wisdom of the ages. The Wise Woman carries inner treasures within her, nothing is ever lost, she saves everything and everyone and when you have purified and fully integrated her, she can save your life.

Some key words of the positives and negatives are listed below, together with some of the interests and activities relevant to this Archetype to help round out the picture of its world.

Time: Oct. 21st to Nov. 21st.

Season: Late Autumn.

Quality: One of the three Earth and one of the four Closed states.

Elements: Earth and Air.

Colour: Sand, tan, pale brown, ochre.

Conflicting opposite: The Fool.

Complementary Opposite: The Actress.

Voice: Dull, flat, careful, monotonous voice rising a little, like sand dunes do. She can sound a little breathy due to all the dust.

Body type: Thin, stick like, round shouldered, bent over with the weight of her load of treasure and worries.

Movement: Slow and cautious, bent.

Weather: Cool, dry.

Landscape: Dry, dusty terrain, a desert

Home: Dusty, full, a hoarder, drab old décor, second-hand old furniture, heirlooms and collections, or a traveller living in a caravan or tent.

Music: Dull repetitive music.

Clothing: Drab, often bought from charity shops or acquired free. Grey suits of the business world.

Food: Preserved, dried foods, pickled foods, stores of grain, out of date foods that she can't bear to waste.

Positives: Wisdom, prudence, memory, caring, reliable, common sense, resourceful, useful, riches, measured, assuring, balancing, responsible, has values, saving, care and concern, inner and outer treasure.

Negatives: Mean, miserly, grasping, greedy, boring, closed, exploitative, nosy, suspicious, a worrier.

Career choices and interests: Banker, accountant, financial consultant, gatherer and dryer of herbs, shop keeper, salesman, travelling salesman, market trader, spinner, reclamation, restoration, archivist, researcher, record keeper, genealogy, tax office, archeologist, merchant, insurance, broker, Chancellor of the Exchequer, the economy, business studies, detective, counselling, conservation, antique dealer. All three Earth types may be involved in the fields of social work, community work and caring of some kind.

Reading Materials and entertainment: Financial Times, Wall Street Journal and other money publications. Business and Collectors magazines, antiques and how to re-use items to save money. How to dry herbs, make jams and preserves etc. Will cut out and collect money-off coupons.

Other names: The Old Woman, Old Mother Hubbard, The Crone, Moneybags, The Miser, Skinflint, a Treasure, The Hag, Old Dragon, Spinster, The Wise Old Witch, a fusspot, money bags, Baba Yaga, some aspects of the Goddess Kali.

How to Practice the Wise Woman

Reading the script is beneficial in several ways –

1. It increases your awareness of your Centre.

2. It helps you to identify and recognise the Wise Woman in yourself and others.

3. It gives you control over your Wise Woman.

4. As the script focuses on positive attributes, it helps you to purify your Wise Woman.

5. It gives you the opportunity to add more strands of the Wise Woman in yourself.

6. You can help others to activate it in themselves.

Reading the script only serves as a rehearsal for the real thing - your daily life. When developing the Wise Woman, you will need to follow through by observing your usual behaviour patterns and seeing where you can introduce her energy. Follow positive impulses you get to do something new, such as budgeting your money, organizing your space, doing memory exercises, drying herbs or repairing things rather than throwing them away. The Wise Woman is a Closed state. If you identify with and realise you live a lot in this Archetype, read the script to purify and identify it in yourself. You will understand your own Wise Woman better. If you are weak in the Wise Woman and identify more with her conflicting opposite, the Fool (Fire and Water), you could find yourself resisting and not wishing to rein yourself in. The opposite reaction is also possible, you may enjoy feeling more collected.

Preparing

Round your shoulders a little so that you are gathered round yourself. Wear something of the appropriate colour (pale sandy brown, with grey perhaps) and style, something old, repaired or dull. To help set the scene, play slow, dreary music. Visualize yourself as a white light in the Centre of your circle, reaching down to the Wise Woman to add sandy, yellowish brown to your colours. Keep the awareness that you are the Centre and not the Wise Woman. Getting the stance and the voice right before you begin, and being aware of maintaining them as you read, will help in channelling the energy through.

It's late Autumn. Imagine yourself in the Wise Woman's landscape, a dry, dusty desert with sand dunes and trade routes running through it, or in a small shop surrounded by many items. Your voice is flat and boring, occasionally rising and sounding slightly breathy due to the dust. Let the feeling grow naturally and gradually. Try not to act it as you could become trapped in the act and limit yourself. If this state is unfamiliar to you, focus on getting the voice right, think of your body, become aware of how it feels. You should feel it closing in on itself and becoming tighter. There is a place for everything and sometimes you need to feel loose (the Fool) and sometimes tight, like a knot in a rope that keeps you safely anchored. Tightness only becomes tension when we stay in it for too long.

Persevere and the other Archetypes will accept that your life has improved, you are more resourceful, self-sufficient and are able to access your inner wisdom. The Wise Woman can help you to be rich in every way. Now read the script.

THE WISE WOMAN

Earth and Air

Dull, flat, monotonous voice, breathy, rising slightly, like sand dunes.

I'm the Wise woman, Earth and Air,
Wisdom is mine, I teach you to care,
Memory is stored behind your brow,
I keep it safe, this is my vow.

I look after you all, throw nothing away,
Everything comes in useful some day.
I don't like waste, one stitch in time,
Saves the garment and stitches nine.

The wool that was once on ram and ewe,

My spinning wheel turns into clothes for you.

I'm sober and flat, reliable, steady,

With well-proven methods I'm ever ready.

With common sense and planned routine,

I keep you safe, I'm wisdom's queen.

I gather, store, accumulate,

My memory can all tales relate.

When you would starve in winter's pain,

I feed you from my store of grain,

For I am the bank, full of resources,

Self-sufficient, repetitive courses.

My possessions are many, through commerce I earn,

I've a nose for business, and yours too I'll learn.

I trade, take everything into account,

And calculate the true amount,

Of all you need that you may LIVE,

My wrinkles of wisdom to you I give.

A mine of information, of useful treasure,

I worry, weigh, collect and measure.

And when you would blindly leap o'er the brink,

My prudence will make you stop and think.

I hold, restrain and give assurance,

I am responsible, I bring you balance.

So naught is lost and naught is broken,

My treasures are yours, but for a token.

I know the true value to place on things,

Make use of them all, what savings this brings.

I mine from the earth the treasure of ages,

With my care and concern, I'll make you all sages.

Racial memory also is stored in my jars,

Come lift the lids and see the rewards.

I'm the Wise Old Lady of the woods,

Who can always lay hands upon the goods.

To the innocent who'll help me with my load,

I'll show the paths to my Treasure Hoard.

All I can save, time, energy, effort,

And so to my Old Wives' Tales come resort,

For what is the gem you hold most dear?

It's your Life, so come, lest death draw near.

Come, come, there's not a moment to waste,

Make use of the sands of time, make haste,

My dears, be no more death's old slave,

My dears, it's your very LIVES I'd save.

The Air Archetypes

The Observer

✳︎⊕

Both the positive and negative attributes are given in this description, to help you better recognise the state in yourself and others. When we repeatedly use an Archetype, it cannot fail to exhibit negative traits, as it becomes overused and not balanced by other states. The climates associated with the months of the year were worked out in the Northern hemisphere, so they may need to be adjusted to suit the Southern Hemisphere and take into account unfamiliar weather patterns linked to climate change.

The Observer

Open Air

November 21st – December 21st

One of the three Air and one of the four Open states.

Air and Earth, the metaphysical linking of Mind and Body.

The season of the Observer is November/December, early Winter, his colour is saffron yellow, golden brown, as dry stalks and straw, the mix of approximately two parts of the yellow of Air, his first element, and one part of the brown of Earth, his second.

His landscape is a bare skeletal world, the grass is flat, the leaves have fallen from the trees, stalks are dry and dead, the fields are bare and nothing is hidden by foliage. Many things are clearly revealed and things that were not seen before are made plain. And so he explores the naked facts, sees the bare frame, the bare bones of any situation or subject, revealing people's states, reasons and motives, stripping everything right down, removing all extraneous factors to the true evidence of what is actually there.

The domain of the Observer is space, the earth's atmosphere, the heavenly bodies and the stars, and in you he is situated slightly above and behind your head. The air surrounding the earth and your body is composed of various gases, which are essential for every form of life. It is also space created between yourself and other people, withdrawing and allowing his penetrating gaze to allow you to be objective, to hover

outside of social and emotional connections in a state of pure detachment. Free from the blinkers of likes, dislikes, opinions and experiences, emotional reactions, feelings and moral judgements, he sees with no preconditioned factors whatsoever. The Observer is a discoverer, he uncovers. From high in his Observatory his eyes range across the cosmos, far beyond the horizon, looking at the skies though his telescope, finding new stars and planets, Astronomy, Mathematics and Science, although it is with the Logician that they are developed. Gazing with cool observation at the heavens and all that is happening on the earth, he is uninvolved, indifferent and unmoved, expressionless, the Archetype with the least animation. He seeks to discover the laws which govern the universe, which necessitates objectivity, detachment, separation and independence.

"Open thou mine eyes, that I may behold wondrous things out of thy law." - King James Bible

This is to be impartial, to look on from a distance and to be attentive. It is only by creating distance, breaking with the past and going far away that we can explore and discover. The Observer separates himself from the customs of time and place, never becoming involved in the mundane world, ever viewing it as from afar with nothing to distort his vision. They say that travel broadens the mind. By going to different countries and experiencing their cultures we realise that there are other ways of being, thinking and behaving. In some ancient cultures, students were advised to travel but to stay for no longer than two years in any one country, lest they be conditioned by it. We see Observer and some Fool qualities represented by the oriental sage, the wandering guru, the yogi who is attached to nothing and no one, has no desires or connections.

"Peace is its own reward." - Mahatma Gandhi

Seeing the truth can be uncomfortable, whether about ourselves, other people or society. We prefer to avoid looking at things that disturb our narrow outlooks and will create groups to conspire against it, supporting each other in seeing only what we want to see, denying ourselves the opportunity to be enlightened and truly free.

Peace is not a relationship of nations. It is a condition of mind brought about by a serenity of soul. Peace is not merely the absence of war. It is also a state of mind. Lasting peace can come only to peaceful people." - Jawaharlal Nehru

Removing yourself physically, mentally and emotionally from a situation helps you to see it from a different perspective.

"Taking time to do nothing often brings everything into perspective." - Doe Zantamata

You must have an open mind with no preferences, desires or notions in order to have a true viewpoint on things. His far-ranging, far-reaching eyes bestow the gift of really seeing. The explorer will have some aspects of the Observer and also the Warrior, who has the drive and courage to get out there. The Observer will feature in law, where objectivity is necessary to uncover the truth, and with the Logician he may be a scientist, exploring life in a laboratory with his 'x-ray' vision. It is fascinating that quantum physics now reveals that at the very smallest parts of ourselves we mirror space, we are made up of nothing but space with little twinkling lights. We are stardust. All is energy. 'As above, so below', 'As without, so within' is true.

"We do not see things as they are; we see things as we are." - Anais Nin

All good artists and art teachers will tell you the same thing - it's about learning to see. To see what's actually there and not what we think is there, not what we think we see. A common mistake with beginners is when drawing the face, they give it a flat head, both from the front and in profile. In life we are involved with each other and therefore only usually look at a person's features from the eyes down, which we usually place too high in a drawing. The skull is almost invisible to us, we more or less leave it out. When we study it, we draw an oval shape and learn that the eyes are actually half way down, and in profile the skull extends a considerable distance. When painting a tree, we see that it is not just one colour, there may be many; shades of green, yellows, browns, blue and purple shadows. Training the eye to see is essential, learning to look and represent what is actually there is the basis of good drawing. This illustrates how in other ways we blind ourselves from realities and distort them. Try it, and see if you can surprise yourself with how you start to see more, and to see in a different way in all areas of life. This objectivity is a liberating gift.

"What I dream of is an art of balance, of purity and serenity devoid of troubling or depressing subject matter - a soothing, calming influence on the mind." - Henri Matisse

The Observer bestows the gift of inner peace, so necessary in our busy, demanding lives. The conflicting opposite of the Observer (Air and Earth) is the Actress (Water and Fire), and many women often find the Observer difficult. There is still a social bias to encourage them into the

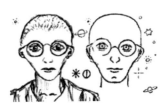
Actress, a state which does come more naturally and easily to them. In addition, they are directed towards their appearance, body shape, fashion and make up, reinforcing conditioned stereotypical roles. Many people who live a lot in the emotional, expressive Actress may run screaming from the room when asked to practice the Observer, shrieking, "It's like being dead!" Well actually, that's not a bad description, for this state does remove you from your interaction with everyone and everything around you. To enter into him creates absolute stillness in body, mind and emotions, rather like being a camera, looking and recording, but high above all the action, withdrawn and distant, fully present in the moment. This appears like the detachment of death. The Buddhists call it a state of Nirvana where one can see through all life without being affected.

"If you are depressed, you are living in the past,
If you are anxious, you are living in the future,
If you are at peace, you're living in the present." -Lao Tzu

To use this state will induce blissful inner peace, tranquillity, calming your anxieties, fears and negative emotions. Meditation is a way of entering the Observer, and a large part of Buddhism and Taoism is an instruction in how to cultivate him. It is of interest that his colour, saffron, is often worn by Buddhists.

"To know Tao, meditate and still the mind." - Loy Ching Yuen
"Peace comes from within. Do not seek it without." - Buddha.
"The sole art that suits me is that which, rising from unrest, tends toward serenity." - Andre Gide

Beginning meditation can be difficult, we meet inner resistance, fidget, can't still our minds, become bored and are aware of aches and pains. Practicing the Observer script is an easier way, gradually adding him to your Archetype repertoire until you find yourself wanting to meditate and finding it easier to return to that peaceful, still place. Retreats are a popular way of getting away from it all, allowing us to gain perspective and be refreshed in a calm and contained atmosphere.

"The quieter you become, the more you are able to hear." (and in this case, see) - *Rumi*

"You can observe a lot by just watching." - Yogi Berra

"Looking behind I am filled with gratitude,

Looking forward I am filled with vision,

Looking upwards I am filled with strength,

Looking within I discover peace" - *Q'ero people of the Peruvian Andes*

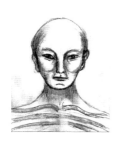

Some cultures of the East and some Christians have gone to extremes in their attempts to fully inhabit the Observer, with prolonged fasting, mortification of the flesh by beating the body, and through various acts such as lying on beds of nails to drive the self out, free of all sensation of the body. (This is not the same as masochism, which is sexual gratification from pain). The Patriarch plays a part here too, inflicting a sense of guilt about the body and so seeking to escape it. Taken to this unhealthy level, there is a complete detachment from life which in itself ceases to matter, so in a negative sense this does become death-like, the skeleton with his hourglass and scythe, an image of this Archetype taken to its limits. Taken to the extreme, movement and taking action become impossible. To a lesser extent, it can be seen in some old people who cease to care for themselves. The Wise Woman (Earth and Air) and the Observer (Air and Earth) share the same two Elements, and neither have the life-giving qualities of Fire and Water, the two dynamics. She is corpse-like and he is a skeleton. We are challenged to inject life into them, which can only be done by balancing them with other states. Negatively, the Observer is callous, impersonal, uncommitted, indifferent and toneless, becoming inarticulate and losing all power of expression. It is not unusual for opposite Archetypes to form relationships and marriages, as 'opposites attract'. You may recognise one partner in the Observer and the other in the Actress. They each have what the other needs, but in some cases, instead of exchanging their qualities, she will complain about his callous lack of emotion and he will accuse her of being hysterical. This is not an unfamiliar scenario.

"We can never obtain peace in the outer world until we make peace with ourselves."

- Dalai-Lama XIV

Using the Observer will give you the ability to truly see truths and yourself as you are now, and the next individual steps to take that will uncover and reveal your true identity.

"The peace in the sky, the peace in the mid-air, the peace on earth, the peace in waters, the peace in plants, the peace in forest trees, the peace in all Gods, the peace in Brahman, the peace in all things, the peace in peace, may that peace come to me." - Rig Veda X

Some key words of the positives and negatives are listed below, together with some of the interests and activities relevant to this Archetype to help round out the picture of its world.

Time: November 21st – December 21$^{st.}$

Season: Early Winter.

Quality: One of the three Air and one of the four Open states.

Elements: Air and Earth.

Colour: Saffron yellow, golden brown.

Conflicting opposite: The Actress.

Complementary Opposite: The Fool.

Voice: He does not normally speak, but for the purposes of invoking him, a toneless, completely flat, quiet, expressionless, disembodied voice, coming from afar, barely audible.

Body type: Skeletal. Centred in the aura slightly above and behind the head.

Movement: He would not normally move and is likely to sit in a meditation pose.

Weather: Cool, airy, clear skies.

Landscape: Sparse, the land devoid of foliage, with everything dying off for the winter season. High up, with an expansive viewpoint of land and skies.

Home: He has no wish for a home, lives in a cave-like dwelling or wanders from place to place. Wherever he lives will contain the bare essentials only.

Clothing: Robes or anything to hand.

Food: Has little interest in food, but if he is fed, he will have plain dishes such as brown rice and a few vegetables.

Positives: Serenity, tranquillity, calmness, restful, peaceful, penetrating vision, objectivity, reveals reality.

Negatives: Cold, callous, distant, devoid of life, unreachable.

Career choices and interests: Yogi, guru, Buddhism, Zen, Taoism, meditation teacher, mindfulness, astronomer, scientist when combined with the Logician, and lawyer when with the Patriarch.

Reading Materials and entertainment: Astronomy books and magazines, television programmes and films about space. Literature about meditation and universal laws.

Music: Space-like sounds.

Other names: The Guru, the Yogi, the Wandering Sage, A Buddhist.

"God grant me the serenity to accept the things I cannot change, the courage to change the things I can, and the wisdom to know the difference." - Reinhold Niebuhr

How to Practice the Observer

Reading the script is beneficial in several ways –

1. It increases your awareness of your Centre.

2. It helps you to identify and recognise the Observer in yourself and others.

3. It gives you control over your Observer.

4. As the script focuses on positive attributes, it helps you to purify your Observer.

5. It gives you the opportunity to add more strands of the Observer in yourself.

6. You can help others to activate it in themselves.

Reading the script only serves as a rehearsal for the real thing - your daily life. When developing the Observer, you will need to follow through by observing your usual behaviour patterns and seeing where you can develop his energy. Follow positive impulses to do something new, such as learning to meditate, looking at people and things and seeing what you missed before, or stepping back when you feel negative emotions. The Observer is an Open state. If you identify with and realise you live a lot in the Observer, read the script to purify and identify it in yourself. You will understand your own Observer better. If you are weak in the Observer and identify more with his conflicting opposite, the Actress, (Water and Fire), you may well dislike him, and will think it's like being dead. Remember that the Observer bestows inner peace, which is a great reward. The opposite reaction is also possible, you might feel beautifully serene.

Preparing

Wear something of the appropriate colour and style (saffron or dull gold), something loose like a robe and perhaps bare feet. To help set the scene, play spacey, sparse sounds or music, nothing emotional. First, visualize yourself as a light in the Centre of your circle, reaching up to the Observer to add saffron yellow to your colours. Let that colour surround you, imagine you are filling up with a golden yellow.

Keep the awareness that you are the Centre and not the Observer. Getting the stance and the voice right before you begin, and being aware of maintaining them as you read, will help in channelling the energy through.

It's early winter. Imagine yourself in the Observer landscape, you are far above, perhaps on a mountain, sitting at the entrance of a cave looking down, even floating slightly in space. This Archetype is associated with the part of your aura slightly above and behind your head, so focus here as you read the script. It is as if you are in the Air, floating slightly above the Earth. All is bare, the leaves have fallen from the trees, the vegetation has died down, it is a bare scene, you see through everything clearly. Sit comfortably, crossed legged if possible, as if to meditate. Your voice comes from afar, with no intonation, barely audible, you hardly move your lips. In this state you would not speak at all but you need to read the script to help you into it. Give it no interpretation or expression whatsoever. Let the feeling grow naturally and gradually. Try not to act it as you could become trapped in the act and limit yourself. Focus on removing as much as you can from your voice and letting a stillness settle in you. You might want to sit up on something to lift you and detach you from the scene.

Persevere and the other Archetypes will accept that your life has improved, you are more serene and objective. The Observer gives you a greater sense of peace and perspective. Now read the script.

THE OBSERVER

Air and Earth

Flat, toneless, disembodied voice, coming from afar, barely audible.

Air and Earth, the Observer am I,

Suspended afar, high in the sky,

I take a step back, withdraw from the scene,

Stripped of involvement, as trees are of green.

In Winter's bareness, lost truths can be seen,

Unblinkered detachment the truth can glean.

With all opinion and feeling shed,

I'm objective to all that is done, that is said.

My distance shows me events from afar,

Shows us all clear, as we actually are,

Through my x-ray vision all is revealed,

Falseness, pretence cannot be concealed.

To my penetrating gaze all is exposed,

I see what is, what is there is disclosed.

An independent view, unaffected by the mass,

Untouchable, incorruptible, my telescopic glass

Makes hidden motives visible, lets no secrets pass,

On bare essentials focused, I see the soil beneath the grass.

Through meditation comes the bliss of inner stillness,

I'm a slim, golden Buddha with infinite patience.

True seeing with clarity, reality uncovers,

Without blindly accepting the viewpoint of others,

I see for myself all that we lack,

And all that we have, in skeletal fact.

Placed far above the presupposed,

I face what is, detached, composed.

Remote in my Observatory I gaze at planets, stars,

Suspended like a camera, recording Earthly wars,

And joys as well, they move me not,

My placid plane remains, come what.

Outside the world of ego, I see virtues, I see flaws,

And put Life in perspective, discover Cosmic Laws.

Outside the world of doing, outside the world of speech,

I see the Metaphysics we need to heal the breach.

My eyes see what to recommend,

To bring illusions to an end.

I am the bare bones, I am the frame,

Upon which to build your own true name.

A cool, serene and tranquil place,

Calm and restful outer space.

I am free from worldly cares,

I am the one who stops and stares.

I open your eyes that you may see,

The Truth that is Reality,

That you may move in clarity,

My gift is peace, serenity.

Universal Laws I uncover,

That the Divine within, you can discover.

Far ranging, far reaching across earth and skies,

I'm the all directional, all seeing eyes.

The Logician

Both the positive and negative attributes are given in this description, to help you better recognise the state in yourself and others. When we repeatedly use an Archetype, it cannot fail to exhibit negative traits, as it becomes overused and not balanced by other states. The climates associated with the months of the year were worked out in the Northern hemisphere, so they may need to be adjusted to suit the Southern Hemisphere and take into account unfamiliar weather patterns linked to climate change.

The Logician

Cardinal Air

December 21st – January 21st

Air and Fire, the metaphysical linking of Mind and Spirit.

One of the three Air and one of the four Cardinal states.

The Logician's colour is the mix of two parts yellow, his first element, Air, and one part red, his second element, Fire, which gives us bright yellow with an orange tinge, the colour of sunshine and amber. The Mind is lit by the Spirit, making it shine brightly. Light in the air is sunlight, the sharp, straight, penetrating beams which chase the darkness away. The Logician's energy comes from the sun, his time is mid Winter, he is centred at the top of your head, the part which the sun strikes first, brightening your mind so it can see clearly to investigate, analyse and gain insight. As this part of the brain reaches upwards to the light, the skull is shaped accordingly, creating an 'egg head'. He is one of the four cardinal Archetypes and therefore extra powerful.

The Winter Solstice falls on December 21st, which is celebrated with fires, torches, lights and the Yule Log, which is the last of the old year from which is lit the log of the new, representing the return of the light, when the days lengthen and the nights become shorter. Rituals to celebrate this have been practiced from ancient times. Christmas is a takeover of the Pagan celebration when the coming of the new light is given a Christian meaning with the birth of Christ. At Christmas, everything shines; the Star of the East, lights on the tree, candles, tinsel, gold, sparkly decorations and bright wrapping papers and cards.

The icon of the Madonna and baby is not original to Christianity, there are images from ancient Egypt showing the Goddess Isis holding the baby Horus who represented the sun, which is almost identical to later Christian images. Ancient Egypt  spanned a period of more than 3,000 years and for much of that time the strongest Archetypes were Mother Nature and the Enchantress, both of whom are body and soul-centred and also Cardinal Archetypes, which is why their influence lasted for so long. Many of their Gods and Goddesses had human bodies with animal or bird heads, relating to the connections with nature, and they also believed in the importance of the dream world and the survival of the soul after death. The Pharaoh Akhenaten was awakened to the existence of the Logician, we see images of him and his wife/consort, (thought to have been Nefertiti), holding up cups to catch the golden rays of the sun. He attempted to introduce the Logician, so that a brighter solar intelligence could be brought to the lunar consciousness of the time. He founded a new cult, but the old ways were too fixed at that time. Now we find ourselves with the opposite predicament, with the Logician ruling the world, Mother Nature being destroyed and the Enchantress dismissed as deluded. During their times, the Moon was considered to be important and people were attuned to it, but now they are called 'lunatics' as if insane. History points to the advent of the Logician. Some seeds of him were planted by Moses who also favoured the Patriarch Archetype, and then came the Protestant reformation in Great Britain from the early 1500s to the late 1600s, which heralded a great surge of the Logician. The Patriarch tried to suppress him, burning him as the free thinker but the Logician prevailed and is now the ultimate authority, insisting on referencing everything to himself; to science and logical thinking, whilst ignoring the wisdom of Water and Earth. The world is addicted to the wonderful technology he has delivered, it is so magical that he has been elected the new God. All must bow down to the scientist and technician. If something is not 'scientific' it is not taken seriously. His victory is almost total. We now live in a world of 'solatics', those who are mad from too much solar consciousness.

His is a landscape of laboratories and factories, where he puts the Worker to use and mass-production takes place; taking precedence over quality. His is a world of skyscrapers, aspiring and urging ever higher upwards towards the sun, his source of power. His buildings are tall, straight, narrow and airy, metal, concrete and glass, far above the ground, separating people into isolating boxes, inhibiting the sense of community. His is a vertical line, looking up into space and down into the atom and, although cut off from nature, there is something insectile about him, his inventions becoming more insect-like in shape, such as flying spy cameras, drones and fighter aircraft. Most insects fly. His focus is in the air and space, reaching ever further up and out. His narrow beam can shine only upon a small part at a time. He has replaced Mother Nature's natural web with a technological one, which connects people from afar, but divides us from those next to us. Originally, the word 'broadcast' described a method of sowing seeds from a basket to ensure wide distribution (Mother Nature). The Logician is a magician, a wizard, but the modern wizardry of his technology and genetic engineering has become a threat to organic life, creating pollutants and poisons that are thrown into mountainous landfills and seas. He is even filling outer space with his discarded rubbish.

"You want to reclaim your mind and get it out of the hands of the cultural engineers who want to turn you into a half-baked moron consuming all this trash that's being manufactured out of the bones of a dying world" - Terence Mckenna.

He has, however, many positive qualities. He is bright and brilliant, he looks into things and examines them, probes and analyses with accuracy in laboratories, law courts, surgeries and any other places where questions are asked and investigations carried out. He is clever, intelligent, your intellect, he can 'throw new light' on a  problem, 'bring facts to light', he 'enlightens' you, like 'a light bulb going on in your head,' 'you see the light', he allows you to 'shine', to stand out as the 'brightest'. He is curious, he has an enquiring mind, he follows straight, rational, logical lines, as sunbeams are straight and unbending. He computes, he invents and uses computers, tablets, mobile phones and calculators. Through his investigations, conclusions are reached and new inventions created. His brilliant mind has invented a technology on which the world now depends. Many women were pioneers, such as Hedy Lamarr and Ada Lovelace, but few have received the credit they deserve. Enlightenment comes with insight, he illuminates your mind as he does your environment. At the flick of a switch, let there be light. His thoughts are fast, he likes mental arithmetic, quick calculations and puzzles, he thinks with 'the speed of light'. His new technologies work at an increasingly rapid rate, mass producing them on machines and robots. He sharpens your intellect as you compete to be the quickest and the brightest, a person's worth being measured only by the I.Q. (Intelligence Quotient), with arts, crafts and Emotional

Intelligence relegated to inferior status. His mental processes are rather like those of a computer and now that our 'educational' system is in his service you say your minds are like computers and children are forced along the same lines of study, obliged to choose from a narrow curriculum, with no training in more practical, wiser or artistic subjects which may suit them better. No wonder teenagers are bored and spend much of their time on devices, escaping into the artificial world he has made, or vandalising their neighbourhoods.. He's so bright and quick, speeding your thoughts and machines. Speed is imperative to him; faster internet, faster cars, how fast his rocket ships hurtle through space, nations competing in the 'space race', deluding himself into thinking that once he has ruined the earth he can simply colonise other planets.

The Logician loses touch with the practical world and, together with the Patriarch, can become the 'absent minded professor'. The sun is so bright, he is 'blinded by science'. We are warned not look directly at the sun lest we damage our sight. Now that his importance has been so greatly overrated, his negative side increases. He is superficial, artificial, substituting experience with theory and technique, ruthless as the desert sun with no concern for the needs of the Earth which he concretes over any time he has a chance.

"They paved paradise and put up a parking lot" - Joni Mitchell

He thinks we don't need Mother Nature anymore as he can grow food in his laboratories and force-grow foods with chemicals and GMOs which are killing the bees and many other creatures on whom the web of life depends. He has blinded himself in reaching for and looking at the sun. He has blinded us all with science, and he could destroy all by nuclear fission, burning us as his source of power, the sun, burns. He can set our planet alight, burning it to almost nothing. Global heating is making this increasingly likely. Unless we change, we face human extinction, but Mother Nature will revive and no doubt be happier without us. His separative influence causes so much unhappiness and insecurity, never before have there been so many people, yet so much loneliness as people find communication with others more and more difficult. Many of us are living alone, people seem unable to commune much anymore, other than through machines. His devices are divisive. Having no Water, he has no humanity and doesn't care for it, he is fixed on theory which can take any view, wafting you into nebulous intellectualism where you can easily lose touch with reality and end up with a plethora of concepts, one as good as another. He can analyse and 'prove' anything out of existence, even us.

"The mind is the greatest slayer of the real" - Madame Helena Blavatsky

He has filled our cities with light, blinding us to the stars at night or the cycles of the moon. He has gone to our heads, he dismisses our creative imaginations and the ancient wisdom of our souls, which he has deemed outdated, yet, ironically, his researches and experiments usually come to conclusions that have been around for centuries. He is in fashion, as he rushes us towards his latest gadgetry. We have come to believe that only machines can become more wonderful and are deluded into neglecting the tremendous power and magic in ourselves. In spite of seeing, in part, how his own brain works, he still doesn't make the connections with the real world.

"A typical neuron makes about ten thousand connections to neighbouring neurons. Given the billions of neurons, this means that there are as many connections in a single cubic centimetre of brain tissue as there are stars in the Milky Way galaxy." - David Eagleman

The Logician has given so many of us a more comfortable world, where we are living longer and have more choices, but we must balance him with other Archetypes and prevent him from negating other paths to knowledge while we still have time. He thinks he can do it all himself, failing to recognise that how he sees is dangerously limited and that he needs the input of the other Archetypes to enhance his shining mind. He experiments with life-extending genetics and drugs, and can't see that evolving our consciousness is the only safe and real way. He has the ability to throw light on many of our inner experiences, our dreams, intuitions, instincts and other involuntary behaviours, affording us greater insight into ourselves. If we learn how to use him positively, his cleverness would lead us to our own transformation, inspiring us to aspire and evolve. Our whole bodies and beings need to reach for the light, not just our superficial thought patterns. He can shine brightness on confusion, and light our way, showing us the straightest, fastest paths to our greatness.

Some key words of the positives and negatives are listed below, together with some of the interests and activities relevant to this Archetype to help round out the picture of its world.

Time: December 21ˢᵗ – January 21ˢᵗ.

Season: Midwinter.

Quality: One of three Air and one of the four Cardinal states.

Elements: Air and Fire.

Colour: Bright yellow.

Conflicting opposite: Mother Nature.

Complementary Opposite: The Joker.

Voice: Fast, metallic, robotic voice, like a computer, empty of feeling and emotion.

Face Type: Long and thin with a high forehead and 'egghead' shaped skull.

Body type: Thin and long with little flesh or muscle.

Movement: Robotic.

Weather: Cold bright sunlight.

Landscape: Tall buildings, roads, cars, cities with the earth paved over and many lights.

Home: A laboratory, minimalist style, glass, concrete and metal architecture, square and tall. Any art will be abstract, walls mainly white.

Clothing: Laboratory coat, space suit, clothing with embedded technology.

Food: Fast foods, microwaved, processed artificial food with GMO's.

Positives: Intelligent, bright, clever, brainy, brilliant, inventive, fast, insightful.

Negatives: Blinded by science, unrealistic, artificial, divisive, unfeeling.

Career choices and interests: Scientist, mathematician, lawyer, technician, computer programmer, inventor, space travel, mathematician, nuclear power, nano technology, examiner, modern medicine.

Reading Materials and entertainment: Anything to do with science, technology and mathematics, gadgets, modern medicine, space, computer games.

Music: Technical, artificial, computer-synthesized.

Other names: Egghead, a brainbox, whizz kid, a boffin, a geek, Wizard.

How to Practice the Logician

Reading the script is beneficial in several ways -

1. It increases your awareness of your Centre.

2. It helps you to identify and recognise the Logician in yourself and others.

3. It gives you control over your Logician.

4. As the script focuses on positive attributes, it helps you to purify your Logician.

5. It gives you the opportunity to add more strands of the Logician in yourself.

6. You can help others to activate it in themselves.

Reading the script only serves as a rehearsal for the real thing - your daily life. When developing the Logician, you will need to follow through by observing your usual behaviour patterns and seeing where you can introduce a different way of being. Follow positive impulses to do something new, such as solving puzzles and other brain exercises, learning something scientific or technical or thinking in a more logical way. The Logician is a Cardinal state. If you identify with and realise you live a lot in the Logician, read the script to purify and identify it in yourself. You will understand your own Logician better. If you are weak in the Logician and identify more with his conflicting opposite, Mother Nature (Earth and Water), you could find yourself resisting and not wanting to raise your energy upwards into your head. The opposite reaction is also possible and you might have realisations, like little light bulbs going on in your head. This Archetype awakens your thought processes and is activated by the sun, so it is better to practice it earlier in the day or it may keep you awake at night.

Preparing

Wear something of the appropriate colour (yellow) and style (minimal, a lab coat would do or something space age). To help set the scene, play some speedy, technical, mechanical, computer type music. Visualize yourself as a light in the Centre of your circle, reaching up towards the Logician to add bright yellow to your colours. Keep the awareness that you are the Centre and not the Logician. Getting the stance and the voice right before you begin, and being aware of maintaining them as you read, will help in channelling the energy through.

Imagine yourself in the Logician's landscape, it's mid-Winter, the sun shines brightly, but it is cold. You can imagine standing outside where you are aware of the sun striking the top of your head, or indoors where it is brightly lit, perhaps in a laboratory or other sterile environment. Remember the Logician's elements, Air and Fire, light coming through the atmosphere. It is midday, when the sun is directly overhead, at its strongest and brightest. Stand straight, you feel tall and slim, reaching into space. Your voice is rapid and sounds as if it is coming from a machine, a computer, robotic and metallic-sounding, devoid of feeling and emotion. Let the feeling gro5w naturally and gradually. Try not to act it you as could become trapped in the act and limit yourself. You will notice that your surroundings and your face seem to pale as you lengthen your attention upwards. If this state is unfamiliar to you, focus on getting the voice right. Let it be fast and robotic. Persevere and the other Archetypes will accept that your life has improved, you can think more intelligently. The Logician increases your mental abilities, helping you to grasp things more quickly. He lights up your mind. Now read the script.

THE LOGICIAN

Air and Fire

Fast, metallic, robotic voice, like a computer.

Air and Fire, the Logician am I,
Beams of sunlight from the sky
Strike the top of my head, shine brilliantly,
The sharp, bright light enlightens me.

My keen, intelligent, active mind,
Asks the questions and answers find,
In straight and narrow logical tracts,
My golden beams light up the facts.

Rebirth of the Sun you celebrate

With candles and lights. I investigate,

Invent with my Technology,

The magic of electricity.

I'm the speed of light, devise machines,

Micro-chips and laser beams,

Tablets, iPod, drones and phones,

Probing genes and making clones.

Futuristic android shapes,

Satellites, Wi-Fi, video tapes,

Speeding Rockets into space,

My fast computers lead the race.

My skyscraper world into the sky climbs,

With flashing bulbs and neon signs.

Tall and narrow, airy and straight,

High above the Earth I separate.

I examine, probe and enquire,

To reach ever higher I aspire.

How the universe works I come upon,

As I rationalize, new ideas are born.

I analyse, I'm accurate,

Your darkness I illuminate.

My brilliant, fast, theoretical mind,

Makes you bright, stand out and shine.

I have technique, my clever brain,

In unbending lines insights gain.

As Scientist the world is in my grasp,

But as Wizard I reach for a higher task.

The Way to LIVE I investigate,

My light will lift you, make you great.

My Magician's mind will all problems solve,

Once you aspire to EVOLVE.

The Patriarch

✳☽

Both the positive and negative attributes are given in this description, to help you better recognise the state in yourself and others. When we repeatedly use an Archetype, it cannot fail to exhibit negative traits, as it becomes overused and not balanced by other states. The climates associated with the months of the year were worked out in the Northern hemisphere, so they may need to be adjusted to suit the Southern Hemisphere and take into account unfamiliar weather patterns linked to climate change.

The Patriarch

Closed Air

January 21st – February 21st.

One of the three Air and one of the four Closed states.

Air and Water, the metaphysical linking of Mind and Soul.

The season of the Patriarch is January/February, late Winter, his colour is green, jade, emeralds, the inside of glaciers, the mix of approximately two parts of the yellow of Air, his first element, and one part of the blue of Water, his second.

As the cold Air freezes the Water it turns to snow and ice, particularly in cold high places, giving us snow clad mountain peaks, glaciers and frost in a wintery landscape. The highest mountains are always covered in snow, coldness is associated with height. Silence covers the frozen landscape, the trees are covered in rime, we are in a lofty, pure, white world. At this time of year many animals and birds, such as the arctic fox and hare, the ermine and the ptarmigan turn white. We think of crystals, mirrors, glass, a diamond. To crystallise is to form a pattern, to mirror is to reflect, and to consider and contemplate. When something is frozen it becomes rigid, preserving food, experiences and knowledge. The Patriarch sits in his ivory tower, looking down at all below from his throne, from which he teaches the laws of life and preaches, pontificates and judges. His closed state protects that which is known and true, he freezes and maintains it, rigid around the purity of the Truth.

This is the world of knowledge and learning, and as snow and ice are composed of crystals, his knowledge is crystallised. We associate him with institutions and places where knowledge is preserved in books, in libraries, or relics in museums, wherever laws, theories and dogmas are made, ceremonies enacted, in courts where judgements are passes, convictions are handed down and convictions are held. He is closed and deaf to the words and views of others, he stands in a higher place, he knows the Truth, and all else is mere opinion. As the snow caps mountains, so the centre of the Patriarch's consciousness is the crown of your head, a dome which is reflected in the tops of places of worship such as churches and temples wherein he preaches from his raised pulpit. The Patriarch is structure, his buildings rising high into the sky, spires like icicles, frozen into shape, grand and exalted. He is the Pontiff; to pontificate is to bridge the gap twixt heaven and earth, as we could say that high mountains do, and as his  buildings seek to emulate. Goddesses, Gods and commandments have been associated with mountains, such as .Everest, more properly named Chomolungma, the Tibetan for 'Goddess Mother of Mountains'. It was renamed by the British after the surveyor George Everest. There is Mount Olympus, famous for its twelve Greek Gods and Goddesses and other sacred mountains around the world.

"The high peaks seem to be the aerial for receiving heavenly and planetary messages and energies from above, reconciling them with the forces of the earth." - *Richard Gardner.*

This Archetype is most often to be found in places of learning and religious cults; he is the Archbishop, the Ayatollah, the Priest, the Pope, the Imam, the Druid Chief, the Dean, the librarian, the writer with a wide vocabulary, the teacher, the headmaster, the scribe, royalty, the gentry, nobility (the nobs), the lord and master, the father figure of the main religions, Jehovah, God the Father, represented on earth by a prophet, a pope, a monk, an emperor, a king. There are many Patriarchs whose truths have been contaminated through hypocrisy which is one of his most negative traits, resulting in organized religions and politicians persecuting others and oppressing them. Each have decided that they have the only truth, which must be imposed on others.

"Too often we enjoy the comfort of opinion without the discomfort of thought." - *John F. Kennedy*

This can be seen in Christianity and other religious cults whose image of God is merely the Patriarch. He is the 'bearded old man in the sky'. Followers of these cults have been persuaded that to be Divine is to be like him, and as a result all meaning and vitality is lost and little connection to the Divine is possible. God was made entirely male roughly 5,000 years ago with the patriarchal takeover, a political move which denied women their own Divinity and severed them from their own powers. Jesus himself called them hypocrites, and we can but wonder if he would be happy with what has been done in his name. Were Jesus to appear in any church or similar patriarchal places of worship, I have little doubt that many would call the police and have the dirty hippy carted away. This is a prime example of how an Archetype with too much power can become demonic. A great difficulty has thus arisen about him, in that many who embody him have the form but not the content. They are over-bearing, but have little useful knowledge. Often persons have adopted his authoritative form to teach what is not true, using it for personal power which has invoked a deep dislike of him, but when you have real truths to defend, his form is essential for preserving them. We have all but annihilated his positive qualities in today's culture. The pendulum has swung in favour of the Worker/Slave with the casual 'anything goes' attitude, and standards have fallen. The Patriarch is the custodian of high standards, he ruled until the advent of the Logician, when we rebelled against his stiff, cold dogmas. But, as a result, we have thrown the baby out with the bathwater, condemning ourselves to a society of increasing rudeness, selfishness, lack of good manners, disrespect and sameness. People speak much of respect these days, demanding it but with little evidence of giving it. Being head-centred, he is severed from the body with all its impurities and traces of the animal still active within us, which manifests in the herd instinct, causing people to attack others even slightly different from themselves.

"This holds up your balanced evolution. Animals are narrow specialists, humans on their way to becoming goddesses and gods must absorb all cultures." - Richard Gardner

The Patriarch is the castrated god, avoiding the smelly and unclean body, especially in its lower regions and cannot possibly meet with his approval. His influence has imbued people with shame and guilt about their bodies. He is frigid, anti-sexual and demands that you forgo sexual stimulus while cultivating him, for it distracts from self-development. He dictates that we cover our bodies. This is why priests are meant to be celibate, although many preach one thing and practise another, often going "green with envy" at the fun and enjoyment others are having. Celibacy has its place and is only negative when misplaced, or not by choice.

The Patriarch, when balanced with other Archetypes, is the custodian of universal laws both temporal and spiritual, giving him great and true authority which is awe inspiring, as it is when we look up at a snowy mountain and marvel at its majesty. What he knows is true, and these gems of indestructible truths are stored in the crown of his head. We place crowns on the heads of Kings and Queens to represent authority, the gems in the crowns mirroring the gems of truth they were presumed to possess. Developing the Patriarch will give you inner authority, the ability to see beyond dogma, the ablity to reflect, discriminate, judge, and come to the truth. Without him you cannot make up your mind, but if his grip upon you be too strong, you cannot change it.
"It is the mark of an educated mind to be able to entertain a thought without accepting it" - Aristotle

"You turn if you want to, the lady's not for turning. - Margaret Thatcher.
Margaret Thatcher is a good example of the Patriarch in a woman. Please don't dismiss her altogether, she did many things which caused much dislike for her, but the good she did is little known. She believed she had to be like a man to get anywhere in a patriarchal society. We may not agree with her policies, but she did support women's groups in the background and pointed the way for others to come through.
"Don't follow the crowd, let the crowd follow you" - Margaret Thatcher
Did you know she was an environmental hero? She was the first UK politician to raise the issue when, in the late 1980s, she shocked the Royal Society and the United Nations with her speeches. The issue was taken up by the media and reported by the BBC as 'crackling with environmental passion'. It encouraged many organisations into creating policies on the environment, but of course, the oil companies shut her down. Jonathon Porritt, head of Friends of the Earth in the late 1980s, spoke of the galvanising effect she had on the green debate:
"Thatcher ... *did more than anyone in the last 60 years to put green issues on the national agenda. From 1987-88 when she started to talk about the ozone layer and acid rain and climate change, a lot of people who had said these issues were for the tree-hugging weirdos thought, 'ooh, it's Mrs*

Thatcher saying that, it must be serious'. She played a big part in the rise of green ideas by making it more accessible to large numbers of people".

She had concerns as to the legacy we will leave our children, the pollution, impurities and mess they will inherit. It was obvious to her Patriarch's insight, and she deserves recognition for at least trying to do something about it.

The Patriarch bestows individuality, for just as no two snow flakes are the same, so must you seek and develop your unique true self. He is the ruler, he makes the rules, allowing no deviation. We call a stick that keeps lines in straight order a ruler. He is cold and untouchable, but without him you will never become an individual. To have him well developed means that authority is vested in you, giving you the power to act in your own right, no longer looking over your shoulder to find permission or approval from others. He has high principles, he is the judge and gives you good judgement. He allows you to judge for yourself. He knows and applies the laws, able to discern between the innocent and the guilty and supports the upholding of the law. Depending on the degree of positive development of this Archetype, these laws can be oppressive and punitive or point the way to a well-structured society, teaching us how to refine ourselves and find our innate truths. He gives the commandments, he is as stern, cold and inflexible as the laws which he makes. When these laws are correct, they take you towards more life, and when in power he punishes ruthlessly. There is no excuse for breaking the law. Punishment and reward come in many forms, some call it Karma. We can adhere to a pure diet and be rewarded with health or we can abuse our bodies with too much alcohol, drugs and junk foods and suffer the results. All actions bring a consequence. It is the Patriarch's intent to direct you towards keeping all laws, natural, temporal, and spiritual that you may reach higher peaks of consciousness. He teaches ethics and high morals.

Snow makes things clean and pure, 'cleanliness is next to godliness' All must be kept tidy. Walking in the snow and skating on ice can clear your sinuses and head. Crisp cold air was said stimulate the phagocytes. The Patriarch brings purification with righteousness, correct behaviour and a knowledge of right and wrong, goodness and wickedness. He is the one who will 'clean up your act'. He will criticise faults and mistakes, he is a good critic, able to point out what makes a thing good or bad, whether it be behaviour, an art form or any other endeavour. He is cultured and refined, liking all things created to a high standard and of high quality.

'He who ignores discipline comes to poverty and shame, but whoever heeds correction is honored.' His habitat is clean, he likes order, he gives the orders and when applied to yourself he gives you self-discipline.

"Disciplining yourself to do what you know is right and important, although difficult, is the high road to pride, self-esteem and personal satisfaction". - Margaret Thatcher

He governs good manners so that we may glide smoothly, as on ice, 'oiling the wheels of social intercourse'. 'Manners maketh the man'. He is formal, proper and values respect, demanding it and giving it, something we must extend in order to learn from each other. He will not tolerate impropriety or disrespect. He gives form to things and speaks of behaviour as either 'good form' or 'bad form. He values good structure in architecture, language and society. He is the orator, essential when you need to make a speech at a formal gathering.

He is regal, erudite, cultured, cultivated, learned, scholarly, academic, literary, bookish, highbrow and studious. He reads to learn, and when he writes or speaks, he chooses his words for the greatest import, for what he knows is important. He deplores bad grammar, spelling, punctuation and a limited vocabulary, especially as he has gathered so many words in his dictionaries for our use. We observe the deviation from his structured rules of good language by how people text, type and spell these days. The Patriarch abhors slovenly speech. He is concerned with the word, selecting his words well as he knows that words have great power and he tells us to "Keep your word". You must honour your word, for it is sacred, and to break it is to lower yourself. Keeping your word keeps you noble and honourable. It is an abomination to break one's word, it reveals a weak, dishonourable character. Punctuality and time are significant to the Patriarch. It is rude to be late and to waste other people's time, treating them as if they are of no importance.

"Arriving late was a way of saying that your own time was more valuable than the time of the person who waited for you." - Karen Joy Fowler

The Patriarch is concerned with and measures time, he is a calendar maker and timekeeper. Switzerland is a country which typifies him, known for its snow, glaciers, mountains and cleanliness. It is famous for the precise timepieces made there. He represents quality in all things, beautifully made furniture, furnishings, clothing, objects and cultivation in people. He argues the case for quality versus quantity, something also put forward by Gurdjieff and Gardner.

"All upon this planet has a limited quantum. This applies also to various types of knowledge. Thus if

you have too many people they will have less knowledge. England built up a huge empire on only a fifth of its present population, and there were many great characters among you then. Population must be reduced and controlled if you would cultivate yourselves." - Richard Gardner

Whether you agree with this or not, from the Patriarch's viewpoint there is an urgent need to improve the quality of our beings before we destroy all. Many cultures have the belief that we were once united in a sacred place and should strive to return, but either every cult sells death as the way there, or the notion to rejected it altogether. In his book, 'The Wheel of Life, Richard Gardner has the Patriarch speaking -

"The height of positive knowledge is to teach you how to recreate that which was shattered in you at the Fall, and you will always fall without me. As you should know, my doctrine is based on original sin, The Fall, and all my true teachings are concerned with the means whereby your shattered souls and spirits may be re-integrated. The various pieces of a complete being have been introduced to you in this book. So you see that all maleness and femaleness must be fully developed and totally integrated. No mean task at your present level of development. At present many of your laws are anti-life. As your evolution advances laws need constant revision."

Negatively, the Patriarch is an over-strict disciplinarian, punitive, censorious, disdainful, stiff, brittle, conceited, haughty, aloof, self-opinionated, deaf to others and lacking the warmth of human kindness and understanding. He suffers from self importance, pomposity, self righteousness and hypocrisy. He is dogmatic and non-negotiable, with a false dignity that is easily offended. He is superior, 'holier than thou', sanctimonious, all-knowing, grandiose, pious, high and mighty. We tell him to "Get off your high horse".

"There is nothing noble in being superior to your fellow man; true nobility is being superior to your former self." - Ernest Hemingway

He favours the conservation of tradition and history, but can be over-conservative and the more a person in the Patriarch strives to uphold high minded codes and adhere to traditional standards, the

more cold and inflexible he will be. We had a bucketful of him in the recent past and he still runs a lot of establishments, including the UK Conservative Party, but that should not put you off from availing yourself of the positive qualities he offers. It is unwise to refuse the gifts of any Archetype simply because others have manifested negative aspects of it. Remember that there is also Water in the Patriarch, so within the crystals of the ice there is beauty, elegance and some feeling, as seen in his architecture and beautiful copper plate handwriting.

 Positively he is a benign figure, Father Christmas bringing you a sackful of gifts - individuality, precision, good manners, formality, respect, dignity, inner authority, discernment, purification and good quality of being. He shows you how to be honourable in your dealings, how to use precision and thought in what you say and do. He points you towards what is really important. If you know and can do something really well, no matter how simple, you are already on your way. Knowledge is power and this knowledge will give you power over yourself, the only power that you need and should seek. Self-respect brings you a natural dignity of bearing and a knowledge that, in the most positive sense, YOU are important.

Some key words of the positives and negatives are listed below, together with some of the interests and activities relevant to this Archetype to help round out the picture of its world.

Time: January 21st – February 21st.

Season: Late Winter.

Quality: One of the three Air and one of the four Closed states.

Elements: Air and Water.

Colour: Jade, emerald green.

Conflicting opposite: The Worker/Slave.

Complementary Opposite: The Warrior.

Voice: Lofty, formal, important, carrying, dignified with exact pronunciation, with a slight echo, as if in a dome.

Body type: Erect, stiff with dome-shaped head.

Movement: Dignified, regal, gliding.

Weather: Snow, frost and ice.

Landscape: Snow-capped mountains, icy cold, the land covered in snow, frost and glaciers.

Home: An Ivory Tower, a study, a monastery, a learning institution, university, stately home, manor house, palace. Will own good quality antiques, traditional artworks, heirlooms.

Clothing: Ceremonial robes, formal suits, conventional dress.

Food: Gourmet foods, delicatessen, haut cuisine.

Positives: Individuality, precision, good manners, formality, respect, dignity, inner authority, discernment, cleanliness, purification, high quality, knowledge, pride, honour, elegance, etiquette.

Negatives: Over-strict, stiff, brittle, self-opinionated, self-important, pompous, self-righteous, hypocritical, dogmatic and non-negotiable, self-righteous, superior, judgmental, stern, all-knowing, critical, sanctimonious, pious, deaf, high and mighty, cold and inflexible.

Career choices and interests: Preacher, teacher, writer, critic, script writer, editor, librarian, journalist, clergyman, judge, university lecturer, professor, monk, orator, conservative politician. Facilitates skiing and skating on his ice.

Reading Materials and entertainment: Books of knowledge, the classics, holy books, anything about the law, Debrette's, books about stately homes, history of royalty.

Music: High Church, formal, choral, classical.

Other names: The Hierophant, Archbishop, the Druid Chief, the Dean, the scribe, the Pontiff, the Ayatollah, a snob, the Lord, Jehovah, Yaweh, the Pope, an aristocrat, Father Christmas, Santa Claus when with the Fool, Jack Frost. (Scandinavian legend tells of the son of the god of the winds who brought frost. Named Jokul and Frosti, meaning 'icicle' and 'frost', the names were combined to become Jack Frost).

How to Practice the Patriarch

Reading the script is beneficial in several ways -

1. It increases your awareness of your Centre.

2. It helps you to identify and recognise the Patriarch in yourself and others.

3. It gives you control over your Patriarch.

4. As the script focuses only on positive attributes, it helps you to purify your Patriarch.

5. It gives you the opportunity to add more strands of the Patriarch in yourself.

6. You can help others to activate it in themselves.

Reading the script only serves as a rehearsal for the real thing - your daily life. When developing the Patriarch, you will need to follow through by observing your usual behaviour patterns and seeing where you can develop his energy. Follow positive impulses to do something new, such as gaining more knowledge, public speaking, reading more, writing, learning new words or brushing up on your manners.

The Patriarch is a Closed state. If you identify with and realise you live a lot in the Patriarch, read the script to purify and identify it in yourself. You will understand your own Patriarch better. If you are weak in the Patriarch and identify more with his conflicting opposite, the Worker/Slave (Earth and Fire), you could find yourself resisting and not wishing to become dignified and 'above yourself'. The opposite reaction is also possible, you might feel important and realize just how much you know already.

Preparing

This Archetype is associated with the dome of your head, so bring your awareness there. It is better to practice it during the day but not essential. Wear something of the appropriate colour (green) and style (ceremonial robes, or a formal suit with a green top or tie. To help set the scene, play classical music such as Handel, choral or high church music; anything that sounds dignified, formal and classical. Visualize yourself as a white light in the Centre of your circle, reaching up to the Patriarch to add emerald green to your colours. Let that colour surround you, imagine you are filling up with green.

Keep the awareness that you are the Centre and not the Patriarch. Getting the stance and the voice right before you begin, and being aware of maintaining them as you read, will help in channelling the energy through.

It's late Winter. Imagine yourself in the Patriarch's landscape. You are on top of a mountain, everything is covered in snow and ice, you feel the freshness of the cold air and see the green shades of glaciers below. The light reflects off the snow, you stand tall, above everything and everyone. You are important. Your voice carries authority, it echoes in your head as it does in a domed building. It carries import and significance. Don't rush your speech, concentrate on articulating well, pronouncing all words with awareness of their importance. Your words have power. You can imagine you are giving a lecture or a sermon to help you get the voice, but of course you do not need to actually be in a church or any other patriarchal place. Let the feeling grow naturally and gradually. Try not to act it as you could become trapped in the act and limit yourself. Think of being up high. If you wish, stand on something to raise yourself up and think about how much you know.

Persevere and the other Archetypes will accept that your life has improved. You are no longer threatened by the authority in others, for it is now vested in you. The Patriarch gives you a greater sense of your individuality. Now read the script.

THE PATRIARCH

Air and Water

Formal voice, important, cultured, lofty and dignified, with exact pronunciation.

I am the Patriarch, knowledge is mine,
From my mountain top I bring Words Divine,
In the crown of your head is where I dwell,
Each gem in my crown has a Truth to Tell.

Air and Water form my ice,
As crystallised knowledge, I am precise,
Formal, correct, good manners I teach,
My standards are high, I judge and I preach.

So hear ye and learn, the Master speaks,

These gems of Truth from snow-clad peaks,

Inspiring awe, great knowledge show,

The patterns of Time reflect that which I know.

With honour I speak from my ivory tower,

I honour my word, for words have great power.

Punctual, exact, I do not abuse Time,

For Time is God's grace, within which to climb

To higher peaks, to Evolve, to Live,

The laws of God are what I give.

Obey these laws, learn these lessons,

And know for yourself, not through other persons.

When I grow in you, you will seek,

That in you which is unique,

For no two snowflakes are the same,

I point you towards your own true name.

An individual, not part of the herd,

Authority is yours if you heed my word.

I structure, write, I give respect,

I discriminate, I can select

Right from wrong, with precision,

I make an informed, correct decision.

Raise yourself to a cultivated mien,

Where all is ordered tidy and clean.

Good quality and refinement are mine,

With moral virtue, I am benign.

I have dignity, I am pristine pure,

All that is base in you I can cure.

For when consciousness fell you were filled with flaws,

You will regain perfection through my Laws.

I am the one who gives the command,

That ye shall reach for the Promised Land.

My students, my Eternal Truth,

Is to teach you the laws of Eternal Youth.

I have spoken to you that you may learn

Good from Evil to discern.

If to thine own self you will be true,

The Knowledge of God will dwell in YOU.

The Relationships Between the Archetypes

The Four Open, Four Closed and Four Cardinal Archetypes.

This section is about how the Archetypes relate to each other. To remind you, we see them grouped by their main Element. Each of the twelve Archetypes is composed of two Elements. No Element can exist alone and nor can consciousness arise from just one - fire needs air to burn and water needs a base, no matter how deep the ocean.

They are paired with the three others in turn which gives a maximum permutation of twelve; four times three. It's easy to remember them if you think of the three Fire, three Water, three Air and three Earth ones. Here they are again - .

Fire

Fire with Water (Fool), Fire with Air (Joker), Fire with Earth (Warrior)

Water

Water with Air (Child), Water with Earth (Enchantress), Water with Fire (Actress)

Earth

Earth with Fire (Worker), Earth with Water (Mother Nature), Earth with Air (Wise Woman)

Air

Air with Earth (Observer), Air with Fire (Logician), Air with Water (Patriarch)

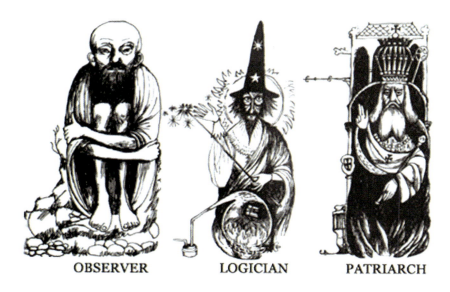

The next thing to know is that each of the four Elements has an Open, a Closed and a Cardinal Archetype.

The Four Open States

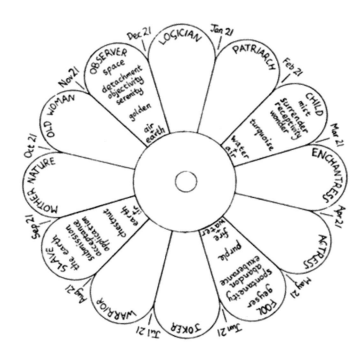

The Four Open States are essential if we are to remain open to change and self-development.

    Open Fire is the Fool, who is open to respond to anything.
    Open Water is the Child, who is open to receive anything.
    Open Earth is the Worker/Slave, who is open to accept anything.
    Open Air is the Observer, who is open to see anything.

The Four Closed States

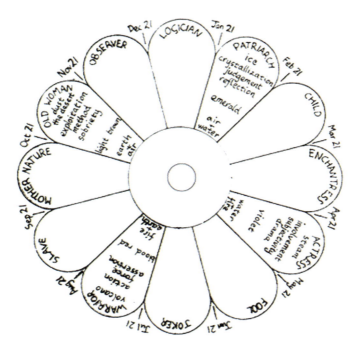

The Four Closed States are essential to protect what we have and have already developed.

Closed Fire is the Warrior, identified with his aims and closed to everything else.

Closed Water is the Actress, closed that she may invoke expressive powers.

Closed Earth is the Wise Woman, closed to all that endangers what we have.

Closed Air is the Patriarch, closed in his knowledge and fixed on the truth.

The Four Cardinal States

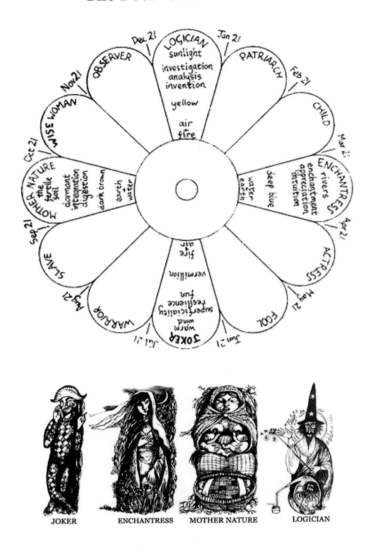

The Four Cardinal States are the most powerful in that I think they can be both Open or Closed.

Cardinal Fire is the Joker who is open to changing the game and fixed on pulling the strings.
Cardinal Water is the Enchantress, open to all feelings and fixed in the guidance of her visions.
Cardinal Earth is Mother Nature, open to nurture all and fixed in her seasons.
Cardinal Air is the Logician, open to new ideas and fixed on a narrow beam of insight.

Grouping them by their Element again, we can see the Open, Cardinal and Closed versions.

Water

The Child is Open, the Enchantress is Cardinal, the Actress is Closed.

Fire

The Fool is Open, the Joker is Cardinal, the Warrior is Closed.

Earth

The Worker is Open, Mother Nature is Cardinal, the Wise Woman is Closed.

Air

The Observer is Open, the Logician is Cardinal, the Patriarch is Closed.

The Six Complementary Opposites

The Six Complementary Opposites

There are six pairs of Complementary Opposites, which we can also call the Natural Merging Opposites, as they blend so easily together. They are always directly across from each other in the circle. They harmonise because, unlike the conflicting opposites, their first elements are the same sex, as are their second. For example, the Actress has Water (Yin) as her first, and the Wise Woman has Earth (Yin) as hers. The Actress has Fire as her second (Yang), and the Wise Woman has Air (Yang) as hers. If you look at the circle, you'll see.

The exception are the Cardinals, the Enchantress with Mother Nature, who have both the female (Yin) Elements, Water and Earth, and the Logician with the Joker, who both have, male (Yang) Fire and Air. The complementary opposites are also both either Open, Closed or Cardinal. Merging opposites frequently manifest in an individual at the same time and he/she can find it difficult to distinguish where one begins and the other ends, but practising each function will define them. Here is a brief description of some of the ways they work together.

ACTRESS WISE WOMAN

The Actress is Water and Fire, the Wise Woman is Earth and Air and both are Closed states. The Actress will get all worked up about any threat to the Wise Woman's possessions, she will shriek at the hint of being robbed, especially if it's her jewellery at risk! The Wise Woman will always make sure the Actress has plenty of jewels, ornamentations, perfumes, toiletries, fancy shoes, outfits and of course handbags, suited to her starring role in the world, sewing and repairing them as needed. She will take care that the Actress does not spend all the money and in return the Actress will make her life more exciting, will dress her up and shift her out of her drabness. Negatively, they can create much anxiety, agitation and emotional outbursts, but positively they are exciting yet sensible about keeping drama in check.

CHILD WORKER

The Child is Water and Air, the Worker/Slave is Earth and Fire and both are Open states. This is the merging of surrender and submission, receiving and accepting. These two together are easy-going, they go along with whatever everyone else wants, impressionable, tolerant, sociable and warm-hearted. They are good workers, like to be of service to others, doing what they're told without having to make decisions. The Slave relaxes the Child and helps to soothe her fears away and the Child brings beauty and faith into the Slave's world. Anything for an easy life, they are easily led, and negatively they can end up in all sorts of messes and find themselves in the hands of bullies, cults and exploiters, but when they find something worth serving, they will do so willingly and beautifully.

ENCHANTRESS   MOTHER NATURE

The Enchantress is Water and Earth, Mother Nature is Earth and Water. These are the two Cardinal females, they have the same two elements, and together are potent. They keep the world going between civilisations, which are called Dark Ages, which is apt as they favour the night and worship the moon. They are natural Wiccans and Pagans. Instinct and intuition are combined in a person with these two, they see the magic of the natural world and in the waters of the earth, growing and working in harmony with them. They are likely to be drawn to interests such as soothsaying, healing and herb magic, and will have an intuitive understanding of other people. Many women, and some men, were murdered during the Witch Hunts for having Enchantress/Mother Nature consciousness, and they are no more encouraged today Femicide is a big issue. If we welcomed them, we would benefit enormously from their powers and abilities. Negatively, they can get bogged down in a sluggish dream world. Positively, their sincere feelings, true understanding, charms and potions bring powerful healing, with a reconnection to the earth and our deeper selves.

WARRIOR   PATRIARCH

The Warrior is Fire and Earth and the Patriarch is Air and Water and are both Closed states. When well-developed, they can be world shakers and changers, with a structured mission and the strength for a powerful campaign. This can be a warrior king, a general, the head of any establishment or business that requires both authority and forcefulness. Together they are chivalrous, like the Knights of Medieval times. Negatively, they can be leaders of an army which marches into a country, taking land, oppressing the indigenous people and imposing a new doctrine. This is the know-it-all-bully, but positively they combine in knowledge and the courage to spread it for the good of all.

FOOL   OBSERVER

The Fool is Fire and Water, the Observer Air and Earth and both are Open states. Together they give us the Wise Fool, one who is open to see and respond to things and receive inspiration. Although able to sit still, this combination is still likely to be tapping a toe or fingers, there will be a restlessness, how much depending on which Archetype is the stronger. They have a fondness of travel and variety, but do not get too involved with any one place or society. Together, they can bring clarity and fun to any situation or project.

The Joker is Fire and Air, the Logician is Air and Fire. These are the two Cardinal males, they have the same two elements, and together they are extremely effective. Resilient, incisive, unfeeling, a witty advocate, able to cope with and trump most arguments. Strong also in using the intellect to manipulate meanings and outcomes, such as the worlds of advertising and statistics. The Joker brings a cheerfulness to the dry Logician, and together they have a sharp mind which works in inventive ways to spark off new ideas and inventions.

The Six Conflicting Opposites

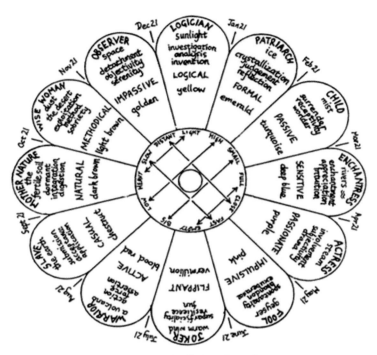

The Six Conflicting Opposites

"It is not our differences that divide us. It is our inability to recognise, accept and celebrate those differences" - Audre Lorde

Two people sitting in a room describe a completely different scene. One will argue that there's a window with views of hills, the other will insist it's a wall with a door and bookshelves. They are both correct, of course, but unless they turn around and see what the other is seeing, they will remain locked in conflict. It is of the highest importance that we reconcile these conflicts if we are to enjoy peace and harmony. We can recognise them within ourselves, between individuals, religions, cultures and nations. Until they are reconciled, there is no chance of mutual acceptance and peace on earth. Opposites attract, but they can also repel. People are drawn together, knowing instinctively that each has what the other needs, yet all too often are unable to exchange their Elements, and so become increasingly frustrated, wanting the other to become more like themselves but failing to realise that it works both ways. Conversely, they may take an instant dislike to each other and become bitter enemies. By practising the dormant other we can understand each other and become more balanced individuals, finding in ourselves what we need, and consequently exchanging a truer, more dynamic goodwill with others. It may be that some people are so entrenched in an Archetype that they manifest a great deal of its negative aspects. It's best to avoid them and find more positive examples.

The wheel above shows six lines going across the circle, each line pointing to the conflicting opposite archetype. They are always between femaleness and maleness, the opposite sex, Yin and Yang. These worlds find harmony difficult because they have nothing in common, being composed of entirely opposing Elements. Fire and Water are opposites, as are Air and Earth, so as we look at each pair, we will see why each one sees the world so differently from the other. Both their first and their second Elements are in conflict, being either male or female, Yin or Yang. In all six conflicting pairs, they make up all four Elements between them, so although they may dislike each other, they also need each other for completion. I mean this in relation to developing and reconciling them in ourselves, rather than always seeking them outside, and I must again emphasise that this does not mean men and women in a sexist sense, but rather the reconciling of opposing aspects of consciousness, whomever they embody. I've given a brief description of how they work together. If you are truly successful in reconciling any two opposites, you will experience a state of superconsciousness with advanced abilities. When Richard Gardner reconciled the Patriarch and the Worker/Slave he found he no longer needed to sleep, he simply rested his eyes for a couple of hours each night and his insights were extraordinary. Alas, it only lasted a year, as he had no one with whom to share his experiences, so he started to sleep for a few hours a night. He did, however, retain that spark of higher consciousness. I never met anyone as perceptive as he. I managed to reconcile a tiny pin head of superconsciousness with the Enchantress and the Joker, being both a professional Tarot reader and Juggler, and it kept me much younger than my years for a long time. Losing Richard, however, was a setback.

OBSERVER   ACTRESS

The Observer is Air and Earth, the Actress Water and Fire, together making up all four Elements. This is a common conflict in couples and in the world. It's distant versus close, detached versus attached, still versus animated. Men (or masculine type women) tend to be more inclined towards the Observer, who is remote, and women (or feminine type men) to the Actress, who is involved. This is a situation that needs balance to bring about understanding. The passionate Actress accuses the Observer of being indifferent and unfeeling, becoming ever more heated in an attempt to get a little emotion out of him, and he accuses her of being hysterical, telling her to "Calm down and stop being so subjective, you're always so worked up about everything." She says "You never say you love me or show it in any way!! I might as well talk to the wall!! You're dead inside!! Dead!!!" I'm sure you'll recognise this scenario. The Observer needs the Actress to help him come to life, to discover his passions and self-expression and she needs him to bring her inner peace and see the bigger picture outside of herself. With objectivity and subjectivity working together as these two are united within you, you would be able to bring benefits to the world with clear-sightedness and passion.

LOGICIAN   MOTHER NATURE

The Logician is Air and Fire, Mother Nature is Earth and Water, making up all four Elements. This conflict is between science and technology versus the natural world, the artificial versus the organic, light versus heavy, analytical against instinctive. To him, she is dull slow and sleepy, with too broad a view, taking her time and doing everything by hand, being 'stuck in the mud', whereas as far as she's concerned he's far too clever for his own good, with a narrow approach which is arrived at too quickly and out of touch with reality. She sees him advancing technology and mass production at the expense of nature through chemically based farming and genetic engineering, with no thought for how it is endangering their home. She complains of the indigestible plastic rubbish he throws into her and he sees her as merely impeding his progress. He cares not how he harms her as his attention is on colonising other planets. With his bright sunlight shining upon her fertile soil, their unification within you will bring your mind and instinct together, enabling you to discover many of the secrets of life and how to use them humanely for the growth and progress of all.

The Patriarch is Air and Water, The Worker/Slave is Earth and Fire, together making up all four Elements. This is the head versus the body, the high against the low. The cold, frozen Patriarch looks down on everyone, particularly the Worker/Slave, viewing her with disdain whilst she sees him as stuck-up and pompous. He is rigid in his icy head and she is warm in her relaxed body. He says, "You are rude, dirty, crude and untidy, socialising with all and sundry, you're an embarrassment. You are uneducated and too stupid to see I am always right. Have you ever read a single book?" She replies, "Get off your high horse and come down to earth a bit, you can't even make a cup of tea, but you think you know everything. You need to relax mate. You'd have no company at all if not for me, you have no idea what's going on in the world." Being in the body, the Slave has no problem with belching, farting, shitting and fucking, whereas the Patriarch likes to pretend he is above such matters. Reconciled, these two will bring together true knowledge which you can apply with practicality, precision and warmth for the social good.

WARRIOR   CHILD

The Warrior is Fire and Earth, The Child is Water and Air, together making up all four Elements. This is the conflict between will and surrender, domination and yielding, hard and big versus soft and small. He says, "You're spineless, wishy-washy, you've no will of you own, you're constantly bullied about by other people and you're too timid and scared to stand up for yourself! You'll never amount to anything." She replies, "You're the worst bully, you're a brute, always bossing me and everyone else about, you're just a big ego who stamps on everything." The Warrior is resolved to reach his target, whether it be for good or not, the Child is aimless, drifting through life, changing her mind at the slightest breeze. When these two co-operate, your Warrior will receive guidance from your Child, which will enable you to direct your own will and take informed action. They will then operate together with dynamic drive focused on a beautiful outcome.

JOKER   ENCHANTRESS

The Joker is Fire and Air, The Enchantress is Water and Earth, together making up all four Elements. Here we have the conflict between flippancy and depth, humour and seriousness, the light and the full, manipulation and sincerity. The Joker keeps you out of your feelings, he is cynical with a good sense of the ridiculous, whilst your Enchantress is sincere, honest, intuitive and aware of the importance of following your feelings. He says, "Always the mystery and the misery, taking it all to heart, weeping and wailing all over the place, why don't you cheer up and see the funny side? Not everything has to have meaning." She replies, "You think you can laugh at everything you unfeeling wind-bag, you're too superficial to know what's important in life. Without my intuition you'd make far more mistakes. Why don't you try love for a change?" The marriage of this pair within you will bring to the surface your psychic abilities and authentic creativity, presenting them to the world with charm, cheerful wit and humour. Reconciled, this pair would be irresistible.

FOOL   WISE WOMAN

The Fool is Fire and Water, The Wise Woman is Earth and Air, together making up all four Elements. This is spontaneity and fun against inhibition and sobriety, leaping to heights versus a flat desert, letting go versus holding on. He complains, "You're such a bore, always counting the cost of everything, worried all the time, same old routine day in, day out, planning ahead, moaning when I bump into things and break them. If the place wasn't so full of old stuff, I'd be able to move about a bit more freely wouldn't I? Why can't you loosen up?" She says, "If it wasn't for me we'd be bankrupt, out on the road with no money, nothing to wear or eat. Someone has to take responsibility because you don't care about anything, you just want to have fun." He says, "He who hesitates is lost", she says, "Look before you leap". It's a delicate balance, knowing when to let go and when to hold on, you need these to be reconciled in order to achieve equilibrium. Then you will have what you need when you need it and can enjoy life to the utmost. Your world will be safe and joyous when you bring these two together.

Regarding the Cardinals, there can also be a degree of conflict between the Enchantress and the Logician which is intuition versus logic, and Mother Nature and the Joker, the substantial and the flippant. This is because their Elements are also of different sexes, but they are not as dynamically opposed as the Enchantress/Joker and Mother Nature/Logician. The Conflicting Opposites can be reconciled as described in the next chapter.

Whilst working on this book, it came to me that it is a truth that if you go far enough in one direction, you arrive at the opposite, in spite of being poles apart. It got me thinking about how this works with the conflicting Archetypes. It has to be something they both do but in completely different ways and from different viewpoints, something that brings them to something the same, where they can merge. I mused on it and did find come connections. The Yin and Yang symbol shows the two dynamic energies containing a dot of the other. The Infinity symbol, a figure eight on its side, connects where the lines cross in the middle, and looking at the DNA, it appears to form a continuous series of Infinity shapes. Perhaps being aware of these connections would make reconciliation of the Archetypes easier. Thank you to Dominic Sladden, who pitched in with some ideas which I've included. This is what I've got so far, some were easier than others.

Mother Nature and the Logician.

The obvious one here is the web, he with his internet, the World Wide Web, and she with her Wood Wide Web, nature connected, with energies running through her in a great web of life.

Both their webs are invisible to the eye, but we can see the results, one on our screens, one in the landscape.

They also relate to smallness, in that she grows life from small seeds and he examines the smallest part of the atom.

The Enchantress and the Joker

Both do magic, he through conjuring, she through sorcery, the moving of energies.

In different ways, they both make things disappear and reappear. He through trickery and illusion, she through apporting.

He makes it appear that people are levitating, she can actually do it.

They both use balls, hers crystal for scrying, his for juggling.

They have curved shapes, she in waves of water, he in flickering flames.

The Wise Woman and the Fool

They both travel, she as the nomad, he as the wanderer. Neither like to stay in the same place, she because of trade, he through responding to something that attracts him. It is now possible for the Wise Woman to establish business premises, but even so, those who succeed in gaining riches often fly all over the world to do so.

They are both featured in fairy stories carrying something, she a load on her back, he with his few possessions tied in a bundle to a stick

They both have balance. She balances the books and keeps everything stored correctly. The Fool is necessary for dancing well, so when he applies himself, he can be great dancer with good balance. Even overweight Fools can be light on their feet.

The Child and the Warrior

Both need to be told what to do. He has to be given his marching orders in order to know what his aims are. He needs other Archetypes for true initiative. Then he will charge off to execute their commands. She drifts from one person, place, idea from another, not knowing where to go or what to do next. In spite of her sensitivity regarding what is happening around her, she needs direction from other Archetypes to steer her out of confusion towards something worthy.

Neither will say no. Both will follow orders.

The Slave and the Patriarch.

Both have an inertness. He through being frozen in ice, she through preferring to lie about doing nothing. Neither willingly move out of their immobility, he by being too rigid, she by being too loose. To get them moving, he needs to get down off his high horse, she needs to get off her arse.

The Actress and the Observer

They both have empty space. He has to be empty of all feeling and reaction, she to allow higher forces to be invoked. They share vacancy as a means to an end; he to see more, she to be more. Stars are significant. She is one on the stage, he looks at them in the sky. They are both starry eyed.

The Reconcilers

The Conflicting Opposites both within and with other people can be reconciled through the use of the four Open states, The Child, Worker/Slave, Observer and Fool. All four can serve as Reconcilers for any of the six Conflicting pairs and are the preferred choice, although I show how other Archetypes could also help to bring greater harmony. The Conflicting opposites are composed of opposing elements, Fire and Air against Water or Earth, Yin against Yan. Harmony is not easily achieved without a Reconciler, which is a combination of the second Element from each Conflicting Archetype. This is easier for them to accept as they already have an Element of the Reconciler in their secondary position. Activating the reconciler on your wheel of consciousness helps you to embrace the conflicting opposite. It doesn't matter if you don't get this all at once, it clicks into place as you see it for yourself bit by bit. Referring to the circles makes it clearer.

"All matter, including you and I, has rhythmic movement within it and our quest should be to create a proper rhythmic harmony within ourselves...you feel happy when you sit near an ocean because your vibrations try to synchronize with the frequency of the waves." - Ed Viswanathan

"That is where my dearest and brightest dreams have ranged — to hear for the duration of a heartbeat the universe and the totality of life in its mysterious, innate harmony." - Hermann Hesse

The Enchantress and the Joker Conflict

Fire and Air against Water and Earth

The Enchantress and Joker are dynamic opposites, Cardinal states and worlds apart, their first Elements being female Water against male Fire. She experiences him as heartless, taking nothing seriously and he sees her as lacking in humour and depressing.

Reconcilers for the Enchantress and Joker

The Enchantress's second Element is Earth and the Joker's is Air, which gives us Earth and Air (The Wise Woman) and reversing them, Air and Earth (the Observer). The open one is the Observer, who provides the Enchantress with the objectivity to get things into better proportion by coming out of her feelings, and the Joker to take a step back and see the consequences of his manipulations. The Wise woman can also help the Enchantress, bringing her out of her dreams and into the material world. She can also teach the Joker to be more caring, but caution is advised, as the Joker and Wise woman together often team up to manipulate and exploit.

The Actress and the Observer Conflict

Air and Earth against Water and Fire

The Actress is a Closed state and Observer is Open. Here we have female Water versus male Air. She experiences him as unfeeling and deadly boring, he views her as hysterical and melodramatic.

Reconcilers for the Actress and the Observer

The Actress's second Element is Fire and the Observer's is Earth, which is Fire and Earth (the Warrior) and reversing them, Earth and Fire (the Worker/Slave). The Worker is the open one, she relaxes the Actress, helps her to come off the stage and blend with other people. She can bring the Observer back into his body and reintroduce him to the practical world. The Observer can then also benefit from practicing the Warrior, who will activate him.

It is strongly advised that the Actress goes into the Worker/Slave and NOT the Warrior, which is Closed, like her, and could be extremely dangerous. Imagine a hysterical Actress together with a rage-filled Warrior. The Actress needs to be well earthed by other Archetypes before she can handle the Warrior.

The Child and the Warrior Conflict

Fire and Earth against Water and Air

The Child is an Open state and the Warrior is Closed. Here we have female Water versus male Fire. The Child experiences the Warrior as a loud, cruel bully and he perceives her as weak, spineless and pathetic.

Reconcilers for the Child and the Warrior

The Child's second Element is Air and the Warrior's is Earth, which gives us Air and Earth (the Observer) and reversing them, Earth and Air (the Wise Woman). The Observer is the open one, he can detach the Child from her fears and let her see the truth for herself. He works well for the Warrior by calming and stopping him crashing about, which allows him to see what he's doing. The Wise Woman can also be good for the Child, she can give her something to care for, like a pet, and close her down to the bombardment of impressions she receives. She can restrain the Warrior, allowing him to weigh up his next move.

The Worker/Slave and the Patriarch Conflict

Air and Water against Earth and Fire

The Worker/Slave is an Open state and Patriarch is Closed. This is female Earth versus male Air. The Worker/Slave sees the Patriarch as a pompous, critical, self-important know-it-all, and the Patriarch looks down on her with disdain, seeing her as dirty, lazy and sluttish.

Reconcilers for the Worker/Slave and the Patriarch

The Worker/Slave's second Element is Fire and the Patriarch's is Water, which gives us Fire and Water (The Fool) and reversing them, Water and Fire (the Actress). The Fool is excellent for the Patriarch, he opens him up, frees his rigidity and melts his ice, so that he can begin to enjoy the dance of life. He stops the Actress from being obsessed with her inner emotions and encourages her to respond to the big wide world. The Actress is good for the Worker/Slave by stirring her emotions, getting her excited about something and getting her off her arse. We see them at work in revolutions, when they are joined by the Warrior, fighting for a cause. (We often see the Patriarch and the Actress together, priests like their fancy frocks and there are many 'As the Actress said to the Bishop' jokes.)

The Fool and the Wise Woman Conflict

Fire and Water against Earth and Air

The Fool is an Open state and the Wise Woman is Closed. Here is female Earth versus male Fire. The Wise Woman frowns upon the Fool's lack of responsibility and inability to take care of anything, and he sees her as a boring nag who doesn't know how to have fun.

Reconcilers for the Wise Woman and the Fool

The Wise Woman's second Element is Air and the Fool's is Water, which gives us Air and Water (The Patriarch) and reversing them, Water and Air (the Child). The Child, the open one, helps the Wise Woman, whose reaction is to care for the Child and by so doing can see the magic of life through her eyes. Grandparents often experience this, basking in the wonderment of their young grandchildren. The Child brings passivity to the Fool, allowing him to experience more of his surroundings, rather than leaping in response to everything. The Patriarch can also help the Fool by slowing him down and bringing him self-control, and he reminds the Wise Woman of her inner treasures, not only her possessions and he will straighten her stoop. He tell us to 'Stand up Straight".

The Mother Nature and Logician Conflict

Air and Fire against Earth and Water

Mother Nature and The Logician are both Cardinal states and have little harmony, their first Elements being female Earth against male Air. She understands him as artificial and dangerous, with his sciences and technologies that are divided from the natural world and to him she is but a 'stick-in-the-mud', opposed to all 'progress' and a fat stupid blob.

Reconcilers for Mother Nature and the Logician

Mother Nature's second Element is Water and the Logician's is Fire, which gives us Water and Fire (The Actress) and reversing them, Fire and Water (the Fool). They both could do with a good jolly up, so enter the Fool, the open one. He is good for Mother Nature, he gets her moving and out and about, and also for the Logician to open him up to new possibilities and to enjoy the flowers. The Actress is useful for modifying the Logician's dispassion, bringing some emotional involvement into his experiments. She also gets Mother Nature excited and brings her forward onto the stage of life.

Neurotic Solutions and Psychological Problems

The Twelve Types of Madness

The term 'neurotic solution' was coined by Karen Horney, a German psychoanalyst, who began to identify some of them. There are twelve, each relating to an Archetype. They are a defensive strategy, we repeatedly use a small part of ourselves as a means of coping with other people, whilst keeping them at bay and not allowing them to come close enough to truly affect us. The term It's like hiding behind a mask, which inhibits the generous giving of ourselves and traps us in a narrow band of consciousness. All neurotic solutions come across as false and therefore can be irritating to other people. When our wheels of consciousness become stuck most of us end up in them. This is why so many friendships and relationships break up, we agree to indulge each other's neurotic solutions until we can't stand it anymore. Practicing our Archetypes and getting our wheels turning will free us from falsity. We have twelve masks and using them all allows us to connect to our real face, our Centre, and be authentic. The previous chapter described how we can heal our neurosis with the reconciling balancing and opposing Archetypes.

Moving from neurotic solutions to madness is largely a matter of degree. Living in a neurotic solution allows a person to still function in the world, but a madness does not. It is more acceptable to say 'mental health issues', but on reflection, we might be better served by saying 'emotional health issues'. In my view, people rarely become 'mentally ill' all by themselves. Their environment, what's going on in their lives, the traumas they have suffered and the support, or lack of, they receive, all contribute. Doing something about the way we collectively live would be far more effective than doctors handing out drugs as the only solution. When we become dangerously stuck in a certain Archetype to the virtual exclusion of any of the others, we can suffer serious psychological problems. The different forms of madness are ways of seeing through each Archetype to the extreme. They are not necessarily wrong in what they are experiencing, but they have become so unbalanced as to become trapped to the point of imprisonment.

True sanity depends on balancing the nature of one state of being with another. To bring someone back from the brink may require not only discovering which medication may be helpful, but also exposure to activities, suitable drama, nature, music, colours or a change of environment will be needed. Frequent practice of a balancing Archetype can then be prescribed, and once an equilibrium is reached the person may go forward to practice other states in the normal way. This work is a gift to those who work in mental health. It clearly identifies the different forms of consciousness and the means to help heal them. This is a brief outline of these problems with a few suggestions as to how they might be approached, although each person will need an individual approach. It would be ill-advised to discontinue traditional medical treatment or other methods being used. There is no suggestion whatsoever that significant changes of treatment should be implemented. The Archetypes and alternative treatments should be introduced carefully and the effects observed before any changes in medication are made, and this only by qualified medical professionals. Each person has individual needs and rates of improvement, therefore the following should be viewed as simply possibilities as to the application of the work. Although the Archetypes can bring magical results, there is no guarantee that everyone will respond. Psychopaths, Narcissists and Sociopaths suffer from a serious lack of the Water Element and it is uncertain as to whether they can ever be cured.

We need to use all the knowledge, skills and experience we have gained so far in all the Archetypes to make progress in healing. Every tool we have has a place and a use.
At times, practicing one Archetype can have the unexpected effect of turning on another. This could be either a joyful gift or a challenge, depending on a person's state of being. We all unfold in unique ways.

⋃ Water Archetypes

The Child Water and Air

The Child's neurotic solution is to become self-effacing, to claim to be insignificant, saying "It wasn't me, I didn't mean it, someone else said it, "I'm incapable of doing it…." Thus, she avoids conflict and taking action over anything. She will be over-apologetic and use a little girl voice to underline her ineffectiveness and disengage from others. Some women use this way of speaking as a means of both not challenging the patriarchal society, and eliciting approval from it.

Going mad in the Child is to feel intense terror as a result of being wide open to every suggestion, inference and impression to the point of catalepsy. She will feel threatened, frozen in fear, and confusion where anything can turn into anything. She may actually be experiencing things as they really are, but those in a less open and innocent state will not see it. In the very young and averagely balanced child, two main Archetypes can be seen to be active - the Child and the Fool. The Child state becomes fascinated by something and the Fool responds to it. It is helpful, therefore, to introduce physical movement. The Fool is the dancer, so appropriate music can be played. Once the person achieves movement through her/his own volition, something to love, such as an animal can be brought in. The Child will need to care for and protect it and so takes a small step towards balance.

The Enchantress Water and Earth

The Enchantress's neurotic solution is to empathise and sympathise with everything, people, animals, even vegetables that are painfully ripped from their roots. She does not want to hurt anyone in case they stop loving her and her dripping feelings annoy others because they appear overdone and insincere.

Going mad in the Enchantress is to drown in hopeless sorrow, where she experiences all the hurts of the world. No one appreciates her and she ends up inside her dismal internal picture show. Her feelings are real, there is a huge amount of suffering, but to become trapped there can be soul destroying. Although right about the world's sufferings, living with these feelings constantly is overwhelming and can result in 'getting the blues' so badly she'll want to kill herself. The world will be too depressing and painful for her. Bringing in the Observer (Air and Earth) can still these depressing inner images and soothe her feelings, helping her to look outwards. As she begins to feel less depressed, her opposite, the Joker (Fire and Air) can be brought in to cheer up. Learning to juggle and joke telling are often successful ways of lightening her up and stretching her perception.

The Actress Water and Fire

The Actress will employ a highly emotional state as a means of fending off and avoiding disturbing or unwanted experiences. She will make everything about her, and people will back off for fear of her shrieking dramas and tantrums.

Going mad in the Actress is hysteria. She will be stuck in her own personal drama, thinking only of her starring role and dazzled by her stage lights. Other people (the audience) are sitting in the dark, no one can reach her or affect her. She will scream for hours to get the attention she wants and is incapable of calming down, to the point of needing sedation. Using the Worker/Slave (Earth and Fire), will start to relax her and bring her down to earth through massage, practical jobs and physical contact. Then a creative outlet for her emotions must be found. Art is a means to get her to really look at something outside of herself whilst still being able to express herself. This will allow her opposite, the Observer (Air and Earth) to begin to develop.

↑ Fire Archetypes

The Fool Fire and Water

The Fool's neurotic solution is to be everybody's friend and a jolly, well-liked chap. He repels others with his loud guffaws, laughs and mimes. There is a restlessness that constantly moves him on, never staying anywhere long enough to make real connections.

The traditional image of The Fool's madness is the 'village idiot' who has nothing, loses everything and sees no point in anything. He lives in total witless spontaneity, living in the 'now' and unable to cope with living in the world. These types were once described as 'touched', originally meaning touched by the Divine. These days we no longer value this open state and so there is no opportunity to gain from his experiences. He is put somewhere where he can be 'looked after' or is left homeless. He could easily be a flasher, exposing himself frequently and at certain women who will probably be in the Wise Woman, who might need to be shocked into arousal, although I certainly don't advocate this approach. He's actually going through the right motions but in the wrong place at the wrong time to the wrong people, which makes it abusive. Patients with Bipolar Disorder may have episodes of poor impulse control and high levels of disinhibition, exacerbated by drugs and alcohol, which can increase the risk of criminal activity, and research shows that they are at a higher risk of committing suicide. The Child can slow him down by catching his eye and making him look at things and the Patriarch can freeze his relentless movement. Once he is still, he can be balanced by his opposite, the Wise Woman (Earth and Air) who teaches him how to care.

The Joker Fire and Air

The joker is used as a neurotic solution to avoid deeper feelings, nothing is taken seriously, everything and everyone is a joke to be sent up and manipulated. Prisoners and those with stressful occupations, such as police, medics and rescue services, employ him to sidestep painful emotions with black gallows humour.

Madness in the Joker is to be terrified of the deeper feelings, the soft underbelly and all is just one big sick joke. It is to become trapped in extreme cynicism where nothing has any depth or intrinsic value. The laugh is on him, as his sniggering isolates him and prevents any meaningful connection with other people. Some comedians have gone so far into his extreme that they swung the other way and ended up committing suicide. Meditation through the Observer gives him a chance to contemplate the benefits of other states and then his opposite, the Enchantress (Water and Earth), can be used to reawaken his feelings in positive ways.

The Warrior Fire and Earth

The Warrior uses aggression as a neurotic solution, keeping others at arm's length with the threat of conflict. This is to be argumentative and cruel to the feelings of others. Madness in the Warrior is outbreaks of uncontrolled violence, rage, going berserk, flailing around in all directions and requiring sedation. Before drugs were used, it was straightjackets and padded cells. Teaching him meditation with the Observer (Air and Earth) will calm him down, or using the Wise Woman and giving him something to care for and protect will awaken him to gentleness and love which will allow his opposite, the Child, to be practised. In some prisons the inmates, many who have committed violent crimes, are given dogs to look after and train. One project is to work with rescue dogs. A behaviourist helps with training and socialising the dogs with a view to getting them a home. It's amazing how these prisoners change once they've experienced the love of a dog.

⊕ Earth Archetypes

The Worker/Slave Earth and Fire

The neurotic solution of the Worker/Slave is to put up with everything in the hope that it will get better or go away. This is to think that there is nothing you can do about anything and so avoid having to engage with others. You just have to put up with it. Politically, the rise of the Worker/Slave is a reaction against authority, the Patriarch (Air and Water), her opposite. There is an upsurge of dramatised emotions, the Actress (Water and Fire), in the oppressed workers. They rise against the Patriarchal oppressor, create revolution and overthrow him with the Warrior. Political prisoners have been known to cover their cells with shit.

Madness in the Worker/Slave is to be really in the shit. There will be outpourings of the crudest language with many rude swear words - fuck, cunt, shit, arse, piss, bugger, cock, dickhead etc.- and such persons are likely to excrete into their hands, lie in the filth and become slothful. They will smear excrement everywhere, including over themselves and may well eat it too. Involving such people in drama will encourage the expansion of their script, and then they can be eased into practicing the Patriarch, who is the script writer and can also get them clean. People who desperately need this Archetype can, to a lesser extent, be like this too, as they reach to earth themselves.

Mother Nature Earth and Water

The neurosis of Mother Nature is to compulsively nurture everyone in the hope that they will be nice to her. She will forever be offering people food, cups of tea and comfort. This is a kind of mothering that can be smothering.

Madness in Mother Nature is to become inert, dull and unable to respond to anything new, reacting only to what is familiar. She will become slothful, can be seriously overweight and immobile, become obsessed with the connections between things, such as how a butterfly taking off in one country can affect the weather in another, or how saying that word allowed a horse to be conceived in China. Those who are ignorant of this state will not be able to understand and will dismiss her views and not see that she could possibly be right. She will become overwhelmed by the great patterns on the web of life, all these connections like weeds choking the garden. She needs her opposite, the Logician (Air and Fire) to work things out rationally, but first we might introduce the Fool who can loosen her up, and once she's moving, new ideas can be introduced, allowing her access to the Logician. The Actress may also help her to express herself and become excited about something.

The Wise Woman Earth and Air

The Wise Woman's neurosis is to be riddled with suspicion about everyone and she approaches everything with undue caution. She keeps others away through her anxieties as to what people may take from her as she turns the keys in her many locks. She constantly looks out of windows to see what threats lurk and resists any kind of change. She can be very mean and will walk a mile to a shop to save a penny on an item, rather than buy it nearby for one penny more.

Madness in the Wise Woman is extreme suspicion and paranoia. She is a miser, hoarding and over-filling her house with objects that can be valuable or rubbish. She may suffer OCD, an anxious repetition of a routine, with fear of loss, and some aspects of Autism and Asperger's, where change is upsetting. Trying to remove a single item from her results in extreme anxiety. The first thing to do would be to bring in the Child who needs looking after. This will melt her closed doors and encourage her to give. Love can develop in her for any young creature who needs care. She will need to enter into play with it, which allows the fun of her opposite, the Fool (Fire and Water) to enter.

✳ Air Archetypes

The Observer Air and Earth

The Observer's neurotic solution manifests as silent detachment from the situation and becoming remote. He gives little reaction to people, behaving as if he has not heard or they are not there. Through not noticing people and being callous, he drives them away.

Madness in this state is to have the stillness of death. He will lie on beds of nails and mortify his flesh in order to drive himself out of his body and emotions. He is totally indifferent to life on earth, has no interest in anything and appears as if already dead. We cannot entirely blame him, as he has a lot of true vision and has no wish to engage in the horrors and illusions he sees. He has to be brought back into his body, and the Worker/Slave is the one who can begin his rescue with massage and physical manipulations. He needs to get back in touch with the physical world, so he should be given objects that are pleasant to touch and can be moved around. The Warrior (Fire and Earth) is also helpful in awakening his energy and the wish to do something, which can then move him into his balancing opposite, the Actress (Water and Fire). She will provide the enthusiasm to do things and bring an emotional attachment to his aims.

The Logician Air and Fire

The Logician's neurotic solution is to baffle everyone with science and engage in endless speculation, intellectual discussion and theory. His Air ends up blowing everyone away. Psychological problems ensue when his thoughts become too fast to cope with, truth is lost as analysis and theory take over and frantic calculations go on in his head. He loses touch with reality, as one idea is as good as another and so he drifts off into space. None of his ideas appear to have any realistic sequence or be attached to anything actual and he will be unable to relate to his environment. All four open states can be helpful; the Observer to help him shut off his mind through meditation, the Child to open his eyes to other ways of seeing, the Fool to show him more of the outer world, and the Worker to bring him back down to earth. A dramatising of his ideas (the Actress) could slow them down, make them more real, and then he should be taken to the countryside to meet his opposite, Mother Nature, and be involved in practical matters, farm work and the growing

of plants. This will teach him to slow down, a necessary aspect of his cure.

The Patriarch Air and Water

 The Patriarch's neurotic solution is to let everyone know how very important he is and he becomes offended if he thinks they are taking liberties. He demands respect but does not always give it. He always knows best and is brittle in his dealings. He drives people away by assuming authority in every situation and treats all as his inferiors, making them feel small.

In his cold, frozen state, his madness manifests as self-aggrandisement where he thinks he's God, Jesus, Napoleon, king Arthur etc. He is mad on self-importance and delusions of grandeur. He can also become over-concerned with cleanliness, order, washing his hands repeatedly, avoiding contact with surfaces and insist that everything is placed in a particular order. He imagines that everyone is carrying harmful germs and must be kept away lest they kill him. He can agonise over deciding which is the best way to arrange things into patterns. He needs to be humbled, but first his icy rigidity must be melted. The Fool (Fire and Water) can introduce the heat of movement and bring him into his body where he can begin to embrace his opposite, the Slave (Earth and Fire). He can be given practical tasks to connect him to reality, even though he considers them to be beneath him.
Hyper religiosity and religious psychosis can be serious forms of mental illness, where some patients claim to hear God's voice, telling them to harm and even kill people. This is most frequently connected to Schizophrenia and can be accompanied by paranoia. Research is showing that males are up to three times more likely to develop it than females, although this may be disputed. This is not to say that using the Patriarch causes it, far from it, there are different reasons for the development of this illness; e.g. upbringing, environment, childhood experiences, drug and alcohol abuse and possibly hereditary factors. If a person has always been sweet, kind and pleasant, this behaviour normally continues after diagnosis. If the person has been a problematic child and teenager, then the negative behaviour can worsen. I am no expert, this is only what I have heard and read, but it does seem that these types of mental problems do tend to latch on the Patriarch.

Sequences of Elements

The Sequences of Elements and how they work in people was the first aspect of this work that was explored and defined by ascertaining which elements were seen to be strongest and which weakest in individuals. It was then advanced to the discovery of the Archetypes. If you're practising the work you don't need to study it. I could have left it out altogether, but decided to include it, as it is a useful aspect and can give deeper understanding over time. Once you know about the Open, Closed and Cardinal states, the Opposites and Reconcilers, and have read the chapters on each Archetype with how to practise it, you have all you need to work on your evolution. I provide some examples of sequences, with illustrations. Our sequences indicate which Archetypes we use, and influence the order in which we bring new ones in, but you may come to know this intuitively without having to analyse it. The subtlety and power of these living elements are so great that the following can only be a rough guide to help us begin to recognise their positions in our make-up. Knowing your sequence helps you to understand how your personal elements work, which are strong and which are weak, and will give you insight about yourself, but I urge you to familiarise yourself with the Twelve States before you immerse yourself in trying to work it out. This is because -

Firstly, the purpose of this work is to shine a light on where you are so far and to give you a practical means of further self-development. To over-focus on sequences carries the risk of further locking yourself in. The Work is like a practical tool bag, with twelve tools with which to build yourself. It should not be used like Astrology or other 'what you are like' systems that can define some of your characteristics, but carry with it the implication that this is you and you're stuck with it. Knowing the Archetypes well and practising them will reveal which Elements you favour and which are under-developed and make it easier for you to see your sequence. We need to keep reminding ourselves that growth is not more of what we are already, it's going in the opposite direction and awakening what is dormant. Turning your Wheel of Life is the way to freedom. Revolve to Evolve.

Secondly, as you awaken latent archetypes in yourself, your sequence will become less significant. You will be learning to develop and balance all Four Elements into an integrated harmonious wholeness, so it doesn't matter if you can't work it out. It's best to regard sequences as signposts, clarifying the direction of further growth. You have an exciting journey ahead. If your Air Element is well developed, you will enjoy exploring the logic of this chapter.

Thirdly, it depends how strongly developed your usual elements are. Some people have well established, obvious elements and some appear to be muddy with little there at all. It may surprise you to know that it is people with underdeveloped elements who may have the easier path to self-development. To feel you haven't developed anything very much at all can be an asset. You won't have the challenge of strong forces conflicting with the new energies coming in. We could compare it to singing lessons. A naturally big voice will often force it out with faulty technique, producing a harsh sound and risking damage to the vocal cords. The teacher has the task of returning the voice to small and then building it up to its full power with the correct, supporting technique. It is easier, therefore, to teach a person with a small voice, as it is already in the correct position to begin broadening, building and raising it.

We should also remain aware that circumstances and environment affect us in relation to our innate make-up. There are differing individual reactions to similar events, even in those with the same sequence. Bearing all that in mind, what do we mean by Sequence of Elements? Basically, it's the order they are in and the way they work.

We speak of the first, second, third and fourth element, the placing of each being significant, revealing an inner pattern of which Archetypes you are likely to be favouring. This is what it means to have the elements in the relevant positions -

The First Element
The Element we have first tends to be in a purer state than the others, we use it with ease, yet it is not always obvious to ourselves or others. We are comfortable with it, it works automatically below the surface, we take it for granted and may wonder why other people have difficulty with it.

The Second Element

The Element we have second is usually suppressed, but well-developed. We call it 'in the box' because we keep it locked up instead of using it. Sometimes it is called the 'dodgy element', because we dodge it in ourselves and others. We fear it because we don't know what it might do, it's been imprisoned for years. Will we be able to control it? The Archetype scripts included in this book, with the chapter on how to practise and use reconcilers, will help you to release it in a safe and manageable way.

The Third Element

Our third Element tends to be over-developed; it dominates the personality and is not in as pure a state as the first. There is something 'third rate' about an element we have third. We tend to identify it by saying, "I am like this, not like that". Quite frequently, persons are to be found using their third element in the kind of work they do and the face they show to the world. It will become purer as you develop other elements. 'Thirds of a feather flock together' is a term I coined, as we tend to gravitate towards others who have the same Element as ourselves in the third position.

The Fourth Element

The fourth Element is the weakest and reaching it is a major step forward towards the completion of the self. Few of us have managed it, but when we do use it, we feel we are 'in our element', we have a sense of fulfillment. The Archetype scripts are designed to help you to develop and balance your four Elements.

It was noticed that it is usual for women to have a female, Yin Element last (Water or Earth), and men a masculine, Yang (Fire or Air), and this is mainly true, but it would be unwise to make it a hard and fast rule, as we don't know what evolutionary changes may be taking place and there are always exceptions.

The illustration below helps to see the condition of the four placements, with the first glowing healthily, the second in the box, the third over large and a bit wonky and the fourth small and feeble.

We'll look at each position and what it means to have different Elements in them.

The First Position - The Purest

Water first is to have true, authentic feelings as opposed to sweet sentimentality. These people can be dreamers, creative, open and receptive and feel more deeply than they ever show, empathetic, intuitive, sensitive and often quietly kind.

Fire first is to be truly effective and able to take considered action on one's own initiative. These people are doers, but don't necessarily make a song and dance about it, they just get things done.

Earth first is to have inner security, realistic and sustaining to others. Earth firsters often don't mind how many people lean on or draw from them. They carry security within and have no need of riches to make them feel stable and safe.

Air first is to be quick on the uptake, bright and clever, taking intelligence for granted rather than identifying with it, or bothering to show it off. These people have no need of academic recognition to prove their intelligence and tend to be mystified by how slow other people's thinking is. This is to possess a true logic.

The Second Position – the Suppressed

Water second (in the box) means that the feelings are suppressed and there will be difficulty in empathizing and communicating with others. These people are often afraid of their own feelings and those of others, so will become cut off, unsympathetic and hard-hearted. They avoid crying, not wishing to open the 'flood gates' and face their inner pain, but also depriving themselves of the deepest joys.

Fire second (in the box) is to be an ineffectual person, one who never really knows what she/he really likes or wants, and is afraid to say so on the occasion when she/he does know. This is due to the fear of having an effect on almost anything or anyone. They rarely act on their own initiative and tend not to develop much of their potential. We often do not know if we are pleasing Fire seconds or not, because they don't react, and when they do occasionally release a little fire, it can be hard to handle, coming out as bad temper, shouting, with kicking of doors and stamping of feet.

Earth second (in the box) is the type of person who shudders at the thought of getting his/her hands dirty and usually tries to remove all traces of earth, choosing décor that is almost exclusively white, concretes over gardens and has to have things immaculately clean and tidy. Due to the suppression of the earth element, there may be dreams or jokes about excrement and similar earthy muck. Earth in the boxers often don't know what is really happening in the world, because the world is earth. Interesting how, as we are in danger of destroying our planet, the fashion for minimalistic white homes is prevalent.

Air second (in the box) is very definitely a non-intellectual. Such persons sense, feel or intuit their way through life, they loathe the air element and become anxious, run away, get a headache, or go to sleep when confronted with intellectualism. They don't like reading or studying or anything that might cause them 'brain strain'.

The Third Position – the Dominant

3

Water third can be dripping with gushy saccharine, saying everything is beautiful even when it is obviously not. This is sentimentality as opposed to sentiment. People like this may appear sympathetic, but you can sense they don't really understand. They like ornamentation and cutsie teddy bears, clamp their hands over their ears at the mention of hunting and slaughter but are happy to eat meat. Some call themselves 'Earth Angels' or claim to come from the 'Angelic Realm' or the 'Star Seed Realm' and suchlike. Some of these give me an image of a beautiful cake, decorated with flowers, hearts and butterflies, but when you cut into it, it's full of maggots.

Fire third persons are often the trouble-makers of this world, reacting to everything, they can let nothing be, let nothing pass. They are constantly active, no matter how pointlessly or ill-considered. They can never sit still and let themselves relax, or anyone else for that matter. We are living in an increasingly fire third world, hyperactive, loud, harsh with fewer opportunities to enjoy our inner lives in peace and quiet.

Earth third people are usually matey, casual and easy going, untidy and not overly bothered with hygiene. They like clubs and clubbing together and are often found in the building trade and the local pub. When they choose to learn skills, they are good artisans, working at a trade with their hands.

Air third is identified with the intellect and has a tendency to baffle him/herself with argument and blind everyone else with science. This is a mental, argumentative type who may have a fast brain but doesn't necessarily understand much. Air thirds are often attracted to academia and the teaching profession. They are the types most likely to dismiss this work without understanding a word of it.

The Fourth Position – the Weakest

Water last is one of the feminine (Yin) ways to fulfillment. This person will seek true love in the hope that the lover will awaken this element in her/him. She/he looks for her/his raison d'etre through love. These types are romantics, ever seeking the soul mate who will complete them. It is possible for Water lasters to find a fulfilling role in the world without finding a lover. A cause, such as children and animals in need, where love can be given and exchanged can achieve it. This is fulfillment through loving.

Fire last is one of the masculine (Yang) ways to fulfilment. Many people can live a frustrating life through never reaching their Fire. In older times initiation ceremonies for youths were designed to help them get into their Fire and to learn how to direct it wisely. If a Fire laster manages to express this element he/she will find the path to self-fulfillment, and is likely to gain recognition through working to change the world in some way. This is fulfillment through doing.

Earth last is one of the feminine (Yin) ways towards fulfillment, which is found in some kind of service to the community or the world at large. To be of service is important, and she/he will not be entirely fulfilled by finding the love of their life, they need for a career too. Not being able to reach their Earth will cause unreasonable fears and the continuation of insecurity and impending disaster, no matter how rich or well supported she/he is. This is fulfillment through service.

Air last is to fulfil oneself through learning and is a masculine (Yang) type. When an Air laster develops his/her Air Element he/she will gather knowledge and is likely to become a consultant, an expert, an authority in a field of knowledge, which is willingly passed on to others. They may also progress to exploring spiritual teachings. This is fulfillment through knowledge.

We can also look at the Elements individually, using the same thumbnail descriptions as above. The more ways we look at things, the better we see them.

Water

Water first is to have true, authentic feelings as opposed to sweet sentimentality. These people can be dreamers, creative, open and receptive and feel more deeply than they ever show, empathetic, intuitive and often quietly kind and sensitive.

Water second (in the box) means that the feelings are suppressed and there will be difficulty in empathizing and communicating with others. These people are often afraid of their own feelings and those of others, so they will become cut off, unsympathetic and hard-hearted. They avoid crying, not wishing to open the 'flood gates' and face their inner pain, but also depriving themselves of the deepest joys.

Water third can be dripping with gushy saccharine, saying everything is beautiful even when it is obviously not. This is sentimentality as opposed to sentiment. People like this may appear sympathetic, but you can sense they don't really understand. They like ornamentation and cutsie teddy bears, clamp their hands over their ears at the mention of hunting and slaughter but are happy to eat meat. Some call themselves 'Earth Angels' or claim to come from the 'Angelic Realm' or the 'Starseed Realm' and suchlike. Some of these types give me an image of a beautiful cake, decorated with flowers, hearts and butterflies, but when you cut into it, it's full of maggots.

Water last is one of the feminine ways to fulfillment for all sexes. This person will seek true love in the hope that the lover will awaken this element in her/him. She/he looks for her/his raison d'etre through love. These types are the romantics of the world, ever seeking the soul mate who will complete them. It may be possible for Water lasters to find a fulfilling role in the world without finding a lover. A cause, such as children and animals in need, where love can be given and exchanged can achieve it. This is fulfillment through loving.

Fire

Fire first is to be truly effective and able to take considered action on one's own initiative. These people are doers, but don't necessarily make a song and dance about it, they just get things done.

Fire second (in the box) is to be an ineffectual person, one who never really knows what she/he really likes or wants, and is afraid to say so on the occasion when she/he does know. This is due to the fear of having an effect on almost anything or anyone. They rarely act on their own initiative and tend not to develop much of their potential. We often do not know if we are pleasing Fire seconds or not, because they don't react and when they do occasionally release a little fire, it can be hard to handle, frequently coming out as bad temper, shouting, with kicking of doors and stamping of feet.

Fire third persons are often the trouble-makers of this world, reacting to everything, they can let nothing be, let nothing pass. They are constantly active no matter how pointlessly or ill-considered, can never sit still and let themselves relax, or anyone else for that matter. We are living in an increasingly fire third world, hyperactive, loud, harsh with fewer opportunities to enjoy our inner lives in peace and quiet.

Fire last is one of the masculine (Yang) ways to fulfilment. Many people, can live a frustrating life through never reaching their Fire. In older, wiser times initiation ceremonies for youths were designed to help them get into their Fire and to learn how to direct it wisely. If a Fire laster manages to express this element he/she will find the path to self-fulfillment and is likely to gain recognition through working to change the world in some way. This is fulfillment through doing.

Earth

Earth first is to have inner security, realistic and sustaining to others. Earth firsters often don't mind how many people lean on or draw from them. They carry security within and have no need of riches to make them feel stable and safe.

Earth second (in the box) is the type of person who shudders at the thought of getting his/her hands dirty and usually tries to remove all traces of earth, choosing décor that is almost exclusively white, concretes over gardens and has to have things immaculately clean and tidy. Due to the suppression of the earth element, there may be dreams or jokes about excrement and similar earthy muck. Earth in the boxers often don't know what is really happening in the world, because the world is earth. Interesting how, as we are in danger of destroying our planet, earth, Interesting how, as we are in danger of destroying our planet, the fashion for minimalistic white homes is prevalent.

Earth third people are usually untidy, not very clean, matey, casual and easygoing. They like clubs and clubbing together and are often found in the building trade and the local pub. When they choose to learn skills, they are good artisans, working at a trade with their hands.

Earth last is one of the feminine (Yin) ways towards fulfillment for all sexes, which is found in some kind of service to the community or the world at large. To be of service is important to someone like this, and she/he will not be entirely fulfilled by finding the love of their life. They have a need for a career of some kind in their own right. Not being able to reach their Earth will cause unreasonable fears and creates the continuation of insecurity and impending disaster, no matter how rich or well supported she/he is. This is fulfillment through service to others.

Air

Air first is to be quick on the uptake, bright and clever, taking intelligence for granted rather than identifying with it, or bothering to show it off. These people have no need of academic recognition to prove their intelligence and tend to be mystified by how slow other people's thinking is. This is to possess a true logic.

Air second (in the box) is very definitely a non-intellectual. Such persons sense, feel or intuit their way through life, they loathe the air element and become anxious, run away, get a headache, or go to sleep when confronted with intellectualism. They don't like reading or studying or anything that might cause them 'brain strain'.

Air third is identified with the intellect and has a tendency to baffle him/herself with argument and blind everyone else with science. This is a mental, argumentative type who may have a fast brain but doesn't necessarily understand anything very much. Air thirds are often attracted to academia and the teaching profession. They are the types most likely to dismiss this work without understanding a word of it.

Air last is to fulfill oneself through learning and is a masculine (Yang) type. When an Air laster develops his/her Air element he/she will gather knowledge and is likely to become a consultant, an expert, an authority in a field of knowledge which is willingly passed on to others. They may also progress to exploring spiritual teachings. This is fulfillment through knowledge.

Examples of Sequences

The sequence of Elements represents different parts of ourselves.

The 1st Element dominates the Essence, the Basic Nature. (e.g. with Air 1st we have a thinking nature).

The 2nd Element is repressed or denied. (e.g. with Water 2nd we repress our feelings).

The 3rd Element dominates the personality. (e.g. with Earth 3rd, we will be body centred).

The 4th Element is fulfilment and realisation. (e.g. with Fire 4th this would be through action and achievement.

The following examples, with diagrams, give a brief explanation as to how a sequence might manifest itself as Archetypes in an individual. We look at -

The Essence - the 1st and 2nd Elements. We can call it the Essential Self. This is a naturally used, taken for granted state, often hidden from the person. We admire and are attracted to those with the opposite Elements here, so if we have Air and Water, for example, we will be reach to those who have Earth and Fire here for completion.

The Personality - the 3rd and 4th Elements. A person will develop this state on the way to fulfilment. It is the way someone is orientated and contains the qualities she/he admires and idealises. It can determine the way of life, career choices and interests, but with the danger of negating the Essential Self, leading to frustration and unbalance. It often doesn't show itself until puberty, but can be sooner.

The Harmonics - The 1st and 3rd and 3rd and 1st Elements. We also call these the Usual States, and are the aspects with which the person feels most comfortable and at home. It is the usual behaviour, developed since childhood, and typifies the outlook and the life led. It can speed up our growth when used, but then we must move on, lest we be stuck here.

The Shadow - The 2nd and 4th Elements. *"Everyone is a moon, and has a dark side which he never shows to anybody". - Mark Twain.*
This one lurks in the shadows, and needs to come out into the light. It is a part of us we don't recognise, opposed and alien to the way we live and believe ourselves to be. This may cause us to see

only the negative qualities and we will consciously avoid them. The Shadow must be recognised if we wish to become more complete beings. Its first Element is the one we have 'in the box' in the sequence, position two. Whatever one's shadow self may be, the partners and friends one needs, and is attracted to, are people who have that aspect of their being developed. This knowledge can be useful, but keep in mind that we often correctly intuit the partners we need to balance us.

"Most of the shadows of this life are caused by standing in one's own sunshine."
- Ralph Waldo Emerson

The Fulfilment - The 4th and 3rd Elements. This is what we need to reach to round ourselves off, to know we are truly growing and have reached some level of our purpose. Developing the Fulfilment takes us closer to balancing our Elements.

If it can be seen that, as different persons have their four Elements arranged in differing orders, it follows that these four Elements give rise to two basic Archetypes in each individual, the Basic Nature and the Personality, although it is often the Harmonics we see. How much of these four are actually used will depend on an individual's evolutionary progression. Few people can demonstrate more than two or three.

Example 1

The sequence is Water, Air, Earth, Fire.

☽ ✳ ⊕ ↑

This combination results in a naturally placid type. In the diagram, the left box shows the Elements in their sequential positions and on the right they are shown as the Archetypes. With Fire last, this is a Yang/masculine type.

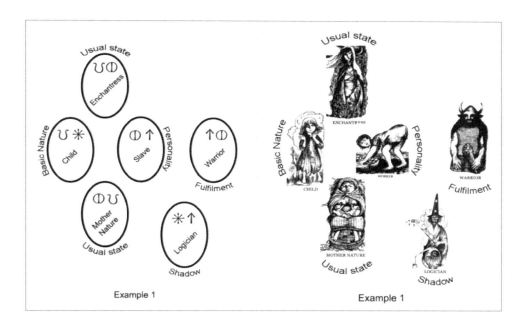

Water, Air, Earth, Fire

***The Essence and the Personality* - The 1st and 2nd Elements/ the 3rd and 4th.** We see these from reading straight across the sequence, giving us 1 and 2, The Child (Water and Air), the Essence, and 3 and 4, the Worker/Slave (Earth and Fire), the Personality. These are two open states. It should become obvious by now that it is ill advised to do what many of us do, which is to get stuck in the second pair of our Elements, the third and fourth (the Personality). Observe also that these two Archetypes always comprise the four Elements, so we can find balance when we know what we are doing.

The Harmonics - **The 1st and 3rd/the 3rd and 1st Elements.**

These are the Usual States. With most of us, our first and third Elements tend to be the more developed, therefore the habitual states in which this person is likely to live are the Enchantress (Water and Earth) the first, and third, and Mother Nature (Earth and Water) the third and first. To put this in musical terms, we do not so much hear a person's basic notes, but rather their harmonics. Thus, we see the four Archetypes to which this sequence of elements gives rise- The Child, the Slave, the Enchantress and Mother Nature. There is no guarantee that all four will be in use, in most people it is mainly two or three.

The Shadow - **The 2nd and 4th Elements.**

This is composed of the second and last Elements, because they are the weakest and least used as a rule. In the shadows in fact. Thus we have the second - Air, and the fourth - Fire, giving us the Logician. The somewhat dull exterior colours of this sequence conceals a bright yellow intelligence as its shadow self, but what is hidden in the shadows will not manifest without cultivation.

The Fulfillment - **The 4th and 3rd Elements.**

This is the reversal of the last two Elements. In this case, Earth and Fire (the Slave) are reversed, giving us the Warrior, bringing fulfilment through action, achievement and effective change.
The person in this example will have some natural charm and intuition, (the Enchantress) and be interested in crafts, gardening, cookery or ecology (Mother Nature). There may be attraction to Paganism, but if she/he does not use the harmonics to any great degree and remains in the Basic Self and Personality, some contentment will be found in practical creativity, as an artisan/worker. To reach the Fire Element, however, brings the Warrior into being, and he/she is likely to become a director or leader of some kind. There will be initial difficulty in achieving this, as we see that the Fulfillment is in conflict with the Basic Self - the Warrior and the Child. The chapter on Reconcilers explains conflicting states and how they can be resolved. We all have our own patterns of growth and working on one Archetype can have positive results on another, so as well as cultivating the reconcilers, having a try at the Actress will enliven this sequence and allow passions and self expression to rise. If the Air is released, here (trapped in the second position, i.e. 'in the box'), this person can become a world changer by knowledge and action. *Doing* brings fulfillment here.

Example 2

The sequence is Fire, Earth, Water, Air.

↑ ⊕ ʊ ✳

This is a very different type from Example 1, with little inner calm, having Fire first, Earth second, Water third and Air last. In the diagram, the left box shows the Elements in their sequential positions and on the right they are shown as the Archetypes. With Air last, this is a Yang/masculine type.

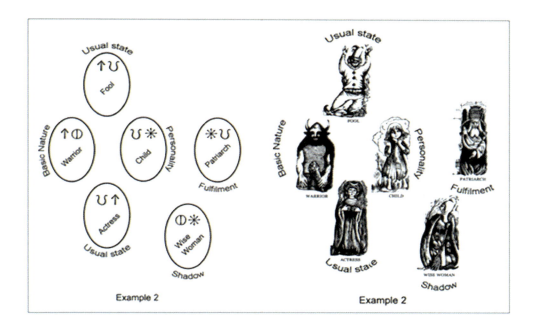

Fire, Earth, Water, Air

The Essence and the Personality - **The 1ˢᵗ and 2ⁿᵈ Elements/ the 3ʳᵈ and 4ᵗʰ.**

Here we see inner conflict, between the closed Warrior (Fire and Earth), and the open Child (Water and Air), this time between the Essence and the Personality. The reconciler, the Observer will encourage peace and harmony.

The Harmonics - **The 1ˢᵗ and 3ʳᵈ/the 3ʳᵈ and 1ˢᵗ Elements.**

These are the Usual States. Relief can be found through performing in the Usual States, the Fool and Actress, which are not too popular in some countries particularly the exuberance of the Fool and the emotions of the Actress, but if he/she is unable to use them, the balance of mind is endangered. The Fool brings fun and dissipates anger and the Actress allows expression and release from inner tension. In this case though, we need to be careful and make sure that a strong Earth archetype such as the Worker/Slave or Mother Nature is also practised, because the Warrior together with the Actress can be a volatile and dangerous combination, both being closed states and lacking in Air, with the likelihood to explode and become hysterical, without the ability to think it through first. It is, therefore, better to stick to an open state here.

The Shadow - The 2nd and 4th Elements.

This is composed of a person's second and last Element, because they are least used as a rule. In this case we have the Wise Woman, (Earth and Air), who brings some Earth, but as she is prone to anxiety, one of the other Earth functions also needs to be introduced. The advantage of the Wise Woman is that she lurks in the shadows, taking care that the inner conflict does not go too far, but she can only help so far before cracks begin to show. Developing her will bring forward her wisdom.

The Fulfilment - The 4th and 3rd Elements.

Fulfillment is in the Patriarch, (Air and Water), the reversal of the second pair of elements (Water and Air), which brings discernment and direction to the Warrior and a sense of inner authority to the Child. He freezes the conflict and through his knowledge allows a new direction. If the Air can be gained, he/she will apply him/herself to learning and study and will find balance and inner peace. The Patriarch will give structure to the Usual States, the Fool and Actress, and allow them to shape their talents into dancing, acting and creative expression in general. The Patriarch could also provide them with good scripts and the Warrior will open doors. What is learned is likely to be passed on in some kind of teaching. Knowing is fulfillment in this case. Through the use of talents, money could be earned, which the Wise Woman in the shadows will invest wisely.

Example 3

The sequence is Air, Fire, Water and Earth.

✳ ↑ ∪ ⊕

In the diagram, the left box shows the Elements in their sequential positions and on the right they are shown as the Archetypes. With Earth last, this is a Yin/feminine type.

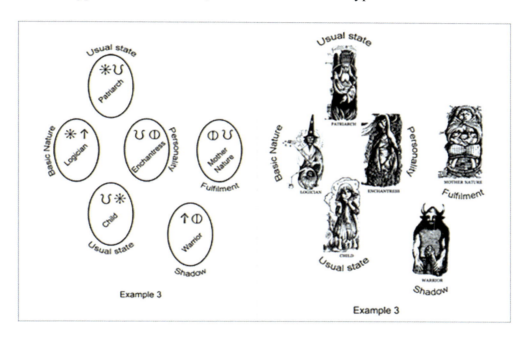

Air, Fire, Water and Earth

The Essence and the Personality - **The 1st and 2nd Elements/ the 3rd and 4th.**
The Logician is the Basic Self, bright and quick on the uptake, like the sunlight shining on the water; she/he is basically intelligent. To be psychic is second nature to her/him with the Enchantress as the Personality. If these people have many unhappy experiences, they can become locked in the negative aspects of the Enchantress, get the blues (her colour is dark blue) and suffer from depression. The Enchantresses will be obvious to anyone with a reasonably good eye for Archetypes, but the Logician may be less apparent. People are likely to be surprised to encounter such intelligence in what appears to be a 'drippy, hippy' type. They can, however, be in some conflict; logic versus intuition, but these are two Cardinal Archetypes and when working together they almost always get

to the truth. Her intuition can show him where to shine his light, so he can explain her prophesies.

The Harmonics - The 1st and 3rd/the 3rd and 1st Elements.

These are the Usual States. In happy circumstances, this woman/man will be the one who, with the Patriarch as one of the Usual Selves, knows a few things. With the Child as the other Usual Self, she/he will tell you all her/his secrets. listen to yours, and will be open to learn and believe in the magic of life. With the help of a Fire Archetype to expand out of the lonely Enchantress and the gullible Child, the two Usual States can come into their own, a performance which can result in the teaching of psychic subjects, writing books or plays and possibly singing, using that aspect of the En*chant*ress. Without Fire, such people run the risk of going through life in the shadows of twilight, feeling frustrated.

The Shadow - The 2nd and 4th Elements.

The Shadow self in this instance is the Warrior, the second and last Element. If the Fire, which is 'in the box', can be released, the Warrior will spearhead campaigns, can be associated with higher realms, teachings, self-development and metaphysics and be extremely effective, armed as he is with knowledge, intelligence and psychic guidance.

The Fulfilment - The 4th and 3rd Elements.

The reversal of the second pair of Elements, is in reaching Mother Nature (Earth and Water) to provide the Earth needed, and to prevent this person from both severe depression and from the blowing of a fuse if all of the above is actualised. To reach the Usual Selves and the Shadow will be very exciting, so Mother Nature is necessary to ground these strong energies. Arts and crafts, working with nature, gardening, looking after children or animals or cooking can bring it all down to earth. Paganism and Wicca can help, particularly the craft aspect of that religion. This person can also be a healer, gaining satisfaction through serving the world and the environment

Example 4

The sequence is Earth, Air, Fire, Water

In the diagram, the left box shows the Elements in their sequential positions and on the right they are shown as the Archetypes. This is a colourful sequence. Being Water last, this is another Yin/feminine type.

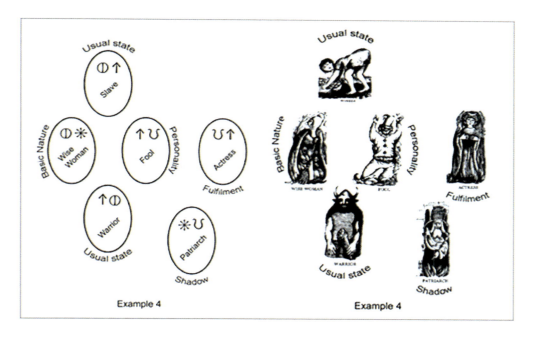

Earth, Air, Fire, Water

The Essence and the Personality - **The 1st and 2nd Elements/ the 3rd and 4th.**
This is another case of one devoid of inner peace due to the conflict between the two basic archetypes, the Wise Woman (Earth and Air) and the Fool (Fire and Water). Being 'Air in the box', this sequence is not noted for its intelligence, particularly if the person becomes too stuck in the Personality, the Fool. In an economically grim environment, the Wise Woman could take over and this person could become the proverbial 'up-tight spinster', with occasional erratic actions from the Fool.

The Harmonics - **The 1st and 3rd/the 3rd and 1st Elements.**

These are the Usual States. The Worker/Slave and Warrior can act as reconcilers as the Slave brings relaxation and the Warrior positive action. The Child and the Observer are good reconcilers too, as the Child gives the Wise Woman something to care for and the Observer calms the Warrior down.

The Shadow - **The 2nd and 4th Elements.**

The shadow is the Patriarch (Air and Water), the second and fourth Elements. Freeing the Air 'in the box' allows the Wise Woman's wisdom to connect with the innate knowledge of the Patriarch, direct the Fool and gain a sense of personal authority, no longer going where the wind blows, as the Fool is wont to do.

The Fulfillment - The **4th and 3rd Elements**.

Fulfillment comes with the Actress, freeing the emotions, creativity and passions, and if she/he can make it to here, she/he can be an extraordinarily good actress/actor. It is not easy to say in which Archetypes this woman/man may end up, it depends on some luck, the environment and the nature of love found in her/his partners. If this is a woman, in a situation where she is kept down she will be used and abused, drawn into unsavoury relationships, initially by her attraction for sexual experiences and forced to bite down on her anger, an aspect of the negative Warrior. If free to use her Warrior, however, she can become an Amazon, and the boot will be on the other foot. If the Fool takes over, she could be a foolish woman losing almost anything she had in the name of love. A similar situation will be seen in the male version, although he is not as likely to be sexually used and may simply end up in frustrating menial work, causing his Fool to drink too much and his Warrior to become aggressive. He will be fulfilled in an area that allows him to express himself in creative ways.

The following is an edited extract from Richard Gardner.

"These days I think of the four elements as comparable to four main strings working a marionette. That would not be so bad, but almost all of us are using no more than two of them most of our lives. Few of us are men and women for all seasons. To correct this, education will have to be replaced by cultivation. When looking at one another, the overall state of the individual must be taken into consideration, because how his or her sequence of Elements manifest depends on many factors. For

instance, have they done any work on themselves? What effect is the marriage or other partner/s having upon them, in the sense of which of their elements are being constantly affirmed or denied? Whether any given Element in the person is in a good or bad state, is it expressing itself positively or negatively? To what degree has an Element been cultivated? And of course, with which Element is the person most identified? as this can be the major cause of his or her imbalance.

Water third in a person expresses itself differently in a Fire first person compared with say, an Earth first person and so on. Every little vital stroke and where it is placed has its considerable effect. There has been and can be endless discussion about all this. It can do more harm than good. What counts is seeing something as it really is. Any time we have succeeded in doing this we shall know, because such truth is quick in its effects! We can change one another with it.
Some people who have become aware of the Elements decide they must have them all 'in the Box', that is, lying undifferentiated in the grey mass of the centre inner circle with nothing cultivated to a recognizable degree. With such persons it is harder to see the sequence of their elements, but they can cultivate any they desire. Their humility gives a sound basis for their further growth. Those with no hope are on the opposite end of the scale. They tell you that all the elements are working in them. If this were true they would be goddesses and gods. If we do not recognize our limitations and roughly where we are at, our further evolution is most unlikely. We are not likely to change or improve anything if we have the illusion that it does not need changing or improving. Perhaps it is clear by now that if we do not know ourselves and capitalise on our innate assets, most of our lives are wasted".

- Richard Gardner - The Wheel of Life (1980) published by the Metaphysical Research Group.

♥I've thrown a lot at you in this book, so The Work may seem like a lot to take in, but as you become familiar with your Archetypes, more and more insights will come to you. In your own way, in your own time, you will make this Work your own.

"Discovering who you were meant to be while knowing what you have become is the single moment of awareness and consciousness that will change everything"

- Ross Rosenberg

. . . . The End

So here we are at the end of the book. It's been a big project, a labour of love, my life's work – so far….

I hope you find help, guidance, healing and life enhancement in its pages and, as you revolve and evolve, go on to shine your own true light far and wide.

It's the final page, but may it be the beginning of a whole new chapter in your own fabulous story.

"I have come to take you out of yourself and take you in my heart.
I have come to bring out the beauty you never knew you had
and lift you like a prayer to the sky." – Rumi

Thank you for reading. Over to you!

The Beginning . . . .

Printed in Poland
by Amazon Fulfillment
Poland Sp. z o.o., Wrocław